Creating the Future School

Schools are often portrayed as being resistant to change, unwilling to teach new material and incapable of organizing themselves in different ways. Taking an international perspective, Hedley Beare argues that there have been changes in the patterns of schooling in recent years, but increasingly radical changes are expected due to advances in information technology, in post-industrial economies and through globalization. These changes are coming, he says, whether schools are ready or not.

This fascinating book is based on the changes a 5-year-old, Angelica, will see in her lifetime. It is divided into two parts: the first describes how schools are viewed by society; the second considers practical responses that schools can make to keep up with change. *Creating the Future School* predicts that the career of teaching will change and the work of the professional educator will differ significantly from what has been the traditional teaching role in the schools of the twentieth century. The book addresses principals, senior members of school staff, teachers, governors and policy-makers.

Hedley Beare is Professor Emeritus of Education at the University of Melbourne. As founding CEO he helped establish and then headed Australia's two most recently created public school systems. He has written extensively on the future of schooling and educational policy. His publications include *Education for the Twenty-First Century*, co-authored with Richard Slaughter, and *Creating an Excellent School: Some New Management Techniques*, co-authored with Brian Caldwell and Ross Millikan, both published by Routledge.

D0862156

Student Outcomes and the Reform of Education
General Editor: Brian Caldwell
*Professor of Education, Dean of the Faculty of Education,
University of Melbourne, Australia*

Student Outcomes and the Reform of Education is concerned with the reform of public education and its impact on outcomes for students. The reform agenda has gripped the attention of policy-makers, practitioners, researchers and scholars for much of the 1990s, with every indication of more to come with the new millennium. This series reports research and describes strategies that deal with the outcomes of reform. Without sacrificing a critical perspective, the intention is to provide a guide to good practice and strong scholarship within the new arrangements that are likely to provide the framework for public education in the forseeable future.

School Effectiveness and School-Based Management
A Mechanism for Development
Yin Cheong Cheng

**Transforming Schools Through Collaborative
Leadership**
Helen Telford

The Inner Principal
David Loader

The Future of Schools
Lessons from the Reform of Public Education
Brian Caldwell and Donald Hayward

Beyond the Self-Managing School
Brian Caldwell and Jim Spinks

Designing the Learning-Centred School
A Cross-Cultural Perspective
Clive Dimmock

Creating the Future School
Hedley Beare

Creating the Future School

Hedley Beare

London and New York

First published 2001
by RoutledgeFalmer
11 New Fetter Lane, London EC4P 4EE

Simultaneously published in the USA and Canada
by RoutledgeFalmer
29 West 35th Street, New York, NY 10001

RoutledgeFalmer is an imprint of the Taylor & Francis Group
© 2001 Hedley Beare

Typeset in Times by Taylor & Francis Books Ltd
Printed and bound in Great Britain by TJ International Ltd,
Padstow, Cornwall

British Library Cataloguing in Publication Data
A catalogue record for this book is available from the British Library

Library of Congress Cataloging in Publication Data
Beare, Hedley.
Creating the Future School/Hedley Beare.
p.cm. – (Student outcomes and the reform of education)
1. Education–Forecasting. 2. Educational change. I. Title. II. Series.
LB415.B44 2000
370'.1'12–dc21   00–36780

ISBN 0–415–23868–4 (hbk)
ISBN 0–415–23869–2 (pbk)

This book is dedicated to the three women who have profoundly shaped who I am:

To my mother Amy
whom I knew for only six years of my life
but who in that time grounded my value system and nature.

To my daughter Bronwyn
who died of leukaemia at age 24
after receiving my donation of bone marrow;
the text of this book was completed on the eighteenth
anniversary of her death
– if she had been given a future, she would have been 42.

And to my wife Lyn,
my lifelong companion and confidante,
my professional partner,
sounding board on all things,
soulmate
and inspiration.
She has heard with patience and kindliness
most of the text of this book
talked across the breakfast table.

Contents

List of figures   ix
Acknowledgements   xi

1 The myth of the unchanging school   1

PART I

**The big picture: why schools are being compelled
to change their ways**   **9**

2 From an old world-view to a new   11

3 From a society of factories to a society of knowledge
   workers   23

4 New ways of knowing: implications for curriculum   36

5 The networked universe   54

6 From bureaucracy to enterprise networks   65

PART II

Looking at the practicalities: how will schooling change?   **83**

7 Schools which break the mould   85

8 Choosing what future to have   99

9 Building a manifesto for the school as a provider   113

10 On reporting outcomes   128

11 Reworking the curriculum within a new mindset   144

12 Teachers for the school of the future   166

Contents

13 A new kind of school   186

      Bibliography   194
      Index   203

Figures

6.1 The networked organization for a knowledge-based society   73
10.1 The several audiences for feedback and reporting   135
10.2 Calibrating the measuring stick   140
10.3 An outcomes-reporting protocol   141
11.1 A three-dimensional grid to consider how a learning task
      contributes to cognitive, cultural and personal development   161
12.1 The professional mind-map Part 1   174
12.2 The professional mind-map Part 2   175
12.3 The professional mind-map completed   176

Acknowledgements

A book which tries to paint a big composite picture must inevitably draw upon many extant sketches of the component parts, many of which have been published already. I am grateful to have the consent of those who have allowed me to incorporate here many of the ideas and wordings which I have used elsewhere.

The book came together as the result of my time as a Visiting Scholar in Education at Aoyama Gakuin University in Tokyo, where I delivered a series of lectures on the future of schooling. That posting gave me the opportunity to assemble much of the material contained in this book. I am particularly grateful to my friend and colleague of many years, Professor Takeshi Sasamori, for his encouragement.

The book builds on (and therefore in some instances has had to re-use) some of the material contained in *Education for the Twenty-First Century*, which I co-authored with Professor Richard Slaughter and which was published by Routledge. In the same way, I have drawn on my opening synoptic chapter in *The Primary School in Changing Times*, edited by Tony Townsend and published by Routledge in 1998.

I was able to systematize my thinking about the emerging shape of schools and schools systems, about the new roles for teachers, about the nature of the future for this generation of schoolchildren and about the intricacies of planning by writing a set of monographs on these topics. I am grateful to the Australian Council for Educational Administration (ACEA) and the Independent Association of Registered Teachers in Victoria (IARTV) both for publishing these works and then for allowing me to use the raw material in them for this present book.

I am most fortunate as an Emeritus Professor to have been given a congenial base to work from in the Centre for Applied Educational Research (CAER) in the University of Melbourne. I could not have succeeded with the production of this book without the resources of the Centre. I wish to acknowledge the collegiality I have enjoyed with the members of the Centre, and in particular the help of its Director, Professor Peter Hill, and its Executive Officer, Tim Jones.

Acknowledgements

Much of this book has been generated through my activities on the staff of the Faculty of Education at the University of Melbourne. The contributions to my thinking from fellow academics and from the senior educators who make up our postgraduate degree candidates have been huge. I am particularly blessed when I have close colleagues like the current Dean, Professor Brian Caldwell. My Assistant while I was a full-time professor, Ms Trudy Lingwood, has been a constant help to me.

Finally, my wife Lyn has been a true partner in the composition of this book and in helping me to fine-tune the ideas contained in it. She is herself a remarkable educator and professional companion, with the incisive wisdom born of years as a resource centre librarian and teacher librarian and from a lifetime of engagement with books. She more than any other has been instrumental in the generation of this book. It is impossible for me to thank her adequately.

1   The myth of the unchanging school

The popular view is that the modern school as we have known it has been remarkably resistant to change. For the whole of the twentieth century at least, the school took children at age 5 or 6, put them into class groups composed of children of the same age, put each class in charge of one teacher, and allocated students and teacher to a self-contained classroom. There the pupils were led through a curriculum based on the notion that human knowledge is divided into 'subjects'. The curriculum has been graded from the elementary (or rudimentary) through to the very complex, and the children advance 'upwards' through it in lockstep over twelve years of study. The schools are ranked according to this upward progression by being labelled kindergarten or preparatory, elementary or primary, junior secondary or middle school, senior secondary, and then tertiary or higher or post-secondary. In all cases, too, the staff 'teach', implying that they are transferring knowledge in which they have special expertise to 'learners' who are relatively ignorant. Schooling has therefore been concerned with a systematic and progressive transfer of knowledge from expert to novice.

Furthermore, the schools look the same. The traditional school is set in a large geographical area called 'the school grounds' or a campus (which is Latin for an open plain), and fenced in to imply that it is a self-contained institution. The formal instruction is conducted in sets of relatively large buildings consisting of rows of classrooms opening into long passageways which are designed to control or at least co-ordinate student movement. If one allows for varying degrees of artifice and architecture, school buildings tend to look the same the world over.

The impression, then, is that schools do not change much, in fact that they have not radically changed over many decades. In spite of dramatic developments in society and the world, schools seem to go on doing the same things in the same way with the same results and with variations in student performance being the consequence of the same things. Dale Mann quotes the President of the Xerox Corporation:

'I can't think of any other single sector of the American society that has absorbed more money by serving fewer people', and yet schools remain as they have always been – chalk and teacher talk, 9 to 3, September to June.

(Mann, 1992: 217)

Mann pointed out that in 1992 the 'average reading achievements of students in the age 9, 13 and 17 years' had shown no increase over the previous seventeen years; 'the national trends appear as flat lines'. Yet, he says, 'Had schooling advanced at the same rate as computers have since 1950, the twelve years of kindergarten through [to] senior high school could be accomplished in ten minutes for three cents' (Mann, 1992: 228).

But there *have* been changes, many of them far-reaching, since primary and secondary education became universal in industrialized countries during and after the nineteenth century. The current predictions of radical, deep and pervasive changes to schooling are not simply because of the arrival of the twenty-first century. Rather it is because there are structural and framework changes in progress – new ways of viewing knowledge, new ways of conceiving of planetary systems, new patterns of interactions across the world, new meaning and definitions for the world of work, new approaches to birth control, child-bearing and child-rearing, and powerful new information technology which not only speeds up access to the volume of information, but in many ways supersedes print materials and the traditional techniques of publishing. It is obvious that schools had to adapt, and indeed are already adapting. In the process, however, they may well be forced into remaking themselves into shapes which bear little resemblance to the patterns of the traditional school.

What the emerging school looks like

It is already becoming clear what schools, at least those in the so-called developed countries, will look like as the new century unfolds.

* Schools are becoming self-managing, partly self-funding and are being encouraged to operate as stand-alone enterprises.
* They receive funding from government (and often from several levels of government) on the basis of the fact that they agree to teach the key learning or core areas of skill and knowledge, with appropriately negotiated outcome measures. There is a growing tendency to put a bounty on the head of each enrolled student and the school to be paid an 'education credit' (or voucher) when the child is enrolled. The educational purchasing power of the child is calculated on certain indices of need (Ross and Levacic, 1999).
* Other users-pay revenues are becoming available to the schools, and their money is now being earned and spent in diversifying ways. The premises in which schools operate, for example, are likely to be built or owned by

another business enterprise, and then leased to the educational user or provider. Put simply, more of the school's work will be done in rented space or facilities.

- Schools, both public and private, are tending to select their own staff, and not all of the staff involved with instruction and learning are called teachers. Most of those employed are likely to be on contracts, which are agreements to deliver certain services or to perform certain functions for an agreed price. So the new professionals do not draw salaries as such, but favour project-based employment rather than permanent employment in one school, system, or firm.

- Schools are becoming networked through a rich variety of alliances and interactions. They have formal relationships or compacts with other schools, an extensive set of multi-media connections; and strategic alliances with service agencies. Schools are creating their own actual or quasi-systems which enable them to diminish unproductive competition and threat by co-opting or by co-operating with those vying for the same clients.

- Progressively, the leading schools are global. They build links with overseas providers of learning. They run off-shore campuses.

- And they are accumulating other functions, some of which have not until now been associated with the local school. They provide community facilities (sports halls, theatres, computer centres) for a fee, and raise revenue for themselves by so doing. 'Full-service school centres' are alliances among welfare and community development agencies, community health and private medicine, and recreational agencies. These co-operating agencies adopt a case-mix approach to the school's clients, its students and their families. There is a burgeoning industry in school-based childcare, crèches and out-of-school-hours care; and these are viewed as integral parts of the educating continuum. Many schools are becoming production centres for curriculum and learning materials, or work in conjunction with media outlets, or provide paid consultancies based upon their own staff's expertise.

- Education, especially schooling, is being offered in 'found space' such as the homes of the children and parents; in houses, literally rented; and in facilities which private enterprise builds and leases. 'Home schooling', at least in part, is becoming a major component of education.

As Professor David Hargreaves (1997: 11) of Cambridge University observed:

> Once the myth of a unified [school] system is exploded, then the disintegration of the system to something closer to ... heterogeneity might accelerate .... I believe it will become more difficult over the next 25 years to talk about 'the education system' in the sense of a distinctive, coherent and [state] managed system .... The traditional 'education system' must be replaced by a *polymorphic* educational provision – an infinite variety of multiple forms of teaching and learning.

These developments are already under way, and schools are already changing along these lines. In spite of the appearance of continuity and stability in the way schools operate and the way schooling is delivered, and even if the changes listed above seem radical, they are clearly happening. One factor more powerful than all others is propelling much of the change: namely, costs or (more precisely) value for the dollar allocated to education.

Studies suggest that the dollar allocations for education in real terms have changed little in Western countries since the 1960s; inflation alone accounts for almost all salary increases for teachers in this period; and there are few economies of scale in large school systems. If considerations of funding, costs and value for money are such powerful engines for change, and if there is little more that can be done using the traditional modes of providing schooling, then some new models of schooling are needed which break from the old patterns.

In consequence, we are almost certain to see the acceptance worldwide of the concept of 'education markets' as the basis for planning and practice, with an international trade in education and with some privatized provision of educational services and schooling. Schools will be asked to do things better. They may have to do so within existing resources, or even with fewer but more efficiently used resources.

The cost of providing teachers is an important factor here. Since salaries are the biggest item on any budget, especially education budgets, schools could be forced to become less labour-intensive, with some *instruction* provided by means of sophisticated technology. As teaching becomes more professionalized, schools may use comparatively fewer teachers as we have known them in the past. New categories of 'educator' will develop, the roles will be more widely differentiated and some of the professionals will be much more highly paid. While there may be a demand for more students to be taught to higher performance levels, there could be much less classroom teaching.

So schooling may move towards rapid, tightly targeted, efficient learning – away from universal general education, away from 'developing the whole child', and towards specific, goal-oriented, instrumental learning. It could also become less parochial, moving away from control by local, state or national systems and towards an international exchange of good learning practices and packaged programmes; away from parochialism in curriculum and assessment and towards a kind of educational globalism. The practices of any one school provider will be held up for comparison against the world's best practices.

Not all of these developments are necessarily desirable, and none of them will bring unalloyed good. They are simply trends already in motion. Faced with these kinds of prospects, educators the world over have agonized about how they should plan for the future of schooling. Few see merit in preserving schools like museum-pieces from the past. All realize that schooling is a future-oriented business, since teachers are responsible for preparing young people to be confident, comfortable, and able contributors to a society which is still coming into existence. Ideally, schools should be anticipatory communities, modelling the conditions in the emergent world which young people are about to enter as adults.

But when the United Nations, for its fiftieth year, declared 1995 as the Year of Tolerance, it seemed to be flying in the face of international curricular and policy trends in education. If we judge from school policies internationally, societies appeared to prefer their graduating students to be hard-nosed, earnest and intellectual rather than moral; they would prefer students with mathematical skills (whether they are used to produce weapons of war or effective trade practices); with the ability to read (whether they have the skill of discriminating over whether what they read has any worth); with managerial skills and trading acumen (and not with too many reservations about the dark side of economic policies). Governments appeared to favour rationalism and nationalism, cleverness and cunning rather than the cultivation of too many scruples. 'Useful' subjects seemed to be in favour as the ones which get your country ahead.

Additionally, many of the policies and national plans, especially in the West, looked like a return to the traditional, academic, subject-based curriculum in which mathematics and the hard sciences are most highly favoured. Government after government tried to impose literacy and numeracy testing, competition among schools, rewards for schools with demonstrably good outcomes, the survival of the fittest students, certificates for acquiring useful competencies, a literal trade in education, funding the aspects which breed the skills useful in the world's market-place, and a kind of excellence based on beating your peers. Almost everywhere, it seems, governments agonized about the fact that Japanese students were achieving more highly than their own in mathematics.

Among these policies there was not much enthusiasm for sentiment, human kindness, understanding religious differences, respecting the worth of every person, caring for the globe, being a responsible *global* citizen. Which teachers were rewarded with higher salaries and rapid promotion for teaching these things? For teaching mathematics and science, probably yes. For teaching business studies, perhaps. But tolerance, human worth, care for others, concern for the earth? The best curriculum was deemed to be utilitarian, it seemed, valuable if it is useful.

Those schools policies, it must be admitted, were being driven by economics rather than by the educator profession, and by national rather than local governments. The market economy sponsors competition, beating your opposition, winning, becoming superior to your rivals. Economics talks about self-interest (albeit enlightened), about profits, about survival. Development and expansion imply asking for more; getting things; acquisitiveness; accumulating wealth; becoming rich and often at the expense of others. Global co-operation, doing *without* things, *not* buying things, *not* being a consumer, conserving rather than using up, giving things away, sacrifice and martyrdom, all these sit uneasily with an economic theory which needs a kind of selfishness to make it work.

This view is not shared by the rising generation, and therein lies our hope. When the World Commission on Environment and Development was collecting its evidence for the United Nations between 1983 and 1987, which later emerged as the

Brundtland Report *Our Common Future* (1987), it was confronted by the contrast between the attitudes of the young and those of adults.

> Most of today's decision makers will be dead by the time the planet feels the heavier effects of acid precipitation, global warming, ozone depletion, or widespread desertification and species loss. Most of the young voters of today will be still alive. In the Commission's hearings, it was the young, those who have the most to lose, who were the harshest critics of the planet's present management.
>
> (Brundtland, 1987: 8)

The young generation, at least those among them who are not already alienated, do not have to be convinced about the urgency of treating the earth as a delicately interlocked ecological system which could be lethally wounded by the time they inherit it.

In short, the last two decades of the twentieth century in particular saw a lot of change, a lot of contestation about the aims of schooling, a lot of impositions from interests outside of school, but interests affected by how schools operate and by the kinds of citizens the schools help to produce. Not least has been the debate about what is economically useful, what are the aspirations of individual students, what values underlie the work of schools, what are to be both the tangible and intangible outcomes of schooling, what impacts schools have on the labour market, and about the extent to which schools are responsible for societal well-being.

A story may illustrate the way schools have had to change. A visitor had been watching, fascinated, a skilled lumberjack as he was felling trees in a forest. 'How can you do those things so neatly and expertly?' she asked. 'Well, it's really this axe,' the woodman replied. 'I've had the same one for twenty years. In that time, it has had six new heads and fifteen new handles, but it is still working as well as ever.'

The point of that story is similar to a question posed to me when I became the Chief Education Officer of the school system in Australia's national capital. Canberra High School had been the oldest and most revered government secondary school in the Australian Capital Territory, but it had outgrown its site close to the civic centre. It was therefore moved to a new campus in the suburb of Aranda, to a completely new set of custom-built facilities. After a few years, it had inherited a new generation of students, it had a new Principal and almost all of the staff who had operated from the original site had moved on. The newly established Schools Authority developed new curriculum frameworks, introduced new senior secondary certification, and even changed the structures so that the high schools ceded to senior secondary colleges their Years 11 and 12 students and programmes. To what extent, then, was Canberra High School the same school as the one which had existed downtown? Yet the parents and old scholars spoke of it as though its history was unbroken.

The same question can be asked of schooling in general. Will schools be forced to change so radically, albeit gradually, in the next decade or two that the twenty-first-century school will resemble almost not at all the traditional school inherited from previous decades? That, indeed, is the issue which we address here. This book brings together more than ten years of work on the future of schooling, especially the changes to the nature of schools as they make the transition into the conditions likely to prevail in the early decades of the twenty-first century. The book draws on numbers of papers, conference addresses and talks given in Australia and overseas and also on workshops and R and D exercises. The material has been thoroughly road-tested.

Since the publication of *Education for the Twenty-First Century* (Routledge, 1993) which I co-authored with Dr Richard Slaughter and which has been much cited, I have been under constant pressure to speak and write on the future of schooling and of teaching. Four monographs which I wrote for IARTV and ACEA on this topic have drawn wide attention, namely:

Who are the Teachers of the Future? (IARTV, 1998);
Education for the Third Millennium (IARTV, 1996);
What Is the Next Quantum Leap for School Systems in Australia? (ACEA, 1995);
An Educator Speaks to His Grandchildren: Some Aspects of Schooling in the New World Context (ACEA, 1990).

While I was a Visiting Scholar in the Department of Education at the Aoyama Gakuin University, Shibuya, Tokyo, Japan in October 1998, I was able to coalesce much of this material into a series of formal lectures on the future of schooling. Those lectures have formed the basis for the present work.

This book takes an international perspective, considering the changes likely to occur in the patterns of schooling at the beginning of the twenty-first century, giving particular attention to the structure and nature of the school in the light of the radical changes which have occurred in information technology, in post-industrial economies, and through globalization. It also seems clear that the career of teaching will change and that the work of the professional educator will differ significantly from what were the traditional teaching roles in schools of the twentieth century.

This is a book for anyone concerned about the kind of education which is appropriate for their children who are currently at school. Its purpose is to open the readers' awareness to how profound is the paradigm shift which has occurred both in society and in the way society views its schools. It aims to show that perpetuating many of the traditional patterns of schooling is unwise, and also unfair to young learners. It gives useable advice on how to make the necessary changes in the process of schooling for the future. After this introductory chapter, the book divides into two parts – the first dealing with big picture (or paradigm) changes, the second dealing with the practicalities of the responses schools might make.

There is such avid interest in this topic on the part of teachers and parents in particular, and there has emerged such a fund of wisdom about the 'schools of the future', that it seems appropriate to bring together at least some of the outcomes of this collective search so that they can be used more widely. Our aim is to be both realistic and speculative, never to lose sight of the big picture while attending to detail, to be simultaneously idealistic and practical. If at the end we have helped to change *your* school or have suggested some productive lines for the development of schooling in your area or country, then we will have achieved our purpose.

Part I
The big picture
Why schools are being compelled to change their ways

2 From an old world-view to a new

During the past decade while I was attending conferences, workshops and talks on the future of schooling, I found myself hearing the same things being said over and over again. They were predictions from a wide variety of experts about the trends shaping the world into which this generation of schoolchildren will proceed, and there was a great amount of agreement and common ground. The statistics came from such diverse sources that it is not possible to check them; but if they are even near the mark, collectively they build up a compelling picture about the future in store for the students now at school. Let us imagine, then, that a child who started school this year is telling us about the world in which she will spend all of her life.

'I am the future's child'

Hullo. I am Angelica. I am 5 years old. I really don't have much of a past. In fact, I am the future.

You need to understand what I am learning to believe, how I think about my future, what my world-view is. You and I both want me to be a success in the world which I will enter as an adult and which I will be responsible for. In future days I will admire you for being able to look forward with me and to help me define what I need to learn.

My world is already very different from the one you have grown up in.

On present life expectancy figures, I will live until I am over 80. So I will be alive and well in the 2070s, and my children will live to see the twenty-*second* century. Can you even imagine what the world will be like for them?

Only three of every hundred babies born this year live in developed countries. So wherever I live or work, I will certainly be mixing in a multi-national, multi-cultural and multi-faith setting, and white people could be the ethnic minorities. I will have to think about that when I prepare for a job.

During my lifetime, a planet-wide economic system will operate, controlled not so much by big nations as by big business networks and by regional centres of trade like Singapore, Bangkok, Mexico City, Los Angeles, Tokyo, Buenos Aires and Sydney. By the time I am 30, there will be more people living in Shanghai than there are in the whole of the South Pacific, including Australia, New Zealand and Papua New Guinea.

The Asia/Pacific area will be a strong focus of my world. China already has a population ten times that of Japan, and nearly half a billion Chinese are under the age of 25. The Asian continent (from India to Japan) already accounts for half the world's population. A Hong Kong bank advertises now, 'There are three billion people in Asia. Half of them are under 25. Consider it a growing market.' Those under-25s are my contemporaries. They will be very aggressive in a number of ways, good and bad, over the next few decades.

It will not matter what nationality I have, because my world is smaller, people move about, and most workplaces will be internationalized. My world is likely to be borderless. I will have access to the world economy through credit cards and transnational banks, and it will be easy to travel overseas. I will spend holidays in China, visit South America often, and I will work for periods in Africa. I will probably be employed in an internationally owned firm, and it is likely that in my home we will speak Japanese, Korean, Spanish, English or Chinese as a second language.

In my secondary school courses, we will study the effect on the world's environment of human activity like transport – trucks, aeroplanes, ships, but especially family cars. Every newly developed country wants its own car industry, and every middle-class family wants to own at least one vehicle. Yet car emissions are changing the climate patterns around the world; *our* cars are changing other people's weather.

Half a billion people in Asian countries are middle class like me, and they have the same consumer patterns and the same attitudes as the middle class everywhere else in the world.

By the time I am in my twenties, world oil production will decline because the known stocks of fossil fuel are being exhausted. Power stations as you know them will not last for much longer. After next decade, world demand for petrol will be going up while the production of oil is going down. Where does that leave me?

There will be urgent international action in my lifetime to limit the size of the world's population. When we entered the twenty-first century, there were 6 billion people alive in the world. A hundred years earlier, at the start of the twentieth century, there were just 1.6 billion people on the planet. Almost exactly that number of the present population live in absolute poverty; and only one billion of the world's people can be confident of having three meals a day.

By the time I am 30 years old, world grain production will have become a problem. China alone will need to import around 370 million tonnes of grain annually, yet in 1995 the entire world exports of grain amounted to around 200 million tonnes.

In my lifetime, the world's super-cities could become almost unliveable, the home of only the chronically poor who do not have the personal resources to move out of them. In the 1950s, when my grandmother was born, only two cities in the world, London and New York, had more than 8 million inhabitants, and each was called a megalopolis. In 2015, there will be about thirty-four such cities, half of them in Asia.

Big cities may be dangerous places too, for they are producing dysfunctional societies. They are an inefficient and unequal drain on resources, and they cause some of the world's worst cases of pollution. My generation will have to do something about all of that. If we don't, by about 2020 approximately 90 per cent of the world's population will live in big cities.

When I get to secondary school, the old confrontation between capitalism and Marxism will be largely over, as well as the so-called industrial economy which produced it. The re-aligning of politics and parties is resulting in new political processes and coalitions across the world. Politics, parliaments, and governments will look different from what they are now.

I am told that this year there are in the world 190 million malnourished children under the age of 5; half of them live in South Asia. By the time I am an adult, there will be at least the beginnings of a world-wide social welfare scheme, to which my country will be required to make contributions in money, personnel and facilities. The 'basic human needs' to be the target for everyone in the world include: access to at least primary schooling; access to health care; clean drinking water; satisfactory sanitation; immunization of all children; access to family planning services; universal adult literacy; elimination of severe malnutrition; and radically reducing maternal mortality (death in child-birth).

South America and Southern Africa will soon provide several 'new lions' of world trade. On the other hand, because of soil degradation and desertification produced by human activity, Sub-Saharan Africa will be subject to ethnic wars and struggles for survival, and therefore a world trouble-spot, especially politically as other countries become involved.

Two billion people in my world do not have access to electricity, 65 per cent have no guaranteed supply of clean water, and around 40 per cent struggle to meet *any* kind of water needs. The developed countries have only a fifth of the world's population, but they consume about three-quarters of the world's energy, three-quarters of the world's metal production, and 85 per cent of the world's wood. While they spend about 15 per cent of their budgets on social security at home, they spend only about 0.3 per cent of their GDP on overseas aid. It just can't go on like this. What will happen if all the world demands what my family takes for granted as its right?

Before I was born, global military spending was around one trillion US dollars per annum. That is unacceptable. By the time I leave school, legitimate military and policing activities for the world community will have been taken over by agencies of international co-operation, and peace-keeping forces will be commonplace.

There will also be strong international courts of justice to enforce globally agreed laws.

Environmentally what happens within the borders of one country is no longer solely that country's business. By the time I start work, environmental responsibilities will be enforced internationally. By the time I am 40, the world could be threatened by 'green wars' unless my generation does something to balance up the unequal access to clean water, to good topsoil, to electric power and to food distribution outlets.

While I am in school, and as the result of scientific co-operation like the international genome project, genetic engineering and nanotechnology will eradicate many physical disabilities from the world's population, and will lead to new approaches to food production. Both will be important industries.

Self-programming and artificially intelligent computers will shoulder many of the tasks which are now being done by human beings. I will live in a 'smart home' wired to carry out tasks like electronic shopping, preparation (and delivery) of meals, washing and cleaning, and other household chores.

Human beings are starting to build living platforms in orbit around the earth and will create colonies in space, the developments engineered by means of international co-operation and global consortia.

The sea will concern my generation. More than half the world's population now lives less than a hundred miles from a sea coast. We can't continue to allow sewage, acid sediment, chemicals, fertilizers and toxic spills to pollute the oceans and to poison the sea's creatures. My son will consider becoming a farmer of the sea, because there are now moves to privatize parts of the sea in the same way as people in the past have 'bought' land.

The effects of global warming are already evident. People living in low-lying areas – on some Pacific islands, on large river deltas which are subject to flooding, and on some sea coasts – will try to migrate, often illegally and often in large numbers, to already occupied country above sea level.

Rural industry has already changed. Forty years ago, for example, Australian farmers produced 25 per cent of their country's Gross National Product (GNP) and 95 per cent of its exports. Now it's down to 4 per cent of the GDP, and only 30 per cent of its exports. It employs only 5 per cent of the workforce. The same pattern is evident in other countries.

No wonder there is unemployment around the world, and particularly in developed countries. The jobs are not located where they used to be. So where will they be? The patterns of the industrial economy will have disappeared by the time I start working. In particular, the 9-to-5 working day, the five-day working week, salaried employment based upon hours spent at the workplace, and the regular holidays based upon the seasons (a left-over from the old agrarian economy) will have gone. My work and employment will be based largely upon contracted labour and fixed-term projects for which I will be paid an agreed fee.

The really prosperous nations in my world have small populations and few physical resources. The 'commodities' they trade are non-material, like technical skills, brain-power, and know-how. Singapore is a good example. My richest friends will work with problem-solving skills, problem-identifying skills and in strategic brokerage. They will talk about 'creating value through people'. They will often refer to themselves as knowledge-workers. That's the kind of job I want to have.

Because muscular strength is no longer an important factor in employment – there are machines to lift and move things – women will occupy a large number of the new occupations and senior positions in the world economy. There is already evidence that they can outperform men in these new roles.

When I complete my twelve years of schooling, every one of my classmates will be expected to undertake some form of post-school training – training for a job, training on the job, a vocational qualification of some kind, or a university degree. In-service training, retraining for a different occupation, professional development and continuous study or learning will be facts of life for all my generation throughout all our lives.

Some jobs may be rationed by allowing a person to work at them for only three days a week. Service industries will abound. We will want people to drive and maintain our cars, to manage our homes, to file our income tax returns, and to look after our assets. Tourism and travel collectively are becoming the world's largest industry and globally will employ the largest number of people.

I do not expect to spend all my life in the employment of one company. No company is likely to remain unchanged for that long anyway. For me, 'work' will ebb and flow, and will often be done intensively, in large chunks in a short period of time. I will manage my own career, and I will not leave it to a company or an organization to do it for me. I may change jobs or relocate seventeen or so times during my working life, and at least three of those changes will be major ones. My husband and I will have to juggle jobs and careers, perhaps in different locations.

My generation is not keen to have many babies either. In developed countries, only three women in every five between the ages of 25 and 35 have dependent children; ten years ago, about three-quarters of that group were mothers. And it is mainly the rich who do not want children. The homes with high incomes average less than one child per household; low-income households have nearly three times as many children as the rich do. My generation will have to be concerned about the effect that has on the nature of community.

Although we will have rediscovered the spiritual and the transcendental, and the world will be 're-enchanted', we will be wary of those people who take fixed and exclusivist positions. Fundamentalists of any persuasion (political and religious) will be treated as threats to our security.

In a world like this, it is important for me to know what I stand for. I will look to my school to help me form my values and decide on my system of beliefs. I have to be careful about what I believe and what I take for granted without thinking. I am not sure where my mother and father picked up their beliefs and attitudes. Our family doesn't go to church, tabernacle or temple any more. There is not much religion in my home. I'll have to be more systematic and deliberate about it because of the complex world I will function in.

I am uneasy about changes in families. I am told there is a 40 per cent chance that Mum and Dad will divorce and remarry while I am still at school. I may not grow up with my natural brother or with both my natural parents. I will not know my grandparents very well because our family will move home so often. Many children of my age are growing up in one-parent families.

I already learn as much from television as I do from school. I spend more time with TV than I do with my teachers. I watch each year about 1,400 hours of TV and see 22,000 commercials which tell me what I should value, what I should eat and what sort of behaviour is acceptable. During my time as a student, then, attempts will be made to reconcile TV viewing and education, even to blur the boundaries between them.

Some of my classmates have already spent more time in child-care (12,500 hours) than they will spend in twelve years of schooling. More than half of our mothers work full-time. The rate has doubled over the past ten years.

Because about 85 per cent of the world's output of videos, films, CDs and TV programmes comes from the United States, my classmates and I are unobtrusively absorbing American culture and values. I know that much of it is driven by commercialism and is often not very ennobling. It is not surprising that there is resistance from Asian countries about American and European frames of reference.

By the time I am in my twenties, Chinese and Indians will make up more than half the population of the world. The 'overseas Chinese' and the 'overseas Indians' will strongly influence and may even control the world's networking webs.

By far the world's largest Muslim country is Indonesia, with a population of over 220 million – larger than that of Japan and Russia but still less than India's. I will have to learn about Islam at school. And because the 'tigers of Asia' are largely Confucian economies, I will be taught in primary school about those characteristics of Confucian societies which produce economic success and community cohesion. A lot of the older textbooks used around the world were Eurocentric in their thinking and are out-of-date. My schooling must teach me about living comfortably in a multi-cultural, multi-national, multi-faith world.

The way we use computers is gently refashioning what my generation thinks about knowledge – what it is, how it is accessed, how knowledge is produced, who owns it. 'Finding out about things' is taking on new meanings and methods for us. I will do a lot of my learning in non-school locations with my lap-top computer. I am connected to the Internet, I have my own e-mail address, and some of my teachers will be located overseas. At school, we communicate every week with schoolchildren in other countries.

Computers are changing the way my schooling is arranged. We have access to an enormous amount of information, and we can consult almost any library and government department in the world. We can find out things through the computer that even our teachers know little about. So we have a different view about knowledge and studying.

The old way of learning – by steps and stages, by the sequencing of learning into one best path, by the traditional, scientific approaches, by having the curriculum divided neatly into subjects – is already passing. Knowledge for me is a web of interconnections where I access interesting information from many angles. Words like 'subjects', 'classes', 'grades' and 'promotion' do not make much sense to me. Schools will not be organized that way by the time I leave primary education.

I will study Shakespeare, Wordsworth and Milton, some Buddhist texts from India, the Greek tragedies, some of the novels from South Korea, the history of China and the politics of South America. Do you know what an international curriculum looks like, and how it can be taught?

Most of the stories I know about have come from films or television or videos. I do not read a lot of storybooks. I am discouraged in many incidental ways from spending time with books. I do not write nearly as much as my mother and father do.

I will not sit for 'final examinations' at the end of my last year at school. That seems a rather silly notion to me. My performance as a student will be routinely checked against national and international benchmarks throughout my schooling. I can choose my assessments and which certificates I present for. The really good universities in the world are all international, and are not restricted by the country they happen to be located within. I want to study in a university or college like that.

There will be a users-pay approach to a lot of education. My mother and father will have to consider what kind of an education they are willing to buy for me. There is already a world trade in good educational practices.

My school will have comparatively fewer teachers than yours had, but they will be better paid and more highly qualified. My school will hire more adults (technical, computing, tutoring, evaluating) to supplement our school work, and some of my teaching will be done by sophisticated technological devices.

My school says I need to be a global citizen. I know what that means. I hope you do.

My views about the planet and the universe are probably very different from yours. To me the planet is not a machine. It is alive. It is a single, complex, living organism, and I have to nurture its health and growth. That fact has changed the way my family and I live, it influences local and world politics, it is changing my system of beliefs and my values, it influences what I buy, sell, and eat, and it is a strong factor in my choice of occupation and where we choose to live.

All these things I have talked about are the raw materials I use to weave my life together. I want to be hopeful and happy and comfortable about my future. It doesn't help me if adults keep telling me gloomy things about the future. Education is all about hope, isn't it? Your schooling was.

Most of all, I want to be wise over what to believe about me and my world. I want to know what the wisest people on earth believe. I want to know how to be a success with my life. I want the world to be a beautiful place for *my* grand-children. My school-teachers are very important to me because they tell me how to deal with the future – the long, long future.

So do you know what to teach me? Do you know what I need to learn? And do you know *how* to teach me? Are you confident that you can design a curriculum which will equip me to live in my world?

My name is Angelica. I am 5 years old. And I am sitting in one of your classrooms today.

The power of world-views and belief systems

What becomes obvious from this description of Angelica's future is that her daily life – made up of things like her life-style, her decision-making structures, her choices of occupation and marriage partner – are founded on how she views her world, on the beliefs and basic assumptions she has formed. *Every human being on earth has a world-view and a set of beliefs*. When a group of people share common elements of their world-view, when they agree about 'the way the world is', then they create a culture. Some views are shared widely across the world and out of those universally held assumptions develops a period in history – the Renaissance, the Industrial Revolution, the post-modern world. In short, world-views and belief systems are basic to living; and they also change.

Peter Drucker has written that somewhere in the middle 1970s the world moved out of the old mindset which had been formed from the Industrial Revolution, and into a post-industrial world, a new landscape where the patterns of thinking and acting are radically different from what they were (Drucker, 1989: 3). If that is so, then the entire population of students now in primary school, secondary school and university have lived the whole of their lives in the period when that new world-view was forming. It is the agenda for contemporary education.

A lot has been said about a curriculum consisting of knowledge and the learning of skills which are *useful* – for the government and society as much as for individual students. Instrumentalism has produced the competencies movement; it has affected curriculum content, producing concepts like 'key learning areas', as though learning is not legitimate unless it is information-driven and packaged into traditional subjects. It has produced the National Curriculum movement, core learnings which every citizen should acquire. It has driven the outcomes approach to schooling, a concentration on tests, the publication of school-by-school results and 'league tables'. These are all control devices to force schools to concentrate on material and utilitarian outcomes, and some of them can be backward-looking.

But all of us, and especially parents, know that quality education involves far more than just learning useful things. Schools become famous when they are also able to provide great teaching, to foster the magic of learning, and to build in young learners a profound sense of responsibility, and wonder about the cosmos. Parents will go to great lengths – personally, financially, geographically – to place their children with educators who are inspiring, who are creative persons, who are aware of the transcendent, who are capable of being stunned by wonder, fascination, dread, who can handle what Rudolf Otto calls 'a clear overplus of meaning' (Otto, 1950). Those teachers provide an education which transforms the learner.

At least three aspects of transformational learning are important factors determining the future of schools and in particular the nature of Angelica's schooling: developing a reliable, enabling belief system; becoming a responsible citizen (which implies citizenship of the world and not merely of a single country); and growing a personal life-story which defines who you are and where your life is going. To paraphrase American Express, Angelica, you mustn't leave school without them.

Learning involves developing a set of enabling beliefs

Every human being believes things. Beliefs are those fundamental, taken-for-granted assumptions which undergird and govern our actions, our thinking, and our living. People may not know how they developed their beliefs, and some of their beliefs can be flawed, silly, inadequate and even dangerous. But everyone has them nonetheless.

Beliefs give us the framework to interpret the world. We also know that beliefs produce real outcomes, because they determine in a thousand incidental ways whether we act in this way rather than that, whether we go to this place rather than to another, whether we give priority to these thoughts and actions rather than to those. By our choices, we bring into existence the very things we believe in!

Furthermore, each of us chooses our beliefs, and then we constantly refine and change them throughout our life. Sadly, we often let others manipulate our convictions about the world. For example, we allow ourselves to believe the arguments of politicians, or we copy what our heroes say or do, we accept what the newspaper and television editors select as the news stories for the day, or we let other people control the agenda of our conversations, and define for us what is and is not important. Learning how to make judgements, how to use discretion, and how to sift for accuracy what we are told by others are important survival skills acquired at school.

Education, then, must concern itself with belief formation. Among other things, it develops the critical faculties, it gives students the methodologies for research and for making judgements, it presents data and information for analysis and understanding. Educators are responsible for developing in their students wisdom like that, and for showing their students how they come to believe what they believe, and how those beliefs impregnate their own daily living (Beare and Slaughter, 1993). Developing beliefs, forming values and fostering constructive attitudes permeates the entire fabric of educating and learning; and is at the heart of any worthy school. Great schools are quite explicit about it. Their 'mission statement' usually expresses their values stance.

Education involves learning to become responsible citizens

Human beings also live in communities. Great schools prepare every one of their students to play a constructive and contributing role in society and for society. It is not an easy lesson to learn because society and 'the powers that be' colonize our thinking and our beliefs in some insidious ways. Wink (1992: 54) gives the following example:

Modern capitalism ... has made wealth the highest value. Our entire social system has become an 'economy'; no earlier society would have characterized itself thus. Profit is the highest social good. Consumerism has become the only universally available mode of participation in modern society. The work ethic has been replaced by the consumption ethic, the cathedral by the skyscraper, the hero by the billionaire, the saint by the executive, religion by ideology.

In just such a way society captures every one of us in its web of meanings. The more international we become, and the more the economies of the world interlock, the more the whole world could become captive to one gigantic hegemony.

Each student, then, will find herself linked within political, intellectual, social and international frameworks which circumscribe her, put demands upon her, and create the boundaries within which she lives her life. Just because she lives in a human planetary society, she is caught up in a minefield of options, responsibilities, duties and compromises. She is communally responsible and morally compromised, simultaneously. A great school knows about this kind of moral incarceration and tries to educate its students about how to cope with being a responsible citizen of the world.

Every student lives out a story, a personal history with meanings

Learning who we are and where we fit into the cosmic order begins in early childhood and is particularly important during puberty, adolescence and early adulthood. Strong cultures have ceremonial rites of passage associated with the stages of growth so that by adulthood each person knows the culture well and where he or she belongs within it. To help that process of induction, every culture from the earliest days of civilization until the present has produced stories, myths, sagas, heroes and heroines to define exactly what makes that culture distinctive. To use the technical term, there is a mythology at work in every society. The fund is always being added to (Campbell, 1972, 1973; Eliade, 1987).

The process of building meanings is not only collective; it is also personal. Every *person* has an individual set of belief-artefacts too. We may not like what makes up our own set of myths, legends, heroes, heroines and symbols, but we have them nonetheless. They are necessary tools. When human beings cannot find the words to convey deep meaning, to talk about the intangible and the noble, or to cope with inexpressible wonder, they have always used the ancient device of inventing stories. Great stories and anecdotes tend to acquire overlays of meaning; some develop into epics; the characters in some of them assume the larger-than-life status of heroes, heroines, goddesses and demigods; and the events in which those characters engage become symbolical of cosmic struggles. Sometimes the stories are based upon actual events to which added significances are attached. Sometimes the stories are invented for the purpose (Yungblut, 1992). Those stories become mythic, part of the mythology. The essential characteristic about a myth is that while the story itself may be fact, based on fact, or fiction, invented for the purpose out of one's imagination, the story's meaning is always *true* for the teller (Campbell, 1988).

My primary schooling was full of stories. Australia was still essentially a colonial society at that time, and the school curriculum tended to copy what was provided in England. We learnt many of the sagas of empire – stories like those of the African explorers Stanley and Livingstone; of General Gordon at Khartoum; of Captain Cook holing his ship on the Great Barrier Reef, and of his being speared to death in the Sandwich Islands; we learnt about Scott of the Antarctic and of Captain Oates who walked out of the tent into a blizzard so that his companions would not be handicapped by his sickness in their dash for safety. The primary school readers carried stories about the Hobjahs, about Hansel and Gretel, about the Three Billy-Goats Gruff, about the Greek legends like the Wooden Horse of Troy, Ulysses and the Sirens, the one-eyed giant Polyphemus, about Julius Caesar crossing the Rubicon. These were European or very British, but at least in that era the important things like love of country, the cultivating of altruism, values formation, the honouring of virtue and respect for others were not left to chance. There was a stock of stories, a set of gods and heroes, a locker-full of images, myths and legends which were held in common and from which we could weave common life meanings. Every viable culture creates its own myths, and every good school teaches its children about them. Most countries have used the common school to pass on the cultural meanings embedded in their operating mythologies.

In an interconnected world, however, with an information super-highway and ever-present television, there is a danger that a single monoculture, largely manufactured in America by producers dominated by a profit motive, will be superimposed across the world. TV sitcoms and newscasts have the power to become the common carriers of meaning. Teachers and parents in particular must be aware of what myths are being invented in their country about their country, what myths they are allowing to be formed in school, and what personal funds of stories children have from which they can weave their own meanings about their world, and more importantly about themselves. Whatever (in their view) makes them feel distinctive will show up in the stories children listen to and tell, and especially about themselves. Young people need to culti-vate the skills to compose their own stories, and especially the 'story of my life'.

To summarize, then, schools do not merely teach useful information or train skills, and it is unlikely that they will ever be allowed to do only that. Much of schooling and a significant part of any curriculum is about intangibles, about dealing with the depths from which we generate our life purposes and aspira-tions. An important part of schooling concerns the formation of constructive and systematic beliefs, the acceptance of social responsibility for the inter-twined and complex task that it is, and the development of stories which convey deep meanings about who we are. With these skills, every student, every Angelica in the world, has to face the emerging world, the world-about-to-be.

Schooling, then, deals with personal formation, belief construction, developing a world-view, and with culture transmission, over and above the acquiring of useful knowledge and enabling skills. Generally speaking, learning of this kind cannot be allowed to become haphazard and will always require the involvement of sensitive and trained adults – parents and professional educators in particular – to oversee the process and to keep it systematic, coherent, and wise. Any plan for schooling of the future must start with a recognition of the importance of a child's world-views and belief systems, and of schooling's responsibility for their systematic development, authentically and without dogmatism or indoctrination.

3 From a society of factories to a society of knowledge workers

To design schools and schooling to meet Angelica's needs expressed in Chapter 2, we must ask what are the significant differences between the way schooling has been provided in the past and the model for schooling which is appropriate in the twenty-first century. That model will be shaped by bigger issues, principally by questions relating to how people conceive of their world and the belief systems they share. Is there a coherent unifying way we can depict the life-space which Angelica is to inherit as an adult? In fact there is.

We already know much about the world-view which will dominate thinking into the early decades of the twenty-first century (see, for example, Brundtland, 1987; Drexler, 1986; Harman, 1988; Ohmae, 1990; Reich, 1992; Kim and Dator, 1994; Zohar and Marshall, 1994) and some of those aspects are the subject of this and the next chapter. The picture is not static, however, and trend lines change. To take a well-known source, in 1982 John Naisbitt wrote *Megatrends: Ten New Directions Transforming Our Lives*, a book widely read, much quoted and often consulted as a basis for planning. Eight years later in 1990 he and his wife wrote a sequel, *Megatrends 2000*, in which they identify ten different trends. They followed with *Megatrends for Women* (Aburdene and Naisbitt, 1993), then *The Global Paradox* (Naisbitt, 1994), and in 1995 *Megatrends Asia: The Eight Asian Megatrends that are Changing the World*. Rather than simplifying the picture, then, the Naisbitts had expanded their list to include two or three dozen megatrends.

On the other hand, some trends are so firmly established that they deliver the inevitable and the predictable. Peter Drucker wrote in 1969 in *The Age of Discontinuity* that had Rip Van Winkle been an economist and had he gone to sleep in 1913, he might have awakened in the mid-1960s to find the world much as he had predicted it would be, in spite of the intervention of two world wars, the Great Depression and widespread industrialization. The world's economic growth continued 'largely along the lines that had been well and truly laid down in those distant days by our grandparents and great-grandparents', said Drucker (1969: 9).

While some predictions stand up better than others, the interesting thing about them all is this. Human beings everywhere tend to put them into picture-language, favouring some metaphors over others in making their explanations about important things. The same picture-language, used over and over again, unconsciously creates frameworks for our thinking and behaviours. Recurring imagery tends to structure what we do, how and what we plan, and how we explain the results. The emotive colour of our favourite words influences our feelings and attitudes. The whole imagery package may channel our assumptions and what we take for granted without thinking about it.

It is also not always recognized that theories, not least our scientific theories, are based upon recurrent metaphors and analogies. For example, for about three hundred years people likened the earth to a machine, or more precisely to a watch – it is inanimate, it works according to certain immutable physical laws, it is an object. The whole planet was deemed to be a thing, to be exploited; and not viewed as a living organism which could die if exploited unwisely and which needed to be nurtured. The machine metaphor led to some remarkable developments, but it also allowed human beings to despoil the planet of which they are a part, to kill off species, to destroy some of the planet's life-support systems, even to threaten the earth's continuing existence. When you attune your ear to the way people talk, especially about the earth, about their society, and about organizations like schools, their recurrent imagery will tell you how they are picturing what is going on and what are their 'working beliefs' (Kaye, 1996: 97–104).

It becomes evident immediately that society, its institutions, and its formal processes tend to conform with the prevailing imagery which is embodied in the *economy* and which is used to explain the economy's operation. At any time in history, there exists a favoured metaphor, almost a one-best-way explanation, to describe how society works. Almost universally, the imagery in that explanation is based on how the majority of people earn their incomes; it determines how society is structured and in particular how schools (which prepare children for life in that society) are operated. The explanatory pattern is repeated across society and becomes what Toffler describes as 'the architecture of civilization', itself a vivid image (Toffler, 1981: 35).

There is growing, widespread agreement that many developed countries are undergoing a major transformation of world-view to rival what occurred when the industrial economy replaced the agrarian, rural, pre-industrial economy. Accompanying that shift is a major change to the explanatory pattern. It has been described as the transition to the post-industrial economy, or to the post-modern state, to the communication age, to the global society. The new world-view and its allied explanations are likely to be widespread across the planet by the early years of the new century.

It would be surprising, then, if the schools which served the *pre-industrial* society did not differ fundamentally from the kind of schools which grew up as a result of the *Industrial* Revolution – and they were. In the same way, the schools in the *post-industrial* economies of the developed world are substantially different in style from the schools which served a society in which manufacturing industry produced wealth and employed most of the people. Schools in the information-rich, internationalized communities of the new century, where information-workers are the newly rich, will differ – will *need* to differ – in several fundamental ways from the schools which people were familiar with in the late stages of the twentieth century.

There are several major consequences to be noted about these major transitions in history, particularly for schooling. First, in each mega-shift, vestiges of the past model remain within the new, and often cause serious dislocations and dissonances as a result. Second, there is always, and especially among parents, a kind of nostalgia for the schooling which seemed to serve them so well when they were young but which belongs now to an outmoded paradigm. To wish those patterns of the past on the students of the present can be cruel and costly for the learning child. Third, when changes elsewhere in society are so rapid, far-reaching and tumultuous and cause such personal anxieties, people long for some familiar conventions to remain as havens of calm and stability. Schools, the guardians of their children and the institutions which impinge through their children on their hopes and feelings, are the institutions to which adults look for assurance, certainty and continuity. And fourth, at those times when the basic assumptions underlying society's functioning undergo the kind of deep-rooted transformation which is labelled a paradigm (or framework) shift, there is always vigorous resistance to those changes from many quarters and interest groups, for the new seems to challenge and perhaps replace the social order which put them at the top of the tree.

Changes to schools and schooling, then, are always accompanied by deep resistances – from conservatives and traditionalists, from the insecure and the threatened, and often from decision-makers whose policy environment is undisciplined, contested and ill-defined. In these circumstances, it is essential to understand the big picture and to know what is driving the changes. Without those theoretical understandings, it is impossible either to make reliable predictions or to lay sensible plans which have a chance of survival.

So it is wise to set out as simply and as coherently as we can exactly what the paradigm changes are which have overtaken schooling. What imagery, held over from a past era, is now dysfunctional and holding schools back from making therapeutic adaptations? Can we assemble in one place the most important factors which are influencing the shape of schooling for the new century?

We attempt such a synthesis in the rest of this chapter and in the following two, with the expectation that doing so will give us a set of design features which can guide future planning. Then in Part Two of this book, we turn our attention to some of the particular and practical implications for a school. The first exercise, then, is to make explicit the essential differences between the pre-industrial, industrial, and post-industrial models of schooling.

Pre-industrial patterns of schooling

Before the onset of industrialization – it has been called the pre-industrial or agrarian society – a large proportion of the population lived close to the land, usually in country towns or villages, and were engaged in occupations associated with pastoral and agricultural industries. There were few large cities, and they existed for commercial, financial, military and governmental purposes. Those who belonged to the agrarian society knew at first hand about the power of nature and the seasons, and how human affairs are at the mercy of the elements. Their daily work patterns were governed by weather and seasons. People shared an affinity and interdependence with animals and birds which is missing from modern societies. The agrarian society would not use a machine image to explain how the world works.

The influence of the Church and religion was strong. Rulers, princes, kings and feudal monarchs were respected, for society was hierarchically bound, as though there was a predetermined order for ruling the earth. In Elizabethan England, for example, the 'divine right of kings' and the class system were accepted as ordained parts of the cosmic order. In the class-bound society which resulted, those who owned land, often by inheritance, were considered the rich upper class. They were wealthy both in that they owned property and in their power to control the work of others. The arts and letters flourished among those landed rich and only among them, for they alone had the leisure and the money for these pastimes. The upper class were also the patrons of social order, and came to be regarded – and to think of themselves – as the born-to-rule.

In such a society, formal education was a privilege for the few. Education was openly elitist because it was privately funded and available only to those who could afford it. Education and schooling, being the preserve of the rich, dealt with the intellectual pursuits to which they alone had access, like litera-ture, languages (especially the classics – Latin and Greek, 'grammar', in fact), history, the arts, philosophy, theology. The education associated with the upper classes eschewed any connection with manual occupations; hand-labour was for the workers, the serfs, the employed; and preparation for those occupations was regarded not as 'education' but as 'training'. Education was about refine-ment; and it was called 'liberal' for it freed the mind and the intellect. It gave rise to the idea that 'academic subjects' are somehow superior to the technical and that 'grammar schools' are deliberately elitist and upper class. Those ideas about education still persist today, even though both the pre-industrial age and the industrial age which supplanted it have both passed. We still tend to asso-ciate some aspects and kinds of schooling with the upper class, with elitism, and with private school education.

An organization in that society, such as a school, naturally borrowed its shape and style from the dominant extant models. Three in particular were used as the models, namely the monastery, the army and the feudal state, and they all have a common mode of organization. The monastery was a place of learning and a natural pattern for the school. There is a superior or abbot called a Principal. The learning children are regarded as novices or catechu-mens. There is a curriculum like a catechism, a body of truth which has to be studied and learnt, some of it by rote. These schools with roots in antiquity insist that the learners wear uniforms resembling the habits worn by monks.

Discipline is fundamental to the monastic form of schooling, with obedience to authority, conformity to good behaviour, and both punishment and penance for infractions as standard elements in the raising of the young novitiates. The academic gown, still worn as ceremonial garb by some teachers and even while they teach in classrooms, is of course derived from the monastic's habit, with the academic hood originally a monk's cowl. With various degrees of severity, many of these characteristics have been kept in place in some of the elite or grammar schools around the world even today. They are like living fossils surviving from an earlier era.

The same could be said of the army analogy, although here it is the feudal (rather than the modern) army which provides the pattern. The idea of knights, chivalry and allegiance to both aristocracy and feudal lords is endemic to the descriptions of some schools. Many schools retain the livery of feudalism – the school shield, embossed with emblems and heraldic crests; a Latin motto; schools hymns or songs; and the regalia of knights and ladies of the realm reflected in the school uniform. The academic 'intellectual' subjects are still favoured as genteel and courtly activity, the mind favoured above dexterity with hand, limb or eye, the practical and technical included only with great reluctance and as though they are somewhat beneath the consideration of the clever. The school is encouraged to operate like a tiny fiefdom (and fees, a word derived from 'fief', are indeed paid). Sporting contests, the 'houses' system, class captains and prefects, and various scholastic ceremonials and assemblies still preserve ideas of the leisure class and a hierarchical society protected by the personal army of the chief. Service to king, country, God and Church are preached as social duties and made the basis for civic and personal responsibility.

In designing schools for the new century, it is prudent to recognize these vestigial, pre-industrial notions about schools for what they are. It may be quite inappropriate and socially dysfunctional to let obsolete ideas about learning based on these concepts continue unchallenged. For example, pre-industrial education has given rise to many of the images we still associate with superior schooling, although we are now inclined to use terms like 'excellence' to describe them. The idea of 'grammar schools' may be still implied even if the title is never used. School buildings and grounds can be made to look like the homes of the landed rich, set in wide, green parks or estates. Many existing (usually private) schools are housed in original buildings which resembled (or even were) the gracious manor houses of the rich.

A compatible cluster of images like this inherited from the society before factories, and which the wealthy, the well-to-do, the upper class and the newly rich strive to preserve in modern schooling, actually may get in the way of good planning and frustrate the development of new forms and more effective models. A lot of the ideas and conventions are unwanted baggage, not only deadweight but unnecessarily costly. One of the first jobs of the educational planner is to debunk or jettison outmoded, taken-for-granted imagery from a previous age which could frustrate an adequate education for a society which functions on quite different premises. Put simply, don't allow that imagery to be used! Replace it!

Production-line schooling

The same must be done with the schooling practices which grew out of the Industrial Revolution and which brought another set of images and symbols into play. Since the seventeenth century, industrialization has come to dominate not only the economies of Europe and North America but the social lives in those countries as well. A cluster of technological advances flowed from the Scientific Enlightenment: the discoveries of scientists like Copernicus, Galileo and Isaac Newton; William Harvey's discovery about the circulation of the blood; the internal combustion engine; the bridge-building technology like that of Brunel; Henry Ford's automobiles and the production line; and the empires of the steel kings like Andrew Carnegie and the Rockefellers. Factory production and the new wealth which came with it changed societies in fundamental ways which could never have been imagined by those who lived in pre-industrial times.

The large-scale manufacturing and employment patterns which were born with the Industrial Revolution were made possible largely by the invention of the steam engine, the internal combustion engine and electricity – by mechanized power, in fact. The crafts of the village were literally manu-facturing, which means in its Latin derivative 'made by hand'. They could now be broken down into their component parts and processes, mechanized and engineered, systematized by experts, put on a conveyor belt, and each part of the production of goods put in the hands of process workers. The production line – the technology for the mass production of commodities – was a huge breakthrough which transformed both work and the patterns of living in society.

To be able to operate at all, the new industrial society required a degree of literacy and basic education in all its production workers, and hence universal elementary schooling arrived. Because it had become a public necessity that no one should miss out, governments made such schooling compulsory, in effect overruling any parents who might want to withhold their children's right to a formal education. Children are cheap labour, and in agrarian communities they could contribute to the family's income by helping their parents on the farm. Becoming a functional citizen in an *industrial* economy, however, required the learning of a consistent set of knowledge and the acquisition of certain basic competencies. (Literacy and numeracy are still referred to as 'basic skills'.) Most of the arguments to justify a common, core or national curriculum, or common 'key learning areas', or compulsory attendance are still the classic ones used at the onset of the Industrial Revolution.

It is important to underline this point. In an agrarian community, the village school is part and parcel of the village culture and central to it. That is still the case in rural communities, and underlies the local outrage when a country school is closed; for to remove the school in large part spells the demise of the country town. The 'common school' builds local identity and a shared culture.

Industrialization can also destroy a sense of community by causing a migration of population, by forming large congregations of people in cities and suburbs, and by coalescing what were local village communities into a nation-state. Wherever industrialization has occurred in the world, larger nation-states form. Every nation-state is then confronted with the necessity to create social cohesion, a common culture (usually incorporating a common language) being the glue to hold the nation together. It has become a universal device for the common school to be made the carrier and nurturer of the common culture. The corollary (and a symptom) is the creation of a national curriculum or something like a set of national goals for schooling.

The big factory, the big corporation which supported it, and big government which regulated the new wealth produced an important new artefact, the large-scale organization, and with it a one-best-way form of management called bureaucracy. Bureaucracy and industrialization grew up together, the one patterned on the other. It is important to understand this connection, for as the world has moved into a post-industrial era in which manufacturing loses its dominance in the economy and the job market, post-bureaucratic organizational forms just as surely develop which overrun or outstrip the bureaucracies at their own game. In the new world order, big government instrumentalities (like education departments) and big, hierarchically bound schools are in the process of unravelling.

The big city is also a product of the Industrial Revolution. Because the people who worked in factories had to be clustered in dormitory suburbs around the places of production, the country's population tended to migrate from the country to the cities. Wherever in the world we find newly industrialized countries (the NICs), there we find burgeoning cities. Some are now called supercities and they have become one of the greatest problems confronting the world today. They are among the planet's worst polluters. They have produced a spate of social problems which would never have emerged in the smaller, pre-industrial villages where everyone knew each other as individuals. The village gave a person multiple associations in the one geographical area; your extended family lived there, you went to church there, you played sport in or supported a local team, you shopped for household food and goods in local businesses. Your local area elected local politicians who had a defined and cohesive community to represent.

The large city exploded all of that. It separated home from work. It dispersed what had been neighbourhoods; indeed it meant that people do not necessarily identify with 'their next-door neighbours'. It has made obsolescent a set of local institutions like sporting teams, churches, shops, banks, political electorates. In many respects it destroyed the rationale for the 'local school'. The post-industrial economy, and especially the information revolution, will undermine the local school even further.

Widespread industrialization also changed the way people thought about money. The village or town markets were one step removed from straight bartering and exchange, but they were now replaced by national and international economies, still called (rather quaintly) the international market-place. Money was now one of the commodities produced by business, and in that context the term 'wealth production' was used – as though money itself was now coming off the conveyor belts of industry. A new wealthy class arose, the so called *nouveau riche*, the captains of industry, which by and large meant manufacturing industry. What were once artisan-created country crafts were now mass-produced in a factory and on a conveyor belt.

Not unexpectedly, the newly rich began to demand the same kinds of privilege the rich-by-inheritance from the agrarian society had once enjoyed, and in terms of education *that* meant the creation of a hierarchy of schools. Between the two world wars, for example, British secondary education divided into grammar schools, technical schools and modern schools, in that order of prestige. The same pecking order has been operating for decades among the older universities, the more recently established red-brick universities, institutes of technology, technical colleges and colleges of further education. Divisions along those lines have become liabilities, disabilities in fact, for educational planning. They have inhibited, for example, cross-crediting, and created fallacious boundaries between vocational, professional and liberal studies.

From the early 1800s, then, Europe, North America and their colonies invented mass education too. Production-line education arrived, in both the literal and the metaphorical sense. When the state began to provide schooling, it was predominantly for the masses, for those who in the past did not have access to the elitist provisions for education – which meant the secondary and tertiary levels. And that distinction has prevailed, unhappily. Private schools still cater for the rich, the intellectual and the academic, for the modern equivalent of the upper class (or the upper 'middle class'), for the born-to-rule (the professional and managerial class) and for the landed rich, for those with new or old wealth. In the industrial economy, 'property' now means more than real estate. *Public* schools, on the other hand, cater for the general populace. Private schools still tend to be situated on large, green estates and in grand buildings, whereas the public schools are urban places, and are modelled on factories, physically as well as scholastically.

The private school is, as we have seen, often still conceived of as a closed community like the pre-industrial village, essentially monastic or feudal; and still based on authority and hierarchy. The underlying model for the public school, on the other hand, was essentially industrial, urban (or more literally suburban), and large. High schools anywhere in the world still operate like city (rather than rural) schools. Their size is still a matter for debate. As in factories, unions have flourished in state schools, but much less so in private schools. To control and administer the state schools, large-scale organizations called education departments were developed; both the large schools and the large departments were run along the lines of the large-scale bureaucracies which ran factory production. The same terms were used, the same ideas, the same control devices, the same framework of analogies and metaphors. It is time now to discard much of that vocabulary, as well as the practices which go with it.

A package of reforms came with those metaphors, as manufacturing and the industrial economy grew strongly between the two world wars. Secondary education was no longer the preserve of the rich and became available in state high schools, funded and run by government. Vocational streams were added to secondary school curricula, apprenticeships expanded in number, technical education became an entity in its own right, and technical high schools were invented. Private grammar schools continued to scorn anything technical. After the Second World War, 'secondary education for all' (universal secondary education) became accepted, university and post-secondary education was made more widely accessible in a way not experienced between the wars, it became available on the basis of academic ability rather than on the ability to pay, and there was growing emphasis in many occupations on gaining a formal credential and the possession of prior (pre-service) training before a person was allowed to practise. Schooling became part of the full-blown, sophisticated, industrially based economy.

Finally, and perhaps of most concern, the content of schooling, the curriculum itself, became modelled on the factory metaphor of the production line. Children were divided into year groups; knowledge was subdivided into subjects; teachers became specialists and credentialled (literally certificated like tradespersons) and ordered into hierarchies; the students were controlled in class groups or batches, moving in linear progression through graded curricula, from easy to more complex, from lower grades to higher grades, 'promoted' (as are workers in factories) up the steps until they graduate at Year 12. There they were checked to see if they conform with societal standards, classified with a road-worthiness certificate called matriculation, awarded a registration certificate, and then let loose on the thoroughfares of the community. It is the factory-production metaphor applied to schooling. Even the private schools adopted the imagery. In an industrial society, they could hardly do otherwise.

It needs to be acknowledged, then, that the model of the primary and secondary schools which came into existence with an education which was universal and compulsory is not only an outgrowth of industrialization but that it adopted the industrial pattern and applied it to learning. The underlying model for its organization was also bureaucratic, conforming with the best, extant model for managing the huge, conformist system which guaranteed a similar level of proficiency in all the 'products' of schooling. In short, the school of the late twentieth century is the result of industrialization and urbanization. It is urban, not rural, in almost every aspect of its orientations.

The transformation stemming from the industrial analogy was not limited to schools. As Toffler points out in *The Third Wave* (1981), the same pattern took over everywhere – in railroads and transport; in the invention of the post office and mass-produced newspapers; in 'the music industry' and theatre; with prisons, hospitals and welfare systems; with the emergence of the emporium, 'department stores' and then the 'supermarket'. A host of voluntary organizations took the same shape – churches, political parties, trade unions, libraries, recreational groups, chambers of commerce. There was a common architecture for society's amenities.

> In ... country after country, social inventions, believing the factory to be the most advanced and efficient agency for production, tried to embody its principles in other organizations as well. Schools, hospitals, prisons, government bureaucracies, and other organizations thus took on many of the characteristics of the factory – its division of labour, its hierarchical structure and its metallic impersonality.
>
> (Toffler, 1981: 45)

So throughout society, and embedded in shops, businesses, communal life and career patterns, what Toffler (1981: ch. 4) calls the 'code' which came with the Industrial Revolution has prevailed, namely standardization, specialization, synchronization, concentration (or massification), maximization (the infatuation with bigness and growth) and centralization. These characteristics are still evident in the structures controlling the curriculum and student learning.

There is a vocabulary in use in schools, then, which is derived from the industrial economy and which has passed its use-by date. The package of images needs to be superseded, even discarded. Is it necessary still to use words like:

- class and grade (as though students are work-teams under a supervising foreman, the teacher);
- departments and faculties, offices and divisions (as though these elements are parts of a bureaucracy still);
- promotion and advancement (as though school still thinks and acts like a trade);
- programmes (or even 'learning programmes'), products, projects, modules (as though the school is manufacturing component parts of something called education)?

Do we wish to perpetuate that pattern into the twenty-first century? It seems obvious that the industrial analogies which schools still use cannot be allowed to continue into a society which is post-industrial and in which those comparisons are not only inappropriate but are substantially dysfunctional. There are plenty of indications abroad to demonstrate the dislocations resulting from that shift in the paradigm – chronic unemployment, youth alienation and religious cultism, to name three. These dislocations did not begin with education nor will they end there, but in a society beyond industrialization schooling needs a new and better logic to justify its practices, and a more apposite language to explain them.

Post-industrialism and the enterprise era

Most developed countries are now in a post-industrial period. For a range of reasons, fewer people are now involved in factory production; manufacturing's share of employment has fallen from near half the population about fifty years ago to around 15 or 10 per cent now. Manufacturing is still producing profits, but employment in manufacturing has been collapsing, while the new occupations and jobs have appeared in the services sector and in the professions.

A new logic for schooling in the post-industrial society was building through the 1980s and 1990s as schools and school systems around the world were subjected to the restructuring or re-engineering movement. It was a confused and at times a destructive period, for often the change agents appeared not to comprehend the organizing logic of re-engineering, and educators were crudely disregarded as being too stolid, too unionized, too unimaginative and too naive to be left in charge of education any longer. Nevertheless, by the early 1990s the rationale for the shape of post-industrial schooling had solidified. In retrospect, one influential book encapsulated the new logic, written by Stanford economists Chubb and Moe and entitled *Politics, Markets and America's Schools* (1990).

The metaphor of the market economy is now widely in use around the world to justify the new policies for schooling. Schools are talked of as though they are private businesses or enterprises providing a product (learning) to a set of clients (students and parents). They are required to contribute to the economic competitiveness of the nation. It is said that they must 'sell themselves', finding a niche in the market and competing for their market share. Schools are forced to be responsive to their local community through a variety of devices which give the consumers choice over which school's services they will buy. Schools are treated as stand-alone enterprises. They are self-managing, with each school having its own single-line budget. School boards or councils not only represent the shareholders (the more usual term is 'stakeholders') but they are the means whereby the school is held accountable. It is assumed that schools will compete for resources (especially governmental funds), that the schools which provide a marketable product will be worthy to survive, and that poor providers (and poor teachers) will go to the wall. The school and its teachers must now monitor their performance outcomes, for they live or die on the quality of their educational services, and the demonstrated value they add to the educational performance of their students. They are expected to be entrepreneurial.

As a result, schools are gaining increased legal and professional responsibilities, with wide discretion over funding, the responsibility to select their own staff and to fill their senior positions from the Principal down, the power to handle the management and upkeep of their physical plant, and so on. A lot of attention is now being given to the managerial role of the Principal, and the qualifications, formal and informal, which a person must have prior to being placed in the role.

The once-centralized educational bureaucracies (whether public or private) have now divested themselves of day-to-day control of individual schools. Instead, they put in place accountability, regular audit, and quality control machinery, and then leave the school alone to carry on its own business (almost literally). They have done away with middle management, downsized, and carry only monitoring functions and global policy-making roles. They have shrunk to being a strategic core. This is the story of most education departments in Australia, the national system in New Zealand, some provincial systems in Canada, and the local education authorities in Great Britain. The combined impact of a denuding of the head office, of making schools self-managing, of shrinking system-provided education services and back-up, and of financial stringency is to smudge the divide between public and private schooling.

This new metaphor which describes schooling in terms of markets and enterprise is powerful in the way it has become the favoured way of explaining the process of learning itself. Governments are now inclined to view education as a product and an exportable commodity. The new metaphor encourages the assumption that education is a personal investment. At the time the Australian government was setting up its Higher Education Contribution Scheme (HECS) in which students could pay up-front fees or defer the repayment until their earning capacity after graduation made it possible, it was stated as justification that only four OECD countries made no charge for tuition in higher education, and that most countries provide a combination of grants and interest-bearing loans to cover tertiary education costs. In short, since education brings personal profits to degree-holders, then a 'users-pay' approach to funding is logical.

The new format does give a better appreciation of what the school is and of the role of its head. If you aggregate the salary bill in any normally sized school of, say, about forty staff members, the capital value of the buildings and equipment, the costs of maintenance and supplies, and its other recurrent expenditures, it emerges as an enterprise with a multi-million-dollar annual turnover. Compared with any other local business, the school is usually the largest enterprise in town. Certainly in any country town or suburb, it is one of the municipality's biggest companies, and it usually occupies the largest piece of real estate in the locality. The managers of these enterprises called school – the Principals – are no longer middle-management, subordinate parts of a big bureaucracy, but rather they are among the most highly skilled and qualified executives (or Chief Executive Officers, CEOs) in the community. The firm they run is much more complicated than any other local business because its purposes are more complex, more public and more politically sensitive, directly affecting daily a far larger proportion of the community than any other enterprise. By its very nature the CEO role in that enterprise requires the delicate exercise of human relations, not merely among the enterprise's own staff but also with a large and volatile set of customers or clients.

The way teachers are employed and deployed changes under this new model. The long-term effect is that new teacher career patterns will evolve, away from a salaried service and into a system in which teachers are paid a market-determined fee-for-service for discharging an agreed professional function, and employed on contracts negotiated by a professional company of which they are principals or partners. The role of the head of school becomes more complicated, of course, and that single position may be converted into a management team containing a congeries of skills, some of them legal and industrial. The convention of a central bureaucracy being the employer of salaried teachers who are then assigned to schools is obsolescent.

Educators and parents may not like the new metaphor. We did not particularly like the factory metaphor either, but we learned to live with it and to make educational sense of it. At least the market metaphor favours a school-centred approach, diminishes top-down control, unpicks the centralization of decisional power, and mutes the hierarchical pyramid which placed learners at the base of the power pyramid, and in the weakest position where the consumer's interests are subservient to the organization. The enterprise metaphor makes us *begin* with the school, and to build out from it the supports it needs to enable it to do its job.

It is unlikely that the market metaphor will remain the only dominant analogy in the Information Age for it is not embracing enough, leaving out of the picture some of the most important factors in learning – like those factors discussed in Chapter 2. For the immediate future, however, it seems likely to be at least one of a group of organizing metaphors for schooling, largely because it gives an easy rationale for political involvements and for the policy community of public education. There are other metaphors from which new organizational rationales and shapes could emerge. We will return to this topic in Chapter 6, for schools will have to be aware of them and make adaptations, some of them profoundly different from their current management formats – if for no other reason than their own survival as an organization!

In summary, then, thus far we have dealt with three megashifts relating to schooling. First, there is vestigial thinking relating to pre-industrial schooling which will have to be discarded because it has outworn its usefulness and is hindering a redesign of schools for the future. Second, there is a set of basic assumptions about schooling and the nature of the curriculum which derive from factory production and manufacturing industry. To preserve that set of images and the practices they have given rise to is an unwanted encumbrance which restricts constructive planning of the future. Third, the post-industrial economy has moulded thinking about schools by constricting policy and planning within metaphors about markets and commercial enterprises. As with the two earlier sets of assumptions, these new explanations are partial and limited. They can be helpful as well as harmful, and like the other two sets, they too can be superseded. But there are several other, overarching factors embodied in the emerging world-view which will profoundly influence the way education is conceived of and spoken about, and to a consideration of them we turn in the next chapter.

4 New ways of knowing
Implications for curriculum

This chapter covers complex territory, but it is necessary for those concerned with schooling for the twenty-first century to confront the material contained here if a more appropriate curriculum is to be designed for students like Angelica. By the end of the chapter several design features should have emerged as well as some understanding of how the content of the curriculum may mutate as a generational mind-change works its way into the patterns of schooling.

One of the first to draw attention to the changed way in which human beings are beginning to talk about their world and their ordinary realities was Marilyn Ferguson in her book entitled *The Aquarian Conspiracy* (1980). As both journalist and author, she had been struck by the fact that new views about the way the world works were emerging simultaneously in a number of relatively unrelated fields; she cites medicine, education, the social sciences, economics, government, psychology, religion and politics. The views were not only fundamentally different from traditional orthodoxies, but they were also consistent with each other across those disparate disciplines, the same over-arching idea worked out in different areas of knowledge. She called it 'the whole-earth conspiracy', convinced that a fundamental shift was occurring wherein people 'found themselves rethinking everything' (Ferguson, 1980: 23, 24).

The Catholic scientist-priest Teilhard de Chardin (1959) was constantly being cited, she found. He had invented the term 'cosmogenesis' to indicate that new ideas were being generated about how the world was formed, replacing the old creation myths which appeared to have gone out of date and which were no longer being taken seriously by most people. He suggested that human beings, seen by him as a palaeontologist as only one of the species inhabiting planet Earth, were capable not only of continuous transformation (as the other evolving species were) but also of a transcendence which made meaning of it all. Ferguson observed that many others were writing and talking about 'the ecology of everything', about connectedness, about what has been termed the 'everything-hangs-together' philosophy. Physicists like Paul Davies (1983, 1992) call it TOE, a 'theory of everything', a new synthesis of what we have come to know about the universe. We discussed this new perception in *Education for the Twenty-First Century* (Beare and Slaughter, 1993: 11–14).

It is of course a many-faceted development, leading to complexities which are difficult to simplify. Indeed the human tendency to classify and codify is itself an act of simplification that flies in the face of the very proliferation and diversification which are the mark of livingness. The point is made cogently in *Disturbing the Universe* (1981), its author, Freeman Dyson, a theoretical physicist, one of the earliest to work on quantum physics and a colleague at Princeton University of Robert Oppenheimer, whose Los Alamos team had developed the atom bomb responsible for ending the Second World War. Dyson wrote that 'species commonly originate in groups called clades', from a Greek word which means a 'branch of a tree' (Dyson, 1981: 222). They break into variations and diversify into adaptations of the original, a branching tree of twigs and variant forms. So, Dyson comments,

> When some climatic or geographical revolution occurs, upsetting the established balance of nature, not just one new species but a whole clade will appear ..., the outcome of an episode of rapid multiplication and diversification of small populations expanding into a new and disturbed habitat.
>
> (Dyson, 1981: 222)

Interestingly, Dyson uses this same analogy to explain what happened when the Roman Empire broke up, when European languages proliferated, and when the Renaissance shook Europe.

Dyson points out that, in biological terms, 'a clone is the opposite of a clade'. A clone is a 'monoglot' (to use his term), someone who can understand or use only one language, and by extension someone who can operate on only one conventional or standard explanation. Clones are therefore 'evolutionary dead ends', he says, whereas 'clades are the stuff of which great leaps forward in evolution are made'. The central problem facing human beings, then, is whether to be a clade or a clone; and how to 'make our social institutions flexible enough to preserve our precious biological and cultural diversity' (*ibid.*: 223).

It is not only a forlorn task but also a counter-productive one to attempt to define (or confine into neat categories) what an expanding, living, clade-like, worldwide culture will be like, or what it will become as the twenty-first century evolves. The important thing is to accept it for what it is, and not to force it into clone-like dead ends of conformity. The fundamental issue underlying our plans for humanity's future, then, 'is not economic but spiritual, the problem of diversity' (*ibid.*: 233), the problem indeed of allowing diversity to occur, to be accepted and to flourish. Diversity signals dynamism and therefore life, conformity signals a system constricted and moving towards death. Schools are no exception. Schooling itself has to be released from cloning tendencies so that it can develop multiple forms and living branches.

Rick Slaughter and I wrote our book about the future of schooling (Beare and Slaughter, 1993) out of frustration that people knew so little about the new outlooks. Asked to assist schools and systems in their planning for the next decade, we found ourselves continually confronted by plans based upon conformist views which were quite clearly going out of date, and quickly. It seemed futile to deal with such plans unless we first confronted the frameworks of outdated thinking which produced them. Without having to try very hard, we could see major trends which are already altering the most basic assumptions about life on planet Earth and about the human community, assumptions which would impact on the purposes of schooling. Although commentators were saying that society was at a major divide in history, schools and school systems seemed not to have grasped in what way the curriculum would be affected by these implied new assumptions about the world, and especially about the nature of knowledge itself. What then are some of these new and major assumptions which will surely change not only what is taught by schools but also how it is taught and the way schools will function?

A new approach to knowledge and knowing

Schools deal with knowledge; it has been the stuff of the normal curriculum. The problem is that there is a standard way of considering both knowledge and the curriculum of schooling which all countries of the world seem to copy as though there could be no other. It has been built on the scientific method, on rationality, on one acceptable way of developing knowledge, of systematizing it and of passing it on. It is mechanistic rather than organic, structural rather than florescent, and is built on the image of the production line. It favours a linear approach to learning, with one component having to be mastered before the next one is tackled; with a logical order to it graded from simple to complex. It is designed on the assumption that there are certain things to be learnt at certain ages of one's life, and therefore on the basis that learnings are age-related and that students should advance through their school programmes in relative lockstep. It has provided a frame of thinking which will have trouble surviving long in the twenty-first century.

This approach to knowledge production, to study programmes and to the curriculum which carries both depends on assumptions developed when the age of Scientific Enlightenment supplanted the medieval view of the world three hundred years ago. At that time, said Capra, 'the notion of an organic, living and spiritual universe [the pre-scientific view] was replaced by that of the world as a machine, and the world-machine became the dominant metaphor of the modern era' (Capra, 1983: 38). Its logic is typical of the Industrial Revolution which, as we have seen in Chapter 3, has fashioned so much of what we take for granted in schooling. Science manufactures knowledge, it was assumed in an appropriate metaphor, by breaking any phenomenon into its component bits; as we study and analyse those pieces, we build up logically, systematically and by synthesis an understanding about the whole. That same, empirical, piece-by-piece approach was applied in Newtonian physics, biology and living organisms, systems theory, medicine, psychology, to economics and political systems and, of course, to education and vocational training. Capra explains:

In the past three hundred years ... we have been driven by the belief in the scientific method as *the only valid approach to knowledge*: the view of the universe as a mechanical system composed of elementary building blocks; the view of life in society as a competitive struggle; and the belief in unlimited material progress to be achieved through economic and technological growth.

(Capra 1983: 12, emphasis mine)

The characteristics of the scientific method have become virtually the underlying creed of modern education (Harman, 1988: 29–33; Beare and Slaughter, 1993: 56–61) whose litany is as follows:

- *Reductionism* Reliable knowledge results from reducing everything to its component parts, and examining each morsel in detail. By building up our knowledge of the individual pieces we will come to an understanding of the whole. Science is therefore reductionist – it reduces a phenomenon to its elements. As a result, scientists become specialists through an ever-increasing concentration on those elements, and therefore by acquiring sophistication about particular subdisciplines. *So this is how schools get their subjects, it is why education developed specialist teachers, and why the curriculum is structured the way it is, cut up into key learning areas.*

- *Positivism* The only safe way to extend our knowledge about the universe, then, is by relying solely on what we can observe. By experimentation and measurement, especially by relying upon the physical senses and the technology which extends them, we arrive at verifiable truth. Only what can be verified is trustworthy and admissible as knowledge. Positivism, a term coined by Auguste Comte, only recognizes facts, positively affirmed through observation and verification, and the laws which govern their interrelations. Put simply, it trusts only the empirical approaches. It tends to reject religious or subjective explanations about phenomena. *This is why science and maths are pre-eminent in the curriculum. And this approach underlies most teaching methods.*

- *Materialism* The empiricist works only with what appears substantial and real, insisting on sensory evidence which can be examined. Even what appears immaterial or intangible has to be converted into examinable data. For example, what we describe as consciousness or awareness is best understood by analysing the physical and chemical processes in the body which produce it. *So the most highly regarded subjects in the curriculum are the empirical ones based on rational analysis. The expressive, the artistic and the discursive are rated lower in importance.*

- *Objectivity* There is a clear distinction between the objective world (which any observer can perceive and which all observers will read in the same way) and subjectivity (which is limited to the privacy of one's own brain and consciousness). What is objective is reliable; what is subjective is unreliable. The subjective can be made valid and the basis for theorizing only if several people report the same condition, confirm each other in their reportage, and therefore verify (or give face validity to) an objective conclusion. *These two characteristics – objectivity and empiricism – provide the rationale for most curricular work in schools.*

• *Rationality* Reason is empiricism's partner. The application of reasoning, rigorous logic, dispassionate (and therefore value-free, or unemotional) rationality, especially when applied to observed phenomena, is the only safe method whereby to advance knowledge or to develop new knowledge. *So values formation has always been an incidental rather than a central part of the curriculum.*

• *Quantitative analysis* It 'stands to reason', then, that qualitative properties are best reduced to quantitative ones, to what can be weighed, measured, rendered objective and assessable. The measurable is safer to handle than the intangible. *These two properties of rationality and quantitative measures explain educators' practices on examinations and assessment, on measuring academic progress, on promotion and certification, and on our concern with outcomes and results.* As a result, the intuitive, the expressive, the unmeasurable, the subjective and the intensely personal have never found a satisfactory place in the curriculum, in assessment or in the public's esteem. As Lovelock commented, 'As is often the way with professions, science more often applies its expertise to the trivial than to the numinous' (Lovelock, 1988: xiv).

Almost everything about twentieth-century schooling, the schooling for an industrial economy, was based on these characteristics of the scientific method. The division of knowledge into subject areas; the way schools examine and assess student achievement and then report it; the division of learning into age-grade levels; the age-grade organization of students into classes or learning groups; the way teachers specialize in subjects; the linear progression in the content included in the curricula; the way schools are organized and the roles are assigned among teachers; the modes of supervision for staff and students – they all follow the inexorable logic of scientism. And almost all schools across the globe have chosen to follow this same logic.

As Ken Wilber (1983a: 23) has pointed out, a scheme for knowledge production built on so small a base and which dismisses anything which was not material was bound to become a nonsense. 'This position on the part of scientists,' Wilber says, using Whitehead's phrase, 'is pure bluff ..., the bluff of the part playing the whole.' And that is the important point. The scientific method has advanced the world's knowledge enormously, and those achievements are not to be devalued, but it is questionable if one paradigmatic approach can exert an exclusive claim on the generation and validation of knowledge (Beare and Slaughter, 1993: 59).

One of the most profound reasons for questioning this narrow approach to science and knowledge production is that the method has begun to recoil on itself, producing counter-intuitive findings which will not fit into science's own tidy, materialistic, mechanistic, reductionist paradigm. The most spectacular example is that of quantum physics, which exploded the rationalistic

Newtonian approaches and has made people question what scientific theory really is. The independent scientist James Lovelock, who invented the concept of Gaia, of one complex living system called Earth of which we are all parts, points out that the words 'theory' and 'theatre' have a common origin.

> A theory in science is no more than what seems to its author a plausible way of dressing up the facts and presenting them to an audience .... A theory that is elegant, inspiring, and presented with craftsmanship is universally appreciated. But hard-working scientists like best [those] theories that are full of predictions .... It matters little whether the view of the theorizer is right or wrong: investigation and research are stimulated, new facts discovered, and new theories composed.
>
> (Lovelock, 1988: 42)

He leads the chapter in which he discusses this matter of theory-building with a quotation from Pareto: 'Give me a fruitful error every time, full of seeds, bursting with its own corrections.' In each of the above quotations, it should be noted, both Lovelock and Pareto have changed the organizing metaphors. When one does that, the theory itself is re-imaged, and that is precisely what seems to be occurring more generally across the world.

There has been a spate of writings from scientists along these lines, questioning science's own certainties and changing its perspectives by reworking its structural metaphors and frameworks. The theoretical physicist Michio Kaku, for example, in his *How Science Will Revolutionize the 21st Century* (1998), argues that one chapter of scientific discovery has closed and that we are making a transition into a new era of scientific work. He speaks of the choreographers of life and intelligence (a dramatic metaphor) and of 'the intelligent planet'. Or consider the case of Professor Gerald Edelman, who won a Nobel Prize for his work on the nature of the human brain. He took to task the scientific community for its use of imagery about machines to describe living organisms (Cornwell, 1993: 4). 'There is a tendency in every age,' he said, 'to compare the brain with the toys that excite us.' The mathematician Leibnitz thought of the mind as a flour-mill, a piece of machinery; early in the twentieth century it was described as a telephone; and until now it has typically been compared with a computer. This mode of explanation, Edelman argued, is 'profoundly mistaken' because that kind of imagery leaves out too much:

> Computer codes simply can't encompass the infinite range of human language, imagination and metaphor; our ability to hold intelligent conversation and create works of art ... or our sense of being individuals .... It's a purely objective, determinist viewpoint that doesn't include *me* .... Physics and computing cannot account for this sense we have of looking out on our world from within.
>
> (*ibid.*)

And then, in a beautiful change of analogy, Edelman asserts that 'each individual's brain is more like a unique and unimaginably dense rainforest, teeming with growth and decay. It is less like a programmed machine than an ecological habitat that mimics the evolution of life itself' (*ibid.*).

Human beings have always widened their knowledge this way, by using imagination, especially by finding new metaphors which release us from images which imprison us. Largely for this reason, various writers have made a strong case for re-establishing the validity of the qualitative dimension of human experience. There are some aspects of human experience which it is simply dangerous not to admit as knowledge.

The quantum porridge

The *old* paradigm, then, is a problem for the modern school's curriculum. When new organizing metaphors for theory, knowledge, and science emerge, then educational institutions will have to adjust how they present knowledge and also develop it. And it is no more significant than in the way we view the universe itself and the planet on which we live. No one has done better this reworking of the explanations about our planet and the universe in post-Newtonian terms than the mathematical cosmologist Brian Swimme in his simple and lucid *The Hidden Heart of the Cosmos* (1996).

There have been some, although not many, attempts to show how new bases for scientific knowings will alter the operating codes of the institutions within society. This book endeavours to suggest some of those likely transformations for schools. Murphy (1997) has attempted a similar exercise for the modern Church, and in doing so has uncovered the knowledge sub-structure on which the new edifices (like schools and churches) have to be built. He states what now is almost the obvious:

> Behind the cultural revolution [of the 1960s–1970s] and the need for paradigm change ... lies the phenomenon of a *dying* worldview and the *birth* of a new one, the death of a worldview based on Newtonian physics and Cartesian thought, and the birth of a quantum worldview.
>
> (Murphy, 1997: 105)

In tracing the movement of assumptions since the 1500s, he points out that Copernicus replaced 'the blind faith and obedience to the mythic worldview' by showing that the earth was not the centre of the universe. Newtonian physics then replaced the notion of the earth as the pinnacle of God's creation with that of 'a dead machine'; God ('a disinterested "watchmaker", the God of scientific religion') simply wound up the clock and then disengaged to let it run according to universal laws. Descartes then shifted the primary focus from the transcendent to the individual, to an 'I-centred culture'. The effect of this movement was unhelpfully to separate elements – the natural from the super-natural, the helper from the patient, humans from nature and the animals, facts from values, the creator from what he or she creates, and so on. This approach forces us to live in a limited, compartmentalized world-view of our own intellectual making.

It is interesting to note that the anthropologist Eliade (1987: 178–9) foresaw the development of the self-regarding, individual-isolating society, and put its development down to the urbanization which is the result of the Industrial Revolution and which divorced people from daily interaction with nature and the land. He called it a 'grave impoverishment':

> The cosmic liturgy, the mystery of nature's participation ... have become inaccessible to [people] living in a modern city. Their religious experience is no longer open to the cosmos. In the last analysis, it is a strictly private experience.

Over the history of the human race, Eliade (*ibid.*: 173) points out, people reproduce 'on the human scale the system of rhythmic and reciprocal conditioning influences that characterizes and constitutes a world [and] defines a universe'. For that reason, the urban dweller has a tendency to see the world as mankind's dominion (that is, under human control) and society as a human artefact, both either methodically or unwittingly produced and ruled over by people; 'the world is no longer felt as the work of God', says Eliade (*ibid.*: 179).

A new understanding of the cosmos, however, has been building for several decades, some say since Einstein's work on relativity, and it has been eroding those compartmentalizations and separations. It burst into flower with quantum physics which 'speaks of the quantum vacuum, the quantum self, particles and waves, non-local effects, timelessness, synchronicity, and intentionality' and which is having the effect of making us revise the 'social, economic, political, psychological, and spiritual implications' (and, we might add, the impacts on the content of schooling) which flow from the new cosmology (Murphy, 1997: 121). Zohar has been one of the most lucid analysts of these effects.

Let us consider two, essentially new, social (as opposed to scientific) realizations stemming from quantum physics. The first is that the self is 'in a creative dialogue with the whole of reality' (Zohar and Marshall, 1994: viii). The self is not a fixed entity looking at another fixed entity called reality; for the two are interacting and changing each other in the very act of co-existence. Connectedness, not separation, is the key to understanding the universe and the space in which we live out our lives. There are 'fundamental forces of relationship that bind the universe together' (*ibid.*: x). Zohar and Marshall talk of the quantum holism which bonds all components of the world and our reality into a whole which is itself interactive. The world changes merely by our observing it. So the 'uncertainty principle' has replaced mechanistic determinism, for quantum leaps can be spontaneous and unpredictable, through 'a kind of instantaneous connectedness between apparently separate things' (Zohar and Marshall, 1994: 35). 'Rather than things moving smoothly through space and time as the result of cause and effect,' says Murphy, 'energy is actually radiated in packets (quanta), and these ... leap from one energy state to another' (Murphy, 1997: 129). Wilber (1983a: 84) puts this new realization well: 'Everywhere we look in nature ... we see nothing but *wholes* [his italics]. Fields within fields within fields, stretching through the common, interlacing each and every thing with each and every other.' He describes it as a 'mandalic map' of the universe which includes us. It should be noted in passing that the organizational design charts of the post-industrial period are inclined to be represented like that, too, in a mandala diagram. It is possible, and probably very constructive, to represent the curriculum in the same way.

In other words, this image of quantum holism has almost unwittingly produced patterned thinking and therefore parallel practices across society. The interconnectedness of a world run by means of computers is one outgrowth. The very image of an 'internet' is consistent with the quantum view; it is after all a network, literally an international network. So also is the environmental movement, in which we envision the whole world dependent upon the preservation of the health of its parts. But there are organizational examples too which Zohar and Marshall address in *The Quantum Society*, subtitled *Mind, Physics, and the New Social Vision.* The pervasive use of teams, they suggest, is a quantum-derived realization that a *group* has a creative edge and an internal dynamic not possessed by the individual members of it separately.

There are, of course, huge implications here for the way schools are organized and run, quite apart from the impacts this kind of thinking will have on the curriculum and how students learn. In the past, for example, we assumed that each student learned separately, and his or her attainments were individually computed and recorded. Certificates of attainment, diplomas and degrees are awarded to individuals. Quantum analogies suggest that there is a huge advantage to be harvested through collective learnings, from branching trees of learning, from a curriculum of clades rather than a cloned curriculum. How will the outcomes of such collective learnings be represented and rewarded? Do you confer a collective degree?

These approaches are an important foil to reductionist science, but they do not erase those approaches. It would be foolish if they were allowed to do so when so much of the world's knowledge has been generated by such processes. But as Wilber observed above, the quantum views do call the bluff of those who argue that there is only one reliable and authoritative approach, especially to knowledge production and to learning. Here is a view for curriculum, for example, which encourages responsiveness; the subject (the material to be learned) changes merely by our looking at it and by our working on it. Knowledge is dynamic and living, not antiseptically cocooned within subject boxes, not pre-ordained. The knowledge familiarly compacted into disciplines and key learning areas is not formed of separate entities but collective, interactive, interlacing with each other. It may help to have the knowledge parcelled and labelled, as the scientific revolution has done for us, but at best this is a useful fiction of what really is.

What emerges, then, is not a wholesale debunking of the traditional approaches to curriculum and subjects. That would be to substitute one arrogance with another. But what it does signal is the need for dynamism and exploration, for experiences to be had before the analysis comes, and then for various explanations and possibilities to be tried on for size. It argues for a curriculum which allows for clumps of learning which can go on without categories put over the findings *a priori*. A lesson in science can just as easily pass for a lesson in language, for example. It argues for an interactive learning environment in which the learner controls many of the levers. It is the educator-as-mentor who accompanies the learning child who keeps system and coherence in the learning discoveries; and that is a demanding task requiring sophisticated professional expertise and some complex theoretical understandings both of the subject matter being explored and of the learning process itself.

A second essential realization from the quantum approaches is that 'what we call consciousness is only one type of consciousness'. 'Everything is awash in a sea of possibilities,' says Murphy (1997: 35, 128). Fundamentally, this is not a linear world; it is open to constellations of happenings and experiencings, many of them with a simultaneity which makes for uniqueness, and which should make us alert to synchronicities of any kind – for they may not come again. To quote Zohar and Marshall (1994: 27),

> The existence of virtual states shows us that we can experience more than one reality at a time, each playing out its individual drama simultaneously with the others. In quantum language, these multiple realities are known as 'superpositions'. We get one reality literally 'on top of' another.

And these, they say, are the norm. 'In both our private lives and our public roles,' they state, we are discovering a 'new *framework* [their italics] for understanding and fulfilling our potential as social beings' (*ibid.*: 7).

To illustrate the point, the geneticist Darryl Reanney (1991: 23) uses the following example. As you are taking off at night in an aeroplane, you look though the aircraft's window and you see the lights beside the runway flashing past you in rapid but linear succession. They seem to be appearing to you one after another, sequenced in time. But when you are airborne and high above the aerodrome, you look down and see all the lights together, all at one time, all in a set pattern which you could not visualize while you were on the ground. Imagine that some people live only on the ground, some only in the air, some only inside the plane. Are they each seeing the same reality? Whose view about that reality is correct?

People the world over now comprehend that there are several viewing stations for reality; there are ordinary and non-ordinary realities. There are also several personalities living within our selves, waiting for our choice to be one or the other. Objectivity and subjectivity are not as easy to separate as we once thought. Larsen (1990: 235) reminds us of the old Zen koan in which 'the roshi asks the student, "Show me your face before you were born."'

We are, in short, in a participatory universe where the human observers help to evoke the reality they observe ('observer participancy', it is called). 'Reality at its most fundamental level is an indeterminate porridge of possibilities', sometimes called the quantum porridge, a 'flux of particles/waves', says Murphy (1997, 132). Our realities are, therefore propositional, depending on the kind of spectacles we use to view what we think we are seeing. In a sociological sense, we manufacture our reality from whatever station we view it from or through whatever explanatory system we choose to impose on it. Furthermore, human beings are not the only such manufacturers, for we must accept our place among all the living beings of whatever kind which make up the universe.

Again, the implications for education are profound, for we are forced at least to review what we have taken to be the certainties and regularities of schooling. It is not the generation of the educators or the parents who will force the rethink of schooling and what education essentially is; it is the generation of learners, breathing the air which envelopes them. They will do the demytholo-gizing and the re-creation, the deconstructing and the reconstructing. It is they who will develop new ways of 'knowing' which for them are authentic and trustworthy. To put the point precisely, people, young people in particular, will grow out of one explanatory system and into others, for as long as they live. They will see it as untenable to accept dogma or outmoded systems of thought or explanation, for reality is responsive to varying explanations and codes. To quote Zohar and Marshall, no single paradigm, and certainly not a mecha-nistic one, can cope any longer with contemporary society (Zohar and Marshall, 1994: 7). And as Tilley puts it, quoting Wiles, 'A statement whose truth or falsity can be determined only in terms of a world-view that is dead and gone can hardly be a statement of direct relevance to subsequent ages' (Tilley, 1990: 13).

Wilber, using obsolescent religious explanations as his analogy, puts this view pungently, in a passage quoted by Murphy:

> Post-mythic men and women have thrown off their childish images of deity as a protective parent, sniveling over their every move, listening to their every wish fulfillment, catering for their every immortality project, dancing to their prayers of magic. Post-mythic men and women did not get thrown out of Eden; they grew up and walked out.
>
> (Wilber 1983b: 83; Murphy, 1997: 58)

Might that not also be the case with the traditional curriculum and its tidy subject containers? If it is, then it may not be easy to describe what systems of thought will replace the superseded ones. It may be that the curriculum has to be stated – at least in part – in terms of inquiry or searching, and not in terms of parcels of knowledge to be learned, or committed to memory. Understandings may be the outcomes of search rather than certainties. At the end of the search, Wilber (1983a: 310) observed, we may not end up with 'final knowledge' at all. The new paradigm is not a way to stop, but a way to carry on .... We might eventually discover that the new paradigm is nothing but the quest itself; the only constant is the search; that Being, as Hegel said, is simply the process of its own becoming.

A return to myth-making

The discussion above brings us to two significant practical developments for schools. The first is that the new ways of knowing and knowledge production give a new entry point for including expressive and imaginative forms as fundamental aspects of the curriculum. And second, the quantum approaches, taken alongside the post-modernism which deconstructs many of the taboos and beliefs traditions from the past, return us to the argument mounted in the second chapter, namely that one of the central purposes of education (or more narrowly, schooling) is to equip the learner with the skills to build a belief system with which he or she can decode and cope with the emerging world order.

The ecumenical theologian Leonard Swidler (1988: 32), who has had to grapple with the difficulties of language in this kind of area, alludes to the problem of expressing 'a deeper reality which goes beyond the empirical surface experiences of our lives'. When we attempt to speak of these matters, we will be forced into using 'transempirical language, that is, metaphor, symbol, and the like'. In terms reminiscent of Wilber's 'category error' (see Beare and Slaughter, 1993: 66–9), Swidler says, 'The mistake we must be cautious to avoid in this situation is erroneously to think that when we speak about the transcendent we are using empirical language. We are not. We can not.' Nor is it possible to be 'reductionistic' (or empirical in the traditional sense) in the way we consider what is 'transempirical'.

In response to the above, there is one well-tried approach whereby human beings deal with the transcendental uncertainties which they find themselves surrounded by and enmeshed within. They resort to story-telling or, more precisely, to myth-making (using the term 'myth' in its technical, not its vernacular, sense). We encountered this topic in the second chapter when we considered the global community with which Angelica was likely to be confronted. At that point we indicated that everyone, literally every human being on earth, weaves a tapestry of beliefs and myths with which to make sense of reality. In short, every young learner has to build his or her own explanatory system for the universe and the building of it usually occurs during the years the learner is at school – indeed, in school.

A mythology, then, is a representation, through language and story, through imagery rather than through propositions, of what the cosmic order is. It is the most widely used explanatory device known to the human race. It has always been part of the schooling within traditional societies, and coming to an understanding of and respect for the prevailing system of myths is part of the initiation which gives one a rite of passage into a culture.

Mythology catches us at the outer limits of our understanding and gives us a method to cope, a means to take the ineffable and to make it intersect with what we deem to be real. As a result, our personal and collective mythologies (we all have them) govern what we think, what we are able to grasp, to act upon, and to achieve. As we stated in the second chapter, myth-making in this respect (like knowledge itself) is part of the essential stuff of schooling.

In their book about the practices of tribal priests (or shamans), Stevens and Stevens (1988: 18–19) tell of an American Indian shaman called Reza to whom two villagers had come seeking guidance about where to locate a herd of wild donkeys.

> Both were told where they could find [the] herd of burros, but one was told the herd had six and the other was told it had eighteen ....Thinking at this point in the story that perhaps Reza's memory wasn't the best, Sandy [the interviewer] ... asked if he had been describing the same herd. 'Yes, same burros, same place' was the reply. 'Not same is how many find,' he offered in his broken English. What the shaman was alluding to was the fact that the first villager could not imagine owning more than six burros. When Sandy asked what would happen if this fellow went to the spot and found the eighteen, Reza answered, 'Man will find only six; it is what he "see".'

In *Educating Psyche: Emotion, Imagination and the Unconscious in Learning*, Neville (1989: 6) observes that 'the original and basic unit of mental activity, which remains the total psyche's preferred way of operating, is the image' – not language, not words, not 'ideas' (whatever they are), but images. The mind responds best to pictures. What we 'see' in our mind's eye is what we instinctively bring into being because it patterns the way we act, think and behave. Not least are the images we carry about in our heads concerning the future.

There is a rich literature about self-image, about the way we continually talk about ourselves and to ourselves. Using the lives of Dag Hammarskjold, Martin Luther King, General George Patton and Charles Ives, James McClendon's (1974) research showed that we tend to model our lives on one or two motifs or self-chosen themes. How we arrive at the model is not always clear, but our self-descriptions, especially apparent in the biographies of great people, reveal how powerfully influential that model is. In a commentary on McClendon's findings, Fischer (1983: 99) observes that 'such images are not peripheral to faith, but that people live their very lives out of them'. The point is that the choice of the model is ours; that the model can be changed (deliberately as well as unwittingly); and that schools ought to help children to acquire the reliable and effective methods to do it.

Imaging, a process as old as human history, involves creating a mind-picture of what we want, a photograph of a plausible future which for us is yet to be. We have convincing and voluminous evidence from all countries, cultures and eras to show that a picture like that, held firmly in the mind and believed in, has the tendency to manifest itself and to become real (Dowrick, 1992, 1993; Johnson, 1986). We use that picture as a framework within which to co-ordinate action and will. By a multitude of unnoticed and unstudied actions and reactions, we pattern our behaviours on that firmly held, taken-for-granted image, and we bring it into existence. What we believe and image is also a lens, bringing things into focus. As Weick (1976) points out, we have superseded the old empiricist's claim, 'I'll believe it when I see it.' The more accurate assertion is, 'I'll see it (only) when I believe it.'

Generally speaking, we only really believe something if we can 'see' it, when we can create a picture of it in our mind's eye, and have no doubts that reality is just like that. Hundreds of elite athletes have trained themselves to peak performance through such visualization, by building a picture about their best self, then investing it with emotion and with what their five senses can image about it, and then by training their body wholistically to reproduce that performance (see, for example, Gallwey, 1976, 1981). This process of visualization has been widely co-opted by management consultants and by organizational leaders under the term 'vision', and the techniques to develop it are powerfully effective, whether used for good or for bad purposes. We all use them, often unwittingly.

The question, then, is what we give credence to. We could not function as human beings unless there was a connected web of things we take for granted without hesitation. Ruth Benedict (1935: 2) was right when she observed that everybody edits his or her reality through a set way of thinking. Harvard medical researcher Herbert Benson (1977, 1985, 1996) has demonstrated that the so-called 'faith factor' has enormous power, allowing us to accomplish almost impossible things, and also bringing into existence what others did not know was there. On this point Neville (1989: 53) makes an interesting observation, in this case concerning healing:

> It appears not to matter greatly what the patient believes in (a favourite doctor, a new drug, a particular form of prayer); the faith in itself has a significant impact on the process of healing. Studies of healing centres such as Lourdes suggest that healing is only available to the faithful; cynics and sceptics fail to reap the benefits.

It is a comment in harmony with what we know from quantum reality.

From earliest times, the shamans or holy-men (a large proportion of whom are women) seem to have made the common discovery that all human beings, indeed all living things, are interconnected in ways which give us multiple options, multiple connections and multiple perspectives. A leading contemporary expert on shamanism, Michael Harner, observed in *The Way of the Shaman* (1990: xiv), 'What most people describe as "reality" only barely touches the grandeur, power, and mystery of the universe.' Human beings, then, choose who they are to be. We can be wild or tame (as Estes' book *Women Who Run with the Wolves* suggests); we can be surface or depth, woman or man, masculine or feminine, light or dark. We have it in our power to *act* as different persons, the same being but wearing different masks. The Latin word *persona* referred to the comic and tragic masks which classical actors held in front of their faces, the word a compound of *sona* (sound) and *per* (through), the 'face through which we speak'.

People can (and do) put on different faces, different personalities, and give themselves a sense of power and liberation by doing so. Note how fascinated we all are with professional actors. Not surprisingly, masks and ceremonial garb play important parts in religious events, in ceremonies of cultural significance, in tribal lore. The practices of the magi, the rituals of the holy men of the tribe, what has been called the shamanic circus (Larsen, 1990: 236), always involve drama, theatre, masks and dressing up, for by these means we can take on the identity of someone else, try on another personality for size, live in various perspectives, and view life from various stances. The American Indian shaman Joseph Rael (1992: 13, 14) has said, 'We can live in alternating realities where the unexpected, the miracle or the afterthought are more the rule than the exception.' He goes on: 'Ordinary reality is made up of overlay upon overlay of alternate realities.' Again, here is a shaman talking like a quantum physicist!

Beliefs, visualization, ideas of connectedness, play-acting and personality tend then to become embedded in, embodied within, narratives and stories. When human beings are confronted by a reality which is hard to describe, and when comprehension teeters on the edge of wonder, then they use the universal device of inventing stories to convey meanings. At the simplest level, they emerge as novels or films or TV serials or stage-plays. Some of them last and survive because they encapsulate so well what human beings know to be authentic about themselves; Shakespeare's plays are like that. Some stories acquire overlays, invent symbolism, or express profundities, or become epics in which the characters assume the status of heroes, heroines and demigods; and the events become cosmic struggles. Sometimes the stories are based upon actual events to which added significances are attached. Sometimes the stories are invented for the purpose. It really does not matter which. The meanings are what is important.

Of growing concern for the community, parents, and teachers, then, is the question of who is creating the myths of modern societies, how those myths are being promulgated, and what collective set of meanings is being legitimized. Clearly, film, television and video libraries are mass-producing stories and images which have the power of myth, and which deliberately create attitudes about the world and about life itself. There are millions of persons generating music and song which carry their own powerful and recurrent messages. As shooting incidents and murders involving young people testify, the consistency of violent depictions on screen and records shapes impressionable people's beliefs. The print media – especially the paperback industry – is producing more books, especially novels, than ever before in human history. Collectively, then, there is a huge, worldwide industry in myth-making. It is generally left to schools, as a formal part of their curriculum, to teach the skills to discriminate, to critique, to appreciate, to classify and to respond.

Stories with mythic qualities begin to impact from early childhood and become particularly powerful as one approaches puberty, adolescence and adulthood and the ceremonial rites of passage into manhood and womanhood, by which time it is assumed that the initiates know the culture well, and have learned to respect and understand it. That modern society has failed to comprehend the fundamental nature of mythic consciousness and of story is all too evident across the globe. *Teachers* almost by default have inherited that role of cultural priest.

Joseph Campbell who, over a lifetime while on the staff at Sarah Lawrence College in the United States, collected, sifted, synthesized and collated myths and legends from around the world, is very clear about the purposes of myth. Every functioning mythology, he found, is a kind of control system which positions its community or its holder in the universe, allowing its adherents to be conducted 'through the ineluctable psychophysiological stages of transformation of a human lifetime – birth, childhood and adolescence, age, old age, and the release of death' (quoted in Sheldon, 1990: 342). Mythologies provide us points of reference, symbols about lasting things, and cosmic explanations (Campbell, 1988: 20). The question is in not whether we have one (we all do), but how robust, healthy and transforming is the mythology we are using at present.

To interpret myths literally (as religious fundamentalists of any kind tend to do) is to miss the point about them, Campbell says. Literal interpretations distort the stories. Simply because mythology attempts to deal with the inexpressible and the ineffable, its only methodology is metaphor – finding word-pictures and apocryphal stories which liken some aspects of the mysteries to things we already know about. The stuff of myths is 'neither places nor individuals but *states of being* realizable within you ..., states of mind that are *not* finally this or that place and time' (emphases mine) (Campbell, 1988: 20–1).

Because the important issue about a myth is whether it explains things credibly, it is bound to accept the cosmology of the day and what people automatically accept as true about the universe. Further, the myth has to be easily understood by its community, for 'a mythological image that has to be explained isn't working', says Campbell (quoted in Sheldon, 1990: 341). Larsen, who worked with Joseph Campbell for over two decades, has written that the myths which people adopt and use are 'empowering structures' which literally have an effect on 'health, vitality, and psychological well-being'. For that reason, the great psychologist Jung came to the realization, 'I simply had to know what unconscious and preconscious myth was forming me' (Larsen, 1990: 13).

There are well-documented methods for unpicking a mythology, a set of images or a belief system and then rebuilding them. Feinstein and Krippner, for example, have a five-phase method to 'unshackle ourselves from outmoded myths', ones which limit us, and to create more self-expanding ones. They comment:

> Education, politics, business, religion, and family are among the institutions that instil the collective mythology into the individual's personal

mythology .... Members of a social group usually do not realise the limitations of the group's world view because it is all they have known.

(Feinstein and Krippner, 1989: 190–1)

We tend not to understand, until we are taught, that cultural myths place boundaries around our awareness.

So how we picture ourselves, the language we use about ourselves and our family, the stories we choose to tell about ourselves or which we allow others to tell, whom we compare ourselves with, what we think we will become, how we define our own universe, these are the raw materials from which we spin our web of myths. The fairly standard and widely used techniques for myth-making include rituals, use of symbols, ceremonials, visualization, various meditative practices, various forms of prayer, affirmations, guided dreaming, shamanic journeying. Most of the techniques have been so well tested over so many centuries that you meet the same familiar ones everywhere you look. The American religious scholar Edward Stevens in his arrestingly titled *Spiritual Technologies: A User's Manual* (1990) lists twenty-eight such techniques, which he appropriately calls 'tools'.

All of the above is an indication why the school of the future will not limit itself to a scientistic, narrowly utilitarian curriculum. In *Educating Psyche*, Neville observes that traditional schools have been dominated by scientism, by rationality, by good, logical, cerebral, non-emotive subjects like mathematics, physics, science and literacy.

> (Because) it is intellect which dominates schooling ... the specifically soul-making subjects – literature, drama, music, the visual and tactile arts – are progressively 'de-souled' as the child proceeds through the school .... When it comes to public examinations which dominate secondary schooling, there can be no marks for being grabbed by a poem, painting or sonata, unless this translates into a motivation to analyse the artifact thoroughly and competently.
>
> (Neville, 1989: 10)

Pioneering work has been done with curricula which engage images, beliefs and myths. For example, in their book *Literacy for Life* Helen and David Dufty (1990: 7) argue that the generation of students now in school needs to grow up with a 'transformed view of the world' and 'educated to see the world in a systemic way': in short, 'to be globally literate'. The curriculum, they argue, ought not to subdivide knowledge into subjects, but should rather bring 'ideas and actions together in meaningful wholes' (*ibid.*: 11). Rather than a 'linear list of ideas', the new approach emphasizes

> the world as a set of connections within a total system. Old dichotomies ... are misleading. You can't possibly deal with issues like the greenhouse

effect without understanding that "natural systems" are inextricably linked with "social systems".

(*ibid.*: 6)

This discussion of the way the curriculum may change may be too complicated, too undefined, to translate easily into the practice of any one school or system, and it is unlikely that teachers or parents will throw away a proven curriculum and replace it with an unproven and apparently unsystematic one. What we have tried to show in this chapter is that the curriculum is not by any means set. It is malleable. It has always changed as the mindsets of its users have changed, and it is at least prudent to be forewarned on the fundamental questionings which the post-industrial, knowledge-based, internationally aware new age of the twenty-first century will bring with it. To hold slavishly to the curriculum which worked in the past is a dangerous tactic for the future.

Conclusion

In summary, then, what lessons have emerged from this chapter concerning the nature of the curriculum for schools in the future? We can list them as a set of propositions as follows:

1   The curriculum is clade-like, branching into diverse learnings and not bounded by subject divisions.
2   The curriculum moves beyond a reliance on the scientific method alone, but without discarding it either.
3   The curriculum introduces the learner to the power of analogy and metaphor, including the way metaphor shapes theory.
4   A curriculum which is based on the notion of the quantum porridge views knowledge as dynamic, not static; and encourages interconnectedness, and studies which jump across the traditional subject barriers; creates a map of learning which looks mandalic in shape, not linear; and encourages the learner to develop different stances from which to view and interpret reality.
5   The curriculum accommodates group or team learning as well as individual learning, and finds a way to give credit for group learning.
6   The search for knowledge is in the final analysis more important than arriving at 'final knowledge'.
7   The expressive and the imaginative are featured across all areas and subjects in the curriculum.
8   The curriculum develops an appreciation of how belief systems and mythologies – both personal and collective – are fundamental to all life and learning; and supplies the learner with the skills to build, hone, change and use a reliable set of beliefs.

A wise community will be insistent that these dimensions of human knowing and acting are put in place and then kept at the centre of the school curriculum.

5 The networked universe

The previous chapter began by showing that schooling has been, and largely still is, deeply patterned on the methodologies of the empirical sciences. While some of this framework needs to be retained if only because we know that it probably works well for certain areas, there has been another fundamental shift in the way we think about knowledge which could have radical implications for the curriculum, the way schools are organized, and the processes of teaching and learning. Put simply, the shift depends on the metaphor of networks, and the living organism as a bonded, interdependent network of parts. As we would expect, this same metaphor is now being used to explain many other aspects of the space we live in. In this chapter, we will consider several of these dimensions, chosen because of their relevance for what schooling is and does.

The living planetary system

As Zohar and Marshall (1994: 7) have neatly put it, 'the whole mechanistic paradigm can no longer cope with contemporary reality'. The previous two chapters have dealt with the fact that about three hundred years ago in Europe, a combination of the Scientific Enlightenment, the Industrial Revolution and European colonization of much of the world led people to liken the universe to a machine which worked on rational lines and by unchanging rules. It was a universally favoured analogy. The world was described as a clock and God ('the Creator') as the clock-maker. Much of theology was teleological. Organizations (including schools) were viewed the same way and were talked about mechanistically; people spoke of their structures and functions; and how to re-engineer them. Schooling was modelled on factories, on the production line, on manufacturing. School architecture followed the factory analogy and schools were even built to look like them. Knowledge was rational, manufactured in the same rule-bound, predictable and conformist way. Science dealt only with things which could be observed and weighed. The whole of creation, indeed, was deemed to run by mechanical and immutable laws.

The most influential criticism of this entrenched view has typically come from those who in the past might have been expected to favour it – from the hard sciences, from the disciplines which have given us such orthodoxies as economic rationalism. For example, the economist Hazel Henderson is scathing about that 'mechanistic, industrial mindset'. In her book *The Politics of the Solar Age* (1988), she says: 'It is now clear to many politicians that the competitive, expansionist, GNP-growth-oriented, resource-intensive industrial system is ... destabilizing to every locality and region on the planet and is catastrophically war-prone' (Henderson, 1988: xxxvi). Our leaders and policy analysts, she says, 'are looking at the world through the obsolete spectacles of macro-economic management and no longer appropriate sets of statistics' (*ibid.*: xxix). They have a 'paradigm problem', she says.

Largely as a result of the critiques of opinion-shapers like Henderson, the assumptions and attitudes of people around the world have undergone a massive and fundamental shift. Put simply, the machine image has been displaced by the metaphor of the living organism. We saw the same shift in metaphor in the citation from Edelman in his description of the human brain. Now the Earth itself is being imaged as a single, living being. Henderson describes it in this way.

> The Solar Age signifies more than a shift to solar and renewable resource-based societies operated with more sophisticated ecological sciences and biologically-compatible technologies. It entails a paradigm shift from the fragmented 'objective' reductionist knowledge and the mechanistic, indus-trial worldview to a comprehensive awareness of the interdependence of all life on earth – what is now well-known as the *Gaia* hypothesis: that our planet is a living organism and we humans are participants (not just observers) in its evolutionary unfolding.
>
> (Henderson, 1988: xxi)

Science is now going that way, towards 'holism'. Reductionist science 'reduced the object of study into smaller and smaller components' and thereby fragmented itself. 'The old mechanistic world view is that knowledge consists of pulling things apart, but emerging concepts say that knowledge derives from looking at how things behave as wholes' (Miller, 1987: 10).

In a much-quoted phrase which has found its way into common speech, Berman (1981) called this process the 're-enchantment of the world', and McDonagh (1986: 77–8) talks of it as freeing the human community 'from the grip of the machine metaphor' and developing 'a new story or myth of the emergence of the Earth' based upon 'modern ways of knowing'. The new mode of viewing our world will show, says McDonagh,

> without a shadow of doubt, that the universe does not run on mechanistic principles .... It shows the old story to be shallow in comparison to the new one's magnificent span of twenty billion years. It also tells us that unless we abandon mechanistic science and technology we place in jeop-ardy the future florescence of this beautiful Earth.
>
> (*ibid.*)

Once the Earth is imaged as a single living organism, with living limbs and members of which human beings are one set, with a life-force which embraces all of its parts and in which its many member bodies interact and find themselves mutually supporting and connected, then our attitudes, modes of explanation and policies all undergo a sea change. For example, says Henderson, just as each village once had its 'commons' (parklands which belonged to everyone), the *world* now has them – they are the oceans, the atmosphere, space and our newest creation, the global economy. For it and the rest of the commons to thrive, co-operative rules are needed with co-operative ownership. We now realize that 'individuals (and countries) are better off if they consider the needs of others and are worse off if they act selfishly' (Henderson, 1988: xxii). So the new metaphor transforms our approach to social responsibility, to our modes of occupying and using land and space, and even introduces a new kind of public morality. It will change a lot of the content of the conventional curriculum.

To use an example, the new world-view forces us to rethink our approach to history, which until now has largely been regarded exclusively as *human* history. Thomas Berry asks in his *Dream of the Earth* (1988: 174) why our histories should deal only with the arrival of the human species. Taking as his example the Hudson river valley in USA, he asks why the impact of human habitation there on the oyster-beds, the hemlock vegetation, the soil and the wetlands is not an essential part of the history. What would the history look like from the viewpoint of the beavers, whose cohabitation of the area is threatened by the destruction of their habitats by this late-arriving species? Using his approach, it would be possible to base at least part of the school curriculum on what he calls 'bio-regional stories', including the histories of the woods, insects, birds and animals, rivers and air, which were here before human beings arrived (Berry, 1988; Kim and Dator, 1994).

Henderson ends her book with this lucid passage:

> The planet is not a spaceship that we humans are 'steering' .... The old-fashioned image has served its purpose, but it encouraged our childish fascination with vehicles, transportation, speed, and power. The maturing understanding, growing out of both scientific research and folk knowledge, confirmed by age-old religious and mythic traditions, is that we are a conscious part of the earth – no mechanical spaceship, but a living planet, a total, teeming, pulsating, living organism.
>
> (Henderson 1988: 411)

This shift from the machine universe to a living universe is already under way and affecting many branches of knowledge, many public policies, the configuration of politics, and so on. How would industrial practices change if mining were seen not as the mechanical removal and processing of dead rocks and minerals from the earth's surface but instead as surgery on the body of a living earth? Already this kind of transformation is apparent in the forestry industry, accompanied by bitter contestation as the paradigms clash.

At base it is a deeply believed-in metaphor shift, with the whole world envisioned as an interconnected living system, a network no less, but alive. Lovelock (1988: 18) has a useful way of depicting it. Any living being is a collection of organs and tissues, each made up of millions of living cells, each of which can live separately, at least for a while. So, Lovelock concludes, 'life is social. It exists in communities and collectives.' Using a term from physics, he declares that any living system is 'colligative', a collection of separable, interactive bits and pieces bundled or tied together and making up the whole. The image will bond a new cohesive approach to the curriculum, to the content of schooling, and to schooling's place in the scheme of things.

Globalization

Globalization is the same idea applied to the economic and social interactions across the globe. Since the early 1990s, influential writers have been pointing out that far-reaching, radical and rapid changes in society were under way, clade-like, not merely among the leaves and branches but deep down among the roots. Peter Drucker's books carried titles like *The Unseen Revolution*, *The End of Economic Man*, and *The New Realities* (a phrase which became part of the vernacular). J.K. Galbraith wrote about the post-capitalist society, as though the old economic verities had been displaced. Charles Handy followed his exposition about the new life of work (*The Age of Unreason*) with *The Empty Raincoat* to explain how human beings would adapt to a redefinition of work. Ken Wilber's *Eye to Eye* was subtitled *The Search for a New Paradigm*. Willis Harman wrote about a 'global mind change', Wolf about 'the search for other worlds' in his *Parallel Universes*. Robert Reich (*The Work of Nations*) predicted the end of the politically independent nation-state. Kenichi Ohmae wrote *The End of the Nation State* in 1995 after putting a new phrase into circulation through the title of his 1990 book *The Borderless World*, in which he speculated about the implications of the newly developing, interlocking global economy. John Naisbitt (who coined the term 'megatrends') added his codicil in *The Global Paradox* by demonstrating that in such a world economy it is the small players and nations, not the large ones, which are positioned to prosper. In short, taken-for-granted assumptions about the world society were being rebuilt. Globalization had become both a reality and an issue.

But coming to terms with globalization is not as easy as at first appears. In 1992, an overseas tour took me to the Philippines and Thailand, to North America, and then to Great Britain and Europe. In moving through the three great trading blocs of the world, it was obvious that the social certainties, habits of thought, and belief-system in each of those sectors were often radically at odds, even while many of them were dissolving. There are on-the-surface similarities and regularities; shopping malls and department stores look the same the world over and the same brand names appear everywhere. The world's thinking and planning are networked, but often in ways that reveal deep-seated incomprehension of cultural differences. Angelica's generation will need to have developed as part of their education an informed, sympathetic and quite complex awareness of the countries which daily affect their life-space. To fashion their new perception about their responsibility as citizens of the *world*, they need an education which is self-consciously international; a curriculum which looks well beyond the borders of their prefecture and country; educational qualifications which are internationally viable; and the confidence to function in an international community in which many belief systems, both religious and quasi-religious, are simultaneously at work. Whether they like it or not, they will be expected to behave like members of a planetary community.

It will also be dangerous for her generation to be chauvinistic, for the interlocking global economy weakens the ability of any one nation-state to control its own affairs, including education. For example, more than fifty of the world's largest economies belong not to *countries* but to multinational corporations – like the huge conglomerate networks which Murdoch and Packer head, or the interconnected companies which made Bill Gates one of the world's richest men. Further, about three-quarters of world trade is accounted for by the world's 500 biggest companies. In the United States, 40 per cent of the exports and half the imports result not from trade between countries, or even among companies, but from intra-company movements, one arm of a corporation trading with another arm of the same company off-shore, or with foreign-based subsidiaries. These activities show up in the countries' trade figures, of course, but it is difficult for any government to monitor, even less to control, these transactions. It is even more difficult to do so when what is traded is not commodities but knowledge, know-how and advice, designs and ideas. Countries struggle to collect taxes on these transactions. It is not surprising that there is universal concern about tax reform, for every social amenity – including schools, hospitals, universities, ambulance services, roads, air and shipping lanes, social welfare services and police – is affected by a nation's ability to raise revenue to pay for these things.

It is also difficult for one country to supply amenities and services to its own citizens when it exists alongside another country whose citizens lack those services. Within a matter of years the world community will have to consider some kind of international social service network. Elements of it already exist in the way countries now contribute to famine relief in Africa; to the problems of refugees in the Balkans and to boat people in Asia; to the aftermath of floods, cyclones, earthquakes and volcanic eruptions; to the AIDS epidemic in Central Africa; to the problem of pollution through smoke haze from Indonesia; to the collective human effect on the ozone layer; to the destruction of tuna fish in the Pacific; or to what might be considered internal politics – such as in the former Yugoslavia, or Indonesia.

In the same way and for the same reasons, *schools* are becoming self-consciously international, especially in the curriculum, because this generation of young learners must become literally world citizens if humanity is to survive as a species. There were some chastening milestones during the 1990s to demonstrate how the world for this generation has changed from that of their parents. For example, 1995 marked the fiftieth anniversary of the end of the Second World War. Very few teachers had even been born by 1945 and therefore had no experience of a *whole world* being at war. It was fifty years from the dropping of the first atom bombs on Hiroshima and Nagasaki, the event which symbolized the arrival of the Atomic Age in which any nation can now trigger the collapse of the world's eco-system. The Vietnam War had ended twenty years before with the fall of Saigon; it was the war which killed the mythology about Western superiority, about colonialism, and about Eurocentric thinking. It was the tenth anniversary of the nuclear meltdown in the Chernobyl power station in Russia, which produced radiation fallout right across Europe, an event which proved that what happens within the borders of one country is not solely that country's business. Civil wars in central Africa, Yugoslavia, north India, Sri Lanka, acts of terrorism which endanger international air flights, the gas attacks in Tokyo's subways, earthquake and famine, and oil spills in seas and rivers demonstrate that it is an interconnected world.

Kenichi Ohmae in his book *The Borderless World* (1990: 19) put it this way:

> Today ... people everywhere are more and more able to get the information they want directly from all corners of the world. They can see for themselves what the tastes and preferences are in other countries, the style of clothes now in fashion, the sports, the lifestyles .... Leaders can no longer keep citizens in sub-standard housing because people know – directly – how others live elsewhere .... They can sit in their living rooms, watch Cable News Network, and know instantaneously what is reported in the United States.

In his prescient book *The Work of Nations: A Blueprint for the Future* (1992) Robert Reich proposed that 'the idea of the nation-state as a collection of people sharing some responsibility for their mutual well-being' was already passé. The global economy had produced an international market-place in which large and small companies buy, sell, lease and franchise component parts and services across the globe, virtually disregarding national boundaries, even using the world's currencies themselves as though they are components to be traded along with goods, services and know-how. The very idea of a national economy, then, was losing its meaning, asserted Reich (*ibid.*: 8). Money can move fast and almost invisibly; functions, production and finance can be shuffled across the globe. As Ohmae (1990: viii) observed, 'Nothing is "*overseas*" any longer.'

Walter Wriston's book *The Twilight of Sovereignty* (1992) put the same view, arguing that national boundaries are becoming increasingly irrelevant, and that the trappings of sovereign power are being leached away. No matter what political leaders do or say, Wriston said, the screens will continue to light up, traders will trade, and currency values will continue to be set, not only by governments, but by the global plebiscite. Indeed, Ohmae (1990: 20) showed that the more we

educate people, the more they become 'global citizens'. The poor and uneducated are anchored to time and place, and are subject to manipulation or
exploitation – political, religious, financial. It is only the citizens of poor countries who are nation-bound and bordered. The rich and the educated become
independent and free. At the point when the per capita GNP exceeds a certain
level (about $US 10,000 a year, he estimated), religion, government, nationality
and sense of locality lose their importance and people become international in
their interests and orientations. For *them*, the world is borderless.

Out of this kind of context, there has developed a global, interconnected
web of enterprises and activities, separable into small parts, interdependent,
and the whole no longer owned by anyone. No one country any longer owns
motor car manufacturing, or footwear and textile production, the computer
industry, or food processing. No one and no country owns companies the way
they did during the Industrial Revolution, when big factories dominated the
economy. There is simply no place for bureaucracy in these enterprises, either
public or private; for bureaucracy belongs with the Industrial Revolution. The
service sector now employs 70 per cent of the workforce in the United States,
60 per cent in Japan, and 50 per cent of the newly industrialized country of
Taiwan (Ohmae, 1990: 15).

Many companies have become loosely connected networks of co-operating
units.

> What is traded between nations is less often finished products than special-
> ized problem-solving (research, product design, fabrication), problem-
> identifying (marketing, advertising, customer consulting), and brokerage
> (financing, searching, contracting) services, as well as certain routine
> components and services, all of which are combined to create value.
>
> (Reich, 1992: 113)

The company does not need to own these contributors to its product; it
merely requires a contract to ensure that they are supplied on time, to the right
specifications and of an acceptable quality. It is more economical for the firm
not to carry these expensive overheads, but to buy contributions when they are
needed. 'In fact relatively few people actually work for the high-value enterprise
in the traditional sense of having steady jobs with fixed salaries' (*ibid.*).

Because this international web of enterprise is so heavily dependent on skill,
knowledge and an educated workforce, probably for the first time in history
education and schooling are at the heart of international well-being, and will
be required to deliver quality learnings. If that is the case, then schools or
school systems can no longer be parochial or insular about their curricula or
about the performance levels of their students, for these school leavers will find
themselves in an international workplace alongside of or in competition with
people from neighbouring countries, and where the jobs themselves (and the
existence of those jobs) depend on international rather than national conditions. Their credentials must have international currency. It is simply no longer

good enough for students to compare their performances only against those of other students in the same year in the same city, province or country. What is learnt in school by young people of their own age in Japan, Canada, South America, Europe, South Korea or India is directly relevant to them. This generation of young people, therefore, must learn to become global citizens through an education and a curriculum self-consciously international.

A new approach to permanence and transience

In schools no less than in the business world, transience has replaced permanence. In *The New Realities* (1990) Drucker listed some of the changes which had occurred in the last quarter of the twentieth century to demonstrate how radically deep and extensive has been the transformation into a new worldview. The following is a précis of the matters which he discussed.

> There is 'no more salvation by society', and Roosevelt's New Deal is now history, no longer believed in. The Russian Empire, the world's last colonial power, has dissolved. The arms race is now seen as counter-productive. We now realize there are limits to government, to what governments can do, and we have moved from a belief in omnipotent government to a belief in privatization. There are new pluralisms abroad which will force us to redefine what we mean by social and community responsibility; and they will tend to be stated in global, transnational terms. There will be a transnational economy that mirrors transnational ecology. Economic development itself has become paradoxical, and economic theory with it. It is now a post-business society, with the decline of capitalism and the rise of knowledge workers. Blue-collar work and unions are under threat, and information-based organizations have supplanted bureaucracies. Management has become a liberal art. Learning has become a continuing core activity for everyone and schools are of fundamental importance.

The list demonstrates a view that nothing has a right to continue to exist if it is non-functional, non-productive and not in phase with the needs of modern times. Success and the right to permanence have been decoupled. In terms of simple operation and survival, many of the world's companies now realize that they can survive only by breaking themselves up into smaller entities. Sadtler *et al.* (1997) argue that large corporations are often worth more dead than alive; their component pieces do better apart, by being sold off or by working autonomously of the large bloc. They talk of the 'unprecedented whirlwind of self-dismemberment' among corporations. Often higher productivity and lower costs are achieved not by doing the job in-house but by leasing out a production or function to another firm which already has the expertise for it. For example, Nike designs and sells running shoes, and only that. The actual production of the shoe, its manufacture, is contracted out, and usually off-shore.

Thus many of the large organizations which we have grown used to in the past are in the process of breaking up into smaller, more vigorous units, held together by strategic alliances and symbiotic arrangements. Brand names and corporate titles sometimes survive the breakup and reassignment of roles and functions, masking how fundamental are the working relationships behind the facade. But there is no sanctity in permanence. What produces the best value determines shapes and structures.

It is usually the organizations in the not-for-profit sectors (like schools, churches, welfare organizations, hospitals, and local institutions) which are the slowest to move, which experience community reaction when they change, and which suffer losses. Their history, their level of community support, their good name and their known modes of operation can obstruct change and actually hasten their demise.

And this is a challenge for schools. Schools have had to learn that they are not so much a set of buildings or real estate but a facility (at times intangible) for providing the core activity of teaching and learning. Schools generally have tried to maintain their operations on one campus; to require their students physically to work on the school's owned premises; to design and control their curricula in-house through their own full-time and salaried teaching staff, working on-campus; and indeed to employ full-time staff rather than mixing and matching excellent skills which they can buy elsewhere at a contract price. Schools tend to operate out of buildings which they own rather than lease; and they purchase rather than lease equipment, which almost immediately becomes obsolescent.

If schools had to pay rental for time and use of physical space, would they keep their buildings and grounds unused during school vacations or at night and weekends? Underused school buildings are everywhere, many wrongly located, many of architecture not worth preserving, many configured unnecessarily for single-purpose usage. When it is now so easy to commute across suburbs and to interact by means of technology, schools tend to tie up their operating funds in physical plant and equipment in unnecessary ways, and they can miss out on access to some of the profession's most skilled practitioners whose services can be leased through contracts.

Even in spite of school closures brought on by demographic shifts, there is still a strong tendency for schools (and their parent populations) to think of themselves as permanent organizations and to put high value on their traditions, their ongoing culture, their past record and their accumulating heritage of former students. The evidence abroad, especially in the international community, is that a longing for permanence can be suicidal as well as unimaginative and unrealistic. Paradoxically, strong institutions may need to practise transience in order to achieve their own permanence and continuity.

Information technology

Probably the most profound revolution of all for a learning institution is the advance in computers and information technology. The huge possibilities for learning technologies and for easy access to information-generating databases from across the globe change the nature of schooling profoundly, including the physical spaces where students learn. Three decades ago, we could not have imagined that a time would come when every child would have access to a television set and a telephone; when every child would be able to use a computer both at home and at school; when everyone would be contactable, wherever they are, by mobile telephone. There is now a growing literature about virtual reality, virtual schools and the virtual organization (Davidow and Malone, 1992; Hedberg *et al.*, 1997; Lipnack and Stamps, 1994).

We shall have to engage the ramifications of the new learning technologies in the second part of this book. It is sufficient here to allude to some of the possibilities and their implications for schooling. It is clear, for example, that:

- Every child will acquire the skills to access digital information in the same way and in addition to the way they now access material in print. 'Literacy' in the sense of reading and writing now means both digital and print.
- Anywhere and at any time, day or night, the child can access the information storehouses of the world. The impact on learning when every child has the equivalent of a 25-volume set of the *Encyclopedia Britannica* physically with her all day and every day is already well known. We know of the assignments she can do, the information she can access, the research skills she can acquire and hone.
- The child can access school from her own home. She also has access to all the digitalized learning facilities in her suburb, town or city. She need not physically 'come to school' so often, especially when her mother or father, working out of their home office, is at home too, and when all her teachers are on-line.
- The standard school day and school year disappear when it is easier to access the Internet after normal working hours. There is no point in preserving the 9-to-5 factory day for schools when factory patterns have been superseded everywhere else in society.
- Schooling is becoming increasingly paperless (it will never be completely so while print skills last) as intra-school communications are computerized, as e-mail access to other students and places is available, as e-books allow even those books in print to be downloaded to a portable carrier.
- Schooling is borderless in that the technology makes for easy contacts which subsume geography, school boundaries and national borders.

Even these few profound changes delivered through the field of information technology have huge implications for the way the school operates (whatever it is in physical terms).

Conclusion

In summary, then, this chapter has dealt with megatrends which are moving schools no less than society's other institutions.

- The new reality images the planet, and probably also the universe, as a single, complex, interconnected, living entity – not a machine but an alive being.
- Globalization is a powerful factor impinging on how we image our world. National borders have become less significant, for this is a borderless world in which one's humanity counts more than one's nationality, where nation-states have lost their powers, and where we all have a collective responsibility for the planet.
- It is a world where change is valued above permanence; where transcendence and meaning are often found in what is fleeting and temporary; where permanence, tradition, and longevity are not necessarily signs of value or success. In that future the role of government is changed, is less relied upon, and often not believed in, and many of the traditional institutions (like schools) have been so slow to adapt that they are in danger of not coping.
- And it is a communicating world in which technology surmounts geography and gives us unimagined access to people, information and things.

From now on, *every* student will have to be encouraged to behave like a global citizen, for education has become part of the borderless world. It is the urgent task of teachers and schools to produce programmes which incorporate the trends enunciated above, designed to produce people who are courageous, robust, well-formed and confident persons. These megatrends may force us to reconceive not only the nature and mission of schooling but also how it is delivered. In the next chapter, we look at the new logic underlying post-industrial, knowledge-based organizations – one class of which are schools.

6 From bureaucracy to enterprise networks

The movement into schooling suited to a twenty-first-century, post-industrial, globalized society should lead to some fundamental changes to terminology. Words like curriculum, class, graduation, programme, levels and streams will either have to be discarded or given new meanings. A lot of school architecture, the ideas about schools literally set in concrete, have to change too. And so will the way schools view and use teachers.

We found in a previous chapter that a post-industrial state is also a post-bureaucratic one. When there is a paradigm change of this magnitude, something fundamental happens to the way society conceives of government and the actions it is appropriate for government to be involved in. A new conception of how agencies like schools, education departments, and enterprises (particularly large ones) are organized and operate comes into play; and a new configuration of resource management (not least, money management) is invented. Even the industrial society's school curriculum was bureaucratic and control-oriented, conceived of as mechanical, logical, ordered and controlled from on high. So how is post-industrial, post-bureaucratic, post-modern schooling governed, controlled, and managed?

A new management model for the delivery of education emerged across the world in the last decade of the twentieth century, based almost universally on how private enterprise works. Its common characteristic is that each unit in the system has managerial autonomy not possible inside a bureaucracy. To understand how the management and control of schools are being remade, then, we need to study the private business model which has been copied (Deal and Kennedy, 1982; Toffler, 1985; Handy, 1985; Caldwell and Spinks, 1988, 1992; Beare, 1990, 1995). The same model is being introduced across the whole range of public administration, and not just in education.

The new logic for government services

Part of the change to the way education and schools are organized and administered results from the new logic for government, a one-best-way based on economics. It has three simple premises:

- *If the private sector can do it, then let them do it.* The private sector can carry out a function more cheaply than a public agency because a private enterprise is dominated by the profit motive. It will perform the function more efficiently, because it is driven by competition and the need for productivity, for getting the most out of the dollar. And it will perform the function well because it must attract (and then hold) customers by giving a superior service.
- *The role of government is to set the frameworks for service delivery*, and not necessarily to supply the service itself. Government exists to create policy, to lay down the principles for a good society, and to regulate, but it should not be in the business of providing goods and services. This approach embodies a belief in small government. When a government sets up a service, it tends to be a monopoly which is not subject to the discipline of competition. So the government is better off acting as the umpire to keep the game clean, disciplined and fair. It causes an automatic conflict of interest if the government is the regulator of a service in which it is also a player or provider.
- *It is legitimate for government to be a provider only when it is a provider of last resort.* Put another way, the government should collect and use tax dollars only when it is obvious that those dollars could not be better used in and by the private sector. It should provide a service only when it is essential to the well-being of society but is unlikely to be provided adequately by private enterprise.

This restated mission of government rests on the idea of the free market and the power of enlightened self-interest. In particular terms, customer choice disciplines every provider by introducing rewards (including continuing patronage) for good service, and almost instant penalty for sub-standard service. The book by the American authors Osborne and Gaebler entitled *Reinventing Government* (1993) neatly synthesized what numbers of writers and practitioners had been advocating for some years. In the 1990s, then, governments of all persuasions sold off the parts of their operations which could just as easily be run *by* private enterprise or *as* private enterprises, including steel mills, banks and insurance companies, power plants, national telephone systems, airlines, metropolitan railways, prisons, garbage collection, fire protection and mail services, and electricity supplies. Privatization became the norm. In the process of divestment, governments around the world freed themselves from the heavy burden of loan servicing (which of course absorbs tax dollars).

The ten operating principles explained by Osborne and Gaebler can be translated so that they apply specifically to schools.

1   *Steering rather than rowing*
    Government should make things happen in education but it need not carry out the functions itself. Hence in many countries schools were made self-managing, were given a lump-sum budget and told to operate with it. In the

process, the distinctions, such as they were, between private and public schools became blurred, and appropriately so (Caldwell and Hayward, 1998).

2   *Empowering rather than serving*

Government should allow those who provide services (in this case, schools) the power to act for themselves. Centralized controls distort the operation of those delivering a service, putting a complication in the way of tailoring the service to what the client wants. Those externally imposed controls need to be minimized where they cannot be disbanded, for they tend to distort the nature and delivery of the service, and sometimes make it more costly.

3   *Injecting competition into service delivery*

Government should sponsor competition among the service providers such as schools and educational support agencies rather than create government monopolies. Schools are therefore expected to compete for their customers. To do that, they must be *different* from each other, success-oriented and aggressively competitive. If it is impossible to see how your school differs from the one across town, then you have not heard the message of the market economy. Competition implies choice; choice implies variety; and variety implies that the user or consumer will make a selection on the basis of demonstrated quality.

4   *Mission-driven government*

Each school is expected to fulfil its educational mission and to focus on that mission as its first and over-riding priority, not to follow a rule-book of government regulations. Therefore, each school needs to define who it is and what it stands for. Rules and laws are not ends in themselves; but a mission is. The government will then insist through external audits and quality checks that the school becomes what it says it wants to be, and achieves the level of student performance it said it would achieve. The school's accountability is based on mission statements and deliberate planning, and then on documented outcomes.

5   *Results-oriented government*

A service agency is judged on its outputs, not by inputs. A school, therefore, must show evidence that it is achieving what it was set up and paid to achieve. Its student learning outcomes must therefore be well documented and defensible, for the sponsorship of learning is one of its prime purposes. If the school achieves its purposes well, an outside regulator or a customer presumably need not be concerned about the methods it used to achieve its ends.

6   *Satisfy the customer, not the bureaucracy ('customer-driven government')*

The schools are considered to be immediately accountable to the public (and especially the learners) they serve. Funding arrangements, especially the subsidies from governments, are therefore remodelled to put purchasing power in the hands of the customer. There are now many extant variations of educational vouchers, including per capita funding and the Victorian (Australia) and Edmonton (Canada) idea of a Student Resource Index, which puts a bounty on the head of each child reflecting the costs of educating that child. The school which enrols the child accordingly receives that level of funds.

7   *Earning rather than spending*
Schools have tended to be spenders and not earners; they are usually called non-profit organizations. The Osborne and Gaebler decalogue suggests that the individual school should be encouraged to earn revenue where it can, rather than merely spend tax dollars. 'Enterprising government' means that the school should act like an enterprise; so regarded, it is a medium-sized enterprise, and by no means small. The school can make money by hiring out its facilities, by selling its staff's expertise in consultancies and professional advisory services, by inventing new uses for the school's resources. Revenue is raised on the understanding that the users pay for the service.

8   *Prevention rather than cure*
As we shall see in the penultimate chapter, education in the industrial economy tended to be formulaic, working to agreed conditions and required standards in the manner of a trade. A truly professional service is expected to be more creative than that. The professional enterprise called school is expected to plan ahead and to take evasive action rather than react to problems after they have arisen. Anticipatory, pro-active and creative, frontier-breaking and corner-cutting – these are the kinds of descriptors which the Osborne and Gaebler approach produces for schools.

9   *Decentralized government*
Big, centralized organizations are as passé as the industrial society which produced them. In the post-industrial, knowledge-based society there is a general movement away from top-down controls both within the school and in the system. The emphasis is on teamwork, professionalism, participation, on sharing responsibility and power, and on a new kind of managerial structure. The heavy-limbed, large-scale, hierarchical, control-driven schools and school systems modelled on the Industrial Revolution's factories have disappeared into history.

10 *And market-oriented schooling*
Government should use the inherent competitiveness of markets to develop the leverage to achieve its public benefits.

Under the new conditions, then, schools, like any other service providers, are to have the same general characteristics – small administration; private rather than public ownership; contracts for a contract price; the principle of users pay; and customer choice. Considerations of social justice do pose problems in such a set of conditions.

Post-modern management for schools

The new management structures for schools and school systems have therefore been modelled upon the successful modern corporation, the flexible conglomerate which keeps central control of the essential and strategic areas but allows entrepreneurial freedom to the operating units which make up the body corporate. Schools and education systems are once again borrowing both the names and the concepts of business, and building the organizational structures which appear to give the flexibility to operate in volatile market conditions and also the means to stay in control of events. It involves paring down big central bureaucracies and reassigning staff; it also involves re-configuring the school itself so that it no longer is bureaucratic and hierarchical in its basic structures. The centre no longer pretends to be the engine of specific, universal control.

These new models are not recent. A new organizational paradigm has been displacing the factory model since the early 1970s, rendering much of the paraphernalia of hierarchy-bound bureaucracy obsolescent and even unworkable. Hammer and Champy (1994: 17), the inventors of 'corporate re-engineering', have written,

> The reality that organizations have to confront ... is that the old ways of doing business – the division of labor around which companies have been organized since Adam Smith first articulated the principle – simply don't work anymore. Suddenly, the world is a different place.

Robert Reich in his seminal *The Work of Nations* (1992: 3) wrote that 'we are living through a transformation that will rearrange the politics and economics of the coming century' and that it will present a 'stark challenge' to organizations. Bill Gates of Microsoft (1999: xiii–xiv, xviii), who has pioneered much of the digital revolution, says that whereas in the 1980s the emphasis was on quality and in the 1990s on re-engineering, 'the 2000s will be about velocity' – the speed of information transmission and transaction – and how organizations cope with such speed.

In summary, then, post-industrial, knowledge-based organizations are radically different in shape and style of operation from those of the industrial society. The societal or political model which required government to be the provider of all essential (and many non-essential) services is out of date and is being supplanted by a new way of thinking. Centralized controls; standardized provisions; equality of access to public services; homogenized quality; awards and regulations which impose conformity and consistency – these have been superseded.

The new logic about government prevails no matter which political party is in power and regardless of which developed country you happen to be in. The model is international, appears to be universally accepted, is justified with the same terminology, and is rooted in the same economic orthodoxies. It undergirds the interlocking, international, monetary and trading systems. It is global. It arrived with the collapse of the Soviet Union, the rejection of communist ideologies as a basis for sound government, the emergence of the Japanese and then the Chinese economies as dominant forces into international markets, the coming-of-age of Asian economies as they confront economic downturn, recession and rebuilding, and the brooding, controlling presence of the international monetary system. It is the result of a newly arrived, powerfully dominant world view which each of us must learn to live with.

The new organizational structures adopt the modes which appear to be successful in the business or private sector. They are based on networks. Since bureaucracy grew out of an economy which was predominantly industrial and for which the major organizing metaphor was the production line, it is to be expected that the post-industrial economy would spawn new forms of organization using the major organizing metaphor of networking. A business which operates on solid bureaucratic lines cannot compete in a post-industrial economy which guarantees survival only to those firms which are flexible and have multiple connections, which can make quick, strategic decisions, which encourage innovation and entrepreneurship, which value creativity rather than conformity, which give their members the power to take local decisions and to exercise initiative, and which regard the people in the organization as partners rather than as property or as 'employees'.

These qualities are also found in those apparently large organizations which are international and multi-faceted. While there are some frameworks, probably centrally devised, which all parts of the network will honour, and while there is a set of priorities which all members of the firm must observe, it is recognized that it would be presumptuous, if not arrogant, of those at headquarters to think they should or even could impose controls on all the day-to-day operations of the firm, or monitor all the activities of its several parts, or make all the strategic decisions for all the company's members.

As Robert Reich pointed out in *The Work of Nations* (1992), we are now dealing with an international web of enterprises. That constellation is so heavily dependent on skill, knowledge and an educated workforce that, probably for the first time in history, education and schooling are at the heart of international well-being, and will be required not only to deliver quality learnings but to be configured appropriately to do it. What we are seeing, then, is an internationalized trade in education, with privatized provision of educational services and schooling, itself copying the international web of other enterprises. Education systems and individual schools are now being required to adopt the fluid, entrepreneurial, organizational patterns which characterize the new growth areas of the economy. Education itself has become an international industry functioning in a borderless world.

The obsolescent organization was based on *control* – hierarchy; bigness and standardization; top-down, centralized command structures; and old-style supervision. The logic for the modern organization is based on *accomplishment of mission*. Even though the context inside as well as outside the organization appears to be fluid and impermanent, it is just such circumstances which impose on the organization's leadership the discipline of clarity of purpose. If one is to stick to the knitting (to use the phrase popularized by Peters and Waterman in 1982) and to concentrate on the activity which the organization is deemed to be expert in, it is essential for everyone in the company to be crystal clear about what is the core business and what are the company's priorities. The trajectory of achieving its mission is usually shown as a series of steps which set the organization on its path and give it the framework to keep monitoring its progress towards the achievement of its prime purposes. The standard process usually looks like the following.

1 *Articulation of mission* Managers must be able to state unequivocally what is the organization's prime mission – why it exists, what are its core purposes, what it plans to do and not to do, in what ways it plans to operate and function. Style, culture, and focus are important considerations from the outset.

2 *Master plan* A long-term plan is then devised, usually covering a period of three, five or seven years, specifying what the organization hopes to achieve in that time, what are its production and operating targets, what are priority areas, what are its proximate, medium and longer-term goals.

3 *An action plan for the year* The organization then draws up a plan for the year, making explicit what are the priorities for that particular year, the production targets, the areas for development for the year, and the timelines.

4 *The action plan is operationalized* The targets are then converted into operational terms, and allocated to particular positions or operational units, together with a statement about acceptable standards of performance. Indicators for measuring performance are negotiated and agreed to, including what evidence needs to be accumulated. The indicators are calibrated against some benchmark considered to embody a satisfactory level of performance.

5 *Mid-cycle reviews* determine how all the component parts are travelling, whether the planned targets will be met, and whether revisions and fine-tuning are required.

6 *End-of-cycle review and the formulation of an annual report for stakeholders* At the end of the year, there is a formal round of reviews, assessing the performance of the whole organization and each of its several parts against the targets set out in the original plan. The cycle usually ends with the construction of a formal annual report, in which the firm gives an account of itself to its shareholders or trustees.

7 *Rewards and incentives* The organization may formally reward high performance to serve as an incentive for efforts in the subsequent cycle. Whether this is done or not, the organization is judged on its outcomes, on what it has achieved, on the basis of data and documented evidence.

This is exactly the process described later in the chapter which relates to school charters, and is principally the reason why the notion of charters came into existence in the first place. Schools are well placed and already skilled to function in this way. When they operate as free-standing, quasi-independent, professional enterprises (the kind of conditions which self-management creates), a set of procedures like these would have to be invented if they were not already in existence. Otherwise, the organization has no acceptable defence against criticism, and is not in a position to satisfy its accountability requirements.

The new organization tends to take a radical approach to resourcing, asking how much it can achieve with the resources it already has, and how it can use those resources in the most creative way. It does not ask to be judged on the size of its budget, but it is concerned that it gets value from the dollars expended. If it encounters resource shortage (and most organizations do!), then it makes sure that the core business is attended to first and that resources are not frittered away on peripherals. It expects to be rewarded for 'value added'. Indeed, it may achieve more by being made lean rather than by being allocated increased funding. Thus Eric Hanushek, in his book *Making Schools Work* (1994), applies the approach to schooling like this:

- Remove from schools any resources not being efficiently used, and contract the service out.
- If schools must have classes, increase their average size and vary the modes of instruction and tutoring.
- Introduce no reforms unless it can be shown that they actually *save* money or are demonstrably cost-effective.
- Employ comparatively fewer teachers, recruited from among the best graduates in the nation, pay them more, but make sure they perform only tasks commensurate with their qualifications and expertise.
- Give teachers monetary incentives for improving the way students perform.

What, then, are the distinguishing features of the organization which has been variously described as a constellation, a federation or a network organization? It was depicted well by Toffler in his book *The Adaptive Corporation* (1985), which analysed how the giant American firm AT&T should restructure to ensure productivity. The organization has a centre or core which retains 'tight control over technical quality, research and development, major investment decisions, planning, training, and coordinative activities' and which becomes 'the intelligence centre of a large constellation of companies and organizations' (Toffler, 1985: 129). It then operates through a spider's web of interconnecting, relatively autonomous, contractual units which deliver goods or services when they are needed, 'just in time'.

Thus there is a relatively small, lean, headquarters (or core) staff. Indeed, the corporation need employ only a core staff, smaller in number, more highly qualified and more synoptic in its roles than the management staff used to be, a group 'whose essential product is leadership' (*ibid.*).

The rest of the firm's activities are conceived of as separable functions. They are defined into modules, and then contracted or franchised out to satellite units or subsidiary firms who supply services or components to the mother company, and usually for a negotiated fee. It is not necessary for the modular operations to be performed by the firm, nor is it necessary for the firm to own all the subsidiaries which handle the modules. Some of them can be mini-firms, some operate as 'firms within the firm', and others as independent entities. The head office or core does not need to concern itself with the internal workings of the subsidiary nor to dabble in its work methods, nor even to own it, provided the service is carried out to the satisfaction of the parent company. Some of the company's best executives may form 'spin-off companies' with venture capital from the parent company and a contract to provide a guaranteed service for a price. (See Figure 6.1.)

Figure 6.1   The networked organization for a knowledge-based society

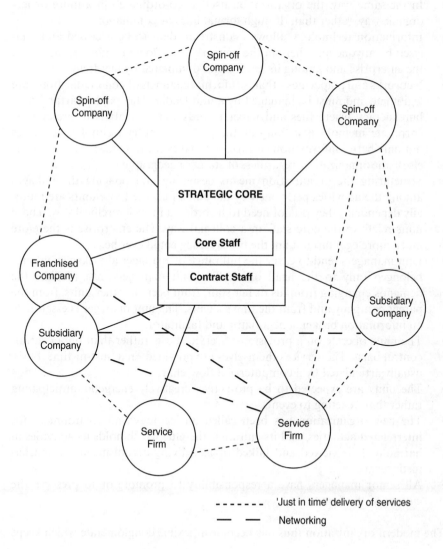

The network organization which replaces conventional bureaucracy thus has the following characteristics:

- It consists of a set of relatively small, relatively autonomous units oper ating inside an umbrella body identified as the corporation or the firm.
- The units are loosely coupled. What goes on inside each unit does not necessarily concern the whole corporation, provided an adequate service is given.
- The unit managers can only operate collegially, they cannot adopt a 'top-down' or 'boss' mentality, because their units are made up of professionalized persons hired on the basis of the expertise they can contribute to the unit's function.
- In the same way, the organization itself is co-ordinated in a more or less organic way, rather than through formal lines of command.
- Information technology allows mainstream data to be accessed and analysed by anyone anywhere in the network. The flow of information within the enterprise and among its parts is not dominated by hierarchy.
- Networks and grapevines – that is, informal channels of communication – are legitimate and must be managed by a unit leader. The 'paper warfare' of a bureaucracy where files and paper records were essential to preserve its corporate memory is a thing of the past. Computer technology provides not only better information storage, but makes the data available to anyone else in the organization, regardless of status or geography.
- Structuring the organization means designing and policing the linkages among the activities performed by the units. Because those units are mutually dependent, they do not need to be ordered in a hierarchical way. Those units relate to the core staff in a collegial way. The enterprise is therefore much more egalitarian than the bureaucracy could ever be.
- Unit managers tend to carry the full range of managerial tasks which once belonged only to the head office. The unit manager must mediate the demands emerging from his or her staff, from peers in other units, from the parent company and from the unit's clients. The unit manager is essentially an information broker, a negotiator and facilitator.
- The units operate on a provision-of-service basis rather than on a central-control basis. The services themselves are provided on a 'just-in-time' basis, usually articulated by a computerized flow-chart.
- The units are expected to be pro-active, creatively energetic, anticipating rather than reacting to events.
- The new organization has been called an 'ecology', an environment for interrelated activities, and its culture is the glue which holds its activities in harmony. It is viewed and talked of as a living organism, not in mechanistic terms.
- All senior managers have a responsibility to promote or to preserve the culture of the firm.

The modern organization thus has become a flexible conglomerate which keeps central control of the essential and strategic areas but allows entrepreneurial freedom to the operating units which make up the body corporate. If we were to apply these principles to the enterprises delivering education, it would probably look like the following. As this organizational model is described, ask yourself, 'Am I describing my school?'

- The organizational pyramid, the typical bureaucratic hierarchy, has been replaced with a network organization, a system of interconnecting, semi-autonomous operating units, each of which is relatively small and whose internal arrangements and modes of operating are self-determined.
- Those units have a contract (either literally or metaphorically) to provide a designated service of a required quality for the enterprise (in this case, the school). It is not necessary for the organization (the school) to *own* all the subsidiary units; they can be spin-off companies, or units to whom a function is franchised out, or firms within a firm (schools within schools), and in those circumstances they are remunerated for doing the job. The parent organization ensures that it gets value for money through an accountability mechanism which uses mutually negotiated performance indicators and a regular audit or set of quality checks. There are formal reporting-back procedures, an agreed format for giving that feedback, and a core unit which handles these regular audits. The units are judged on outputs, on the quality of the services they contribute to the whole.
- There is a 'strategic core', which does not control the units in the traditional sense, but it does co-ordinate them by providing the broad frameworks within which the whole organization operates. That core:

  - makes the strategic decisions for the whole;
  - undertakes long-range planning;
  - co-ordinates and articulates the enterprise;
  - raises the enterprise's global budget, and then apportions it;
  - institutes quality controls;
  - ensures staff development is provided throughout the whole organization;
  - manages the enterprise's (or school's) culture.

- The organization (or school) is organized collegially, not hierarchically, effectively as a federation of sub-systems, with an appropriate internal governance mechanism. It is possible to interchange the parts of the organization without interfering with individual career lines or with the enterprise's well-being.

This new model for management seems particularly well suited to education, for schools are, after all, almost the archetypical 'knowledge organization'.

Meeting the costs

The insistent problem behind all re-engineering of this kind is cost. Education has become so expensive that it is beyond the capacity of governments to finance everything they would like to do in education. Ironically, at the time when higher levels of education are needed to support the kind of economy a country requires to remain internationally competitive, governments appear to have exhausted their options for funding education along traditional lines. Some new devices and policies are emerging.

There are several levels of government and some powerful actors outside education (the business community, for example) which have an intense interest in what happens in education and in schooling. But it is only a sectoral interest, and they are prepared to finance only that part of the educational operation which affects their interests. Education is no longer thought of as an automatic public good, to be funded without question from the public purse. Some elements of it are, but not all of it. What is developing, therefore, is split-level funding, and possibly also split-level provision.

Constitutional powers (or lack of them) notwithstanding, a *national government* tends to be deeply concerned about those aspects of education and schooling which affect the country's economy, the productivity of its workforce, its relationships with its neighbouring countries, and its health (to name four in which it exercises legal authority). The federal government of Australia, for example, has adopted interventionist strategies over the skills of the workforce; it has funded initiatives in migrant education (migration is a national responsibility); and, given Australia's situation in the Pacific circle, it has pushed a national policy about language learning. Where the national government is directly involved like this, it is certain to intervene and is also duty-bound to provide some funding for those areas. A national government will take a keen interest in certain parts of schooling, but not all.

Second, *state or provincial governments* are directly concerned about community well-being, and have shown a willingness to participate in policy formation about and to provide funding for those aspects of schooling which make for social harmony, for the skills of the workforce, for the understanding of political systems and the processes of government, and so on. Thus they support the provision of an education in 'key learning areas', in the domains which make for good citizenship, social responsibility, and a sense of community. In these areas, largely utilitarian and instrumental though their approaches might be, state, territory or provincial governments continue to provide funding, including subsidies for independent schools. The governments at this level seem happy for some schools to be provided at parent expense; they are the so-called private schools. However, it is so socially damaging to have an uneducated populace that governments cannot tolerate such a possibility and have shown themselves anxious to ensure that every child has access to an education in those areas they deem important to society. Where no one else will provide adequate schooling in relation to these aspects, then the state must do so. In this respect, some state-run schools (though at present not all) are substantially 'provisions of last resort'. That is the logic of the market metaphor.

And third, it is now evident that governments are often not particularly interested in funding those educational provisions which are clearly personal, or not essential from their perspectives. Ensuring 'that every child meets his or her full potential' tends to be a *personal or parental* concern rather than a governmental one. The recipient (or his or her parents) will probably be expected to pay for or to subsidize those aspects of schooling; indeed, if they do not, no one else will. To take an example, it may be very desirable for a child to play organized sport, for personal development; but governments are reluctant to meet the expenses for it; and teachers, already overloaded with new roles, are unlikely to provide coaching or supervision without some kind of payment. Notions like education for individual differences, a full education for all and 'education for life' were catchcries of progressive education; but those areas of personal development or personal formation may have to be funded by someone other than government, probably by parents. In the domains which are clearly a 'personal good' for the learner only, some children seem certain to miss out.

What emerges once the metaphor of markets and consumer choice takes hold, then, is that each school can expect to receive split-level funding from a plurality of financing bodies, including different levels of government. It is also probable that as split-level provision grows, some aspects of education which were once associated with schooling will be provided by bodies which until now have not been regarded as 'schools'.

A framework for considering the education sector

The new formats, when applied to education, schools and schooling, produce some new ground-rules. Education has to break itself out of all those constrictive ideas which were inherited from the industrially based society. To make coherent the picture of schooling which has emerged with the mindchange of the twenty-first century, and as an attempt to cohere the ideas which have been covered in Part One of this book, we spell out here a set of nine propositions which embody the logic for the kind of schooling provisions planned for the new century. Some of the propositions may be uncomfortable, and some may change the nature of schooling in ways which the reader may think unfortunate. That may be so. But this is the logic which the new world-view Angelica spoke about in Chapter 2 seems to have produced.

1 Education is an industry, a sector of the economy

It satisfies the definition of an industry, being a 'particular branch of productive labour' (to use the Oxford Dictionary's definition) and providing employment and remuneration for those working in it. Millions of people across the globe earn their livelihoods through their 'productive labour' in education. The sector's 'product' is learning or personal development, for the supply of which people invent programmes. These learning programmes are bought and sold. Some of the outputs of the industry are tangible (like books, computer programs, curriculum materials, examinations and certificates) and some are intangible (like knowledge acquisition, conceptual skills and developed personal proficiencies). Participation in the industry as a worker usually requires formal, pre-practice qualifications. In short, education is an area of systematic, organized work or occupation, and it probably needs to be recognized formally for what it has become, an industry.

2 Education is also a service

That is, the sector consists of providers who supply educational programmes and services. It sells learning, of one kind or another. In general, then, it is a service industry (as distinct from, say, the manufacturing industry).

In some cases, the education industry provides *an essential service*, by definition a service which no person or no community can be left without. Not all the services within the education industry could be labelled 'essential', only a sub-set of them, even in a society wedded to life-long learning. Essential services include health, hospitals, defence, the law courts and systems of justice, and the police. Schools are usually included on the list, although universities are often not. The fundamental point about an essential service is that, no matter how bad or elementary the service is, nothing is as bad as its not being there at all.

An essential service is one which it is incumbent on government to ensure is provided. If a part of education (or, more narrowly, schooling) is an essential service, then it is intolerable for any section of society to be left without adequate access to a school or to schooling. Governments may not necessarily provide the service themselves (although they must do so as a last resort), but it is a government responsibility to see not only that the essential service is in fact provided, but that the service is also of a quality which is deemed by government to be satisfactory. In other words, for an essential service the government must guarantee minimum provision.

3 The government is the regulator of an essential service

Where a service is essential to the well-being of society, it is incumbent on the body which represents the people (the appropriate level of government, that is) to regulate that service – to guarantee both that it is provided and that it meets standards of adequacy. Thus government automatically becomes the regulator of an essential service. It is a function which it can, and often does, devolve to another agency, but it can never sidestep the responsibility.

When the government is the regulator of a service, there can be a conflict of interest when government is also one of the providers, or even the sole provider. The Westminster and American systems get over this problem through the separation of powers – by keeping the legislature and the executive separate (as in the USA), by keeping the legal system (and its police) separate from the political processes of parliament (as in the United Kingdom), or by having the regulators answerable to parliament rather than to the government of the day (as is the case with the role of an Auditor-General). The separation of the role of the service provider and of the regulator has always been problematical with schooling; in Great Britain it led to the creation of Her Majesty's Inspectors (HMIs), educators with the right of entry to any school in the country and whose mandate is not from Parliament but from the Head of State, the Queen.

4 Schooling is a process

Schooling is a process within the education industry. Normally, schooling is considered to be the systematic process provided for young people between the ages of 5 and 18, or from Kindergarten to Year 12 ('K through 12'). It is usually compulsory, at least for part of that K–12 continuum; that is, all citizens who fall into a certain category must undergo the process, and literally no one must be allowed to miss out.

The reasons for ensuring such inclusiveness are at least twofold; first, society cannot function effectively unless everyone in it has been through the process; and second, it is possible for a person to be a fully functioning, responsible and contributing citizen only if he or she has undertaken the process. For example, every person who drives a vehicle on a public road must carry a driver's licence, which testifies to the fact that they have learnt to drive and that they know the laws about the roads. It is a danger to oneself and to the rest of the community (especially its road users) if a person drives while unlicensed to do so.

Thus schooling, as defined above, is a 'compulsory' process, and the act of providing it is an essential service. It is logical to assume that the community (and the government representing it) will provide funding, at least in part, to ensure that the essential service is made available and to guarantee access by everyone to a process which every citizen must have undertaken. In this respect, then, government may not itself be the provider of the services, but it will have to help fund the service, then to police it (that is, ensure that its policies are carried out), and will automatically be a regulator of it.

5 Schools are simply providers of the schooling process

They may not be the only providers, of course, and there may be other effective and legitimate ways of making the schooling process available to users. Thus *school and schooling are not synonymous terms.*

It is also important not to equate 'schools' with 'school buildings'. The premises out of which schools generate or make available to users their learning programmes (which are part of the schooling process) can vary enormously, and probably should. The process itself and its effectiveness or efficacy are not dependent on having a stereotyped set of physical facilities within which to offer schooling. A lot of education and schooling can be, and already is, provided out of rented or 'found' space, and developments in information technology will widen the possibility, and probably diversify the places where formal learning can be undertaken. It will become progressively unlikely that formal schooling can be confined to a single, fenced-in property.

6 Schools are or will become brokers of educational services

The new learning technologies which have made possible the post-industrial knowledge-based society have also inexorably expanded the role of schools-as-providers. We have become used to schools being self-contained, housing all their provisions on one geographical site; but to do that in a technological age which makes learning resources available from all across the globe is untenable. What schools must do now, then, is to garner those resources, to order and systematize them. They will do so on behalf of their clients, putting together components supplied by themselves or by other providers to meet the client's requirements. Schools are therefore not merely 'places of learning'. Rather, they are the articulators of learning, the agents or agencies who make the schooling process accessible and systematic, and who are remunerated for doing so.

7 Every service, including an essential service, has to be paid for

There is a cost for every service or amenity, and it has to be paid for in some way and at an appropriate level. At the least, the payment has to recoup the costs involved. The payment may be carried by the user (when a purely personal gain results from the service), or by the community (through tax dollars) where the process is essential or compulsory. When the benefits are both personal and communal, then a mixed payment is appropriate which shares the provision costs. The basic premise, however, is that education is never 'free', and that someone has to meet the costs of providing it.

8 The term 'teacher' will undergo re-definition as the teaching service professionalizes

'Teacher' is becoming a problematic term. The educator role is certain to evolve into different forms and specializations, principally by the disaggregation of what teachers do and by parcelling those functions in different ways or in different combinations, and also by the development of functions which require more than a one-best-way transmission of knowledge. The obsolescent assumption underlying schooling, education and learning is that it involves the transfer of skill, expertise or knowledge from an expert to a novice, and this action has been known as 'teaching'. It has assumed that there is an expert (a teacher) coaching someone (a student) who knows less about the field than the coach does. 'Schools' therefore have employed 'teachers' to lead novice learners through the schooling process. Information technology will inevitably explode this conception of schooling, or some of it, by making available to learners huge resources of information which they can access and make use of, independently of 'teachers'.

In the past, teachers have been hired both to manage the process of schooling and to provide educational services. They have tended to work from a school base. 'Full-time employment' has been preferred by teachers, and they have been paid standardized, award-based salaries. As private providers who operate in niches within the education industry, teachers are aspiring to pattern their work and careers in different ways. There are no compelling reasons why the stereotype of a teacher should involve the same work patterns for them all, why their appointments ought to be full-time (the term is losing its meaning anyway), why they should be attached to only one school, why their working day should be a standard 8 a.m. to 5 p.m. in a Monday-to-Friday five-day week, or their school duties a standard collage which every teacher is expected to discharge.

The work patterns of teachers can be expected to diversify, especially as the field professionalizes. Some teachers will prefer to negotiate individual packages of functions each of which will attract a fee-for-service rather than a 'salary'. Some teachers will form companies which will operate like (and probably be called) a standard school, and which they will own. Some citizens or societal groups (such as religious groups or coalitions of parents) will form companies or enterprises which also operate like (and are called) a school and which will hire teachers or educators to discharge their functions. Governments may also form such enterprises to run like schools.

The way teachers associate themselves with these educational organizations will vary. Some will choose to be employed on a salary, as is the case now. Some teachers will form themselves into companies which will negotiate and manage on their behalf contracts to provide teaching and other educational services to schools on a fee-for-service basis; some of these contracted teachers will operate like normal 'classroom teachers', but many will choose not to. 'Schools' will hire other personnel to carry out roles which teachers may not wish to undertake or which do not require a person with a teacher's expertise or qualifications. And some teachers and schools – usually the highly able and confident ones – will freelance to provide expert services, either to individual learners or to other providers (such as schools), selling their advice and expertise in areas like curriculum, assessment, pedagogical techniques and new knowledge. In short, the modes of service delivery in education – and in particular with schooling – are diversifying. It is appropriate that they should, and that the approved formats for supplying the process of schooling be able to accommodate such diversification.

9 The funding of education and meeting the costs of schooling will become split-level and more complicated

So who pays for education, and in particular for schooling? The answer depends on which objectives of schooling one has in mind. There are three broad purposes for schooling:

*   *Vocational* Schooling has been seen as the means to lay the foundation for productive employment. It therefore helps to build a skilled workforce and to ensure a robust base for the country's economy. Instrumental and vocational dimensions are found in almost all parts of the curriculum.

- *Societal or communal* Schooling ensures that every young person is adequately socialized and enculturated, so that they are integrated into the community as fully functioning members with a sense of belonging. Schooling contributes to social development, communal harmony, collective well-being. Schooling is the one formal institution remaining with a responsibility for a child's rites of passage into adulthood.
- *Personal* Schooling is undertaken for the purpose of personal formation, to develop one's skills and to improve oneself.

Concerning *education for a vocation*, payment logically should be shared. To the extent that the education contributes to the economic development of the nation, society should contribute to a part of the costs. To the extent that vocationally oriented education increases the individual's capacity to earn an income, the individual should contribute. In a country whose economy is supported through knowledge-based industries, career-long learning is not only to be encouraged but is probably mandatory; and it may enforce such a commitment on its knowledge workers through credentialling: that is, by requiring constant updating of pre-service training. In this connection, then, society may need to use the Keynesian device of contributing to the costs of such training, but then requiring a fair proportion of it to be repaid later out of the recipient's increased earning capacity. The same logic underlies Australia's Higher Education Contribution Scheme (HECS).

Concerning *education which contributes to society's well-being*, and which is made compulsory for that purpose, it seems logical that society should meet the costs out of tax revenue. But it is also obvious that social justice considerations demand that an equal per-capita cost is an inappropriate way to pay the costs. It also raises the issue of the extent to which taxpayers' dollars are distributed among government and non-government providers or schools.

Concerning *education for personal development*, the recipient could be expected to meet the costs of the service, but some consideration has to be made for the ability to pay. Especially is this the case over life-long learning, and the adult learnings which add to the quality of life of a community or society. If life-long learning facilities are affordable only by the rich, the social consequences in terms of bitterness and alienation among those who are not well-off could be severe, socially divisive and communally corrosive.

These nine propositions stem from the discussion in the previous six chapters. They form a basis for planning the kinds of educational provisions which are appropriate for the schools of the twenty-first century, opening up the field for several options, some of which will supersede the ideas embedded in the traditional school. So what happens when we apply these ideas from the first six chapters to the planning and running of particular schools – to your school, indeed? What will the school of the future really be like? More of the same, or none of the same? To those issues we turn in Part Two, where we look at the practicalities.

Part II
Looking at the practicalities

How will schooling change?

7   Schools which break the mould

Principle No. 1   Bring the big picture into focus, and apply it to your particular school.

The dilemma facing those who want to design a schooling process more effective for the Angelicas of the world is that rarely are school planners presented with a blank page on which they can start from scratch. Usually they begin with an already existent school or set of schools, and the best they can do is to adapt and remodel. In short, their task is one of evolution, not revolution. Further, when planners *are* in a position to design something really new, the public acceptance of the new scheme is largely based on whether the new resembles the best of the old. It is very difficult for school planners to break out of the conventions which currently control public notions about schooling.

Even so, plans for the future are best when they begin with an ideal model, a mental picture of how we would like things to be if we had no artificial constraints placed upon us. Because reformers rarely if ever achieve all that they set out to achieve, what emerges is a compromise between what they really want and what it is possible to achieve. Any person, then, who intends to plan a school or a schooling process which meets the needs of the future must go through the intellectual exercise of asking what kind of a school or schooling process they would really build if the circumstances were ideal.

Furthermore, most school planners seem to begin with a school – a single school or school site; they therefore take the context, the wider society, as a given, as unchanging, as a variable which can be held constant while the planning exercise is carried out.

Schools have been slow to comprehend the new scepticism about possessions and the disabilities inherited by owning underused plant and equipment. For example, the capital investment in a normal secondary school, its buildings, equipment and playing fields, would easily account for $10 to $15 million. In terms of hours available in the year (8 hours a day for about 180 days a year), they are formally used for about 17 per cent (or a sixth) of the year. If your school had to pay rental for each of those hours when the school plant is set aside for its exclusive use, would you as a manager be wise to use the facilities at only one-sixth capacity? And even then, do the occupants maximize the use of the space and facility when they do have them exclusively available? Would it not be preferable to sell some of the property, free up some of the investment, and rent premises for at least some of the school's space-needs? Is it not possible to raise revenue by more intensive or alternative use of the premises the school owns? Indeed, why is it that so much of a school's capacity, personnel time and managerial effort is allowed to be siphoned off into what is essentially real-estate management?

Take a second example. A school with a teaching staff of 120 to 140 people (on a full-time-equivalent basis) has an annual salary bill of around $6 million. Add 30 per cent 'on costs', and the school has an annual 'people bill' of around $8 million. If the school could start from scratch without any prior staffing profile to guide it, it would surely be possible to devise a configuration of people and skills which gives greater return for that allocation of people-money.

It is also a curious phenomenon that schools in developed countries are deemed to be owned by the corporate body which owns the physical premises. But who actually owns the enterprise? It is possible to pick up the core business of the school and locate it in other premises. Indeed, it could be broken up into separate but mutually co-operating entities, and the core business provided for a better price, with greater productivity, and with better outcomes. In simple terms, then, the school as an organization for learning should be, if it is not already, in the process of being deconstructed and reconstructed.

Some countries and systems are better placed than others to make the transition. They include those schools and systems which have dispensed with large bureaucratic and centralized structures, which are collegial rather than hierarchical in the way they operate, which have installed the new information systems and which use them naturally in their learning programmes, which can accommodate a curriculum that is networked and branching rather than linear, which foster digital as well as print literacy, which embrace international rather than parochial benchmarks, which encourage mobility and flexibility rather than static and standardized approaches, which have professionalized their teaching service, which try to exploit the creativity of their best personnel, and which have deregulated and freed up their operations wherever they can do so.

The propositions in the previous chapter would suggest that, even for a single school, we must start with the *process of schooling* and what that will be like for Angelica and her contemporaries. Then we need to see the individual *school*, however we may want to image it, as the provider which will broker for Angelica the best schooling possible for her. Most importantly, then, we must not begin the planning with *school buildings*, as though they too are givens. It seems essential to begin by considering, in sequence:

- the schooling process, and what that means in terms of 'curriculum' (what Angelica will learn or need to learn);
- the learning programme, which this 'school' as a professional designer will try to put together for Angelica and her contemporaries;
- which parts of that programme the school will itself supply, acting as a

'provider', and which parts, acting as a learning broker, it will purchase from other providers.

Then the planners will be in a position to define what resources the school needs to assemble as educational designer, provider and broker. It will have to ask what people it needs and the mix of skills it must command within its team; what physical spaces it needs to build, rent or hire; what amenities it must provide for its users, the students; and what organizational framework it must put in place to ensure that its operations cohere, that its operators and operations are effectively co-ordinated, and that its products – the students' learning outcomes – are of a standard worth the purchase. In short, *don't* begin with planning the buildings, or with pre-conceived ideas about what a teacher does.

Plan with a greenfields site in mind

If, then, you were presented with a greenfields site on which a new town or suburb was to be built for approximately 25,000 people, what schools, educational buildings or schooling processes would you recommend constructing, and what rationale for education would you offer the developer? The designs for this twenty-first-century town must incorporate the best thinking not only about schools but also about urban communities of the future. Obviously you would *not* suggest a conventional set of kindergartens, child-care centres, neighbourhood primary schools, high schools and private colleges unless you were convinced that these kinds of educational service centres are the best mode to meet the needs of the next thirty years.

An assignment like this has been relatively rare in the developed world in recent years because of declining birthrates, birth-control measures and the persuasiveness of the arguments for zero population growth. In many Western countries which were involved in the Second World War, a population trough, strung between the high-point 'echoes' of the post-war baby boom, was working its way through primary and secondary schools during the last two decades of the twentieth century, causing schools to be closed rather than new ones constructed. But if you *could* start without the constraint of an inherited plant, existing buildings and dedicated real estate, you are pushed back to first principles. What schooling format and physical provisions would you suggest for this metropolis and dormitory suburb?

The devil is in the detail, of course. In the current world economic climate, whatever proposal is put up must *look* like good schooling, the kind of schooling which will give its students a strong advantage in the world. Unless the facilities themselves look like *schools*, a conservative public is unlikely to be satisfied with them, or to choose to buy a house in the new town.

Modelling like this is a real, not a speculative, exercise. The ideas laid out in this chapter are the result of a school design project like this given to a group of leading educators in Melbourne by the national urban planner Delfin Corporation. This developer has a high reputation in Australia for creativity and a conscience about building not just a group of unrelated houses, but a set of harmonized living spaces which encourage from the outset a sense of community. A piece of land had already been bought for subdivision and was awaiting an integrated design. It was to house a mixed population beyond the fringes of the extended city. The State Education Authority had indicated that it would be sympathetic to giving 'schools' a global budget and a large degree of self-government. It would also support a kind of local education committee to co-ordinate and manage the town's educational facilities. In short, it was thinking about the schools as an interconnecting system, not as a set of isolated, stand-alone enterprises.

On the other hand, the planners had to be realistic and not frighten the horses. People will not relocate to a new suburb if the education provisions look problematical, untried or inferior. A town of 25,000 could be expected to have a school-going population of 4–5,000 students, which in normal circumstances might produce about two Years 7–12 secondary schools and enough students to warrant about six conventional primary schools. There would be some private (non-government) schools among them. The suburb in question would clearly have a high proportion of Catholic residents, and a population of mixed ethnicity. Socio-economic stratification by area was not to be encouraged.

It was a situation ready-made both for the advocates of break-the-mould schooling and for those who argue that information technology will finally explode the notions of 'school', 'learning', 'knowledge' and 'curriculum' as we have come to know them. We have known about the pressure to remodel education at least since books like those of Seymour Papert's *The Children's Machine: Rethinking School in the Age of the Computer* (1993) and James Martin's *The Telematic Society* (1981) and *The Great Transition* (1996) appeared. Most of the aspects of contemporary schooling, we now realize, are derived from concepts which belong with cottage industries (the pre-industrial society) or with an economy heavily dependent on mass production, mass employment and standardization (the obsolescent industrial society).

Many stereotypical things about schools (and the architectural structures they gave rise to) ought *not* to be repeated in this new town. They include:

- *The egg-crate classrooms, as well as the long corridors and cellular ground-plans for buildings which strung those boxes together.* A better use of space is possible, especially because learning and teaching techniques are now much more sophisticated, involving small-group and large-group instruction, and there is individual access to an enormous number of data-banks through the information highway.
- *The notion of set class groups based on age-grade structures.* It is only partly correct to associate certain learnings with certain ages. We need to determine which learnings they are, and then for the rest of the time free the curriculum of artificial straitjacketing. Even so, the learning programme for children and adolescents – even if it is emergent, fed by technology, involves a lot of spontaneous search, and is allowed to be serendipitous –

needs at the end to be systematic, coherent and to cover key areas which all young learners should be introduced to or become proficient in.

* *The division of the school day into standardized slabs of time, with equalized portions of the day devoted to particular subjects.* Especially with extensive computerization, community and international access, and the need for time flexibility and for after-hours access to computers, the school day must surely be reworked. Preferably, any good educational facility – especially one housing sophisticated equipment and amenities – ought to be available on a round-the-clock basis, certainly after school and into the evening, and again early in the morning. It should not be closed up for extended holiday periods either, except for maintenance purposes. More staff are needed for an extended day, and most of them would work in shifts.

* *The linear curriculum, in which there is an apparent one-best-way approach and which sequences 'knowledge' into step-by-step gradations, proceeding from the simple to the complex.* In the technological or information age, the curriculum is likely to become *nodular* (that is, consisting of chunks of learning, the various components of which will have to be unpacked, probably with the help of a teacher or tutor) and *modular* (that is, packages of intense learning which are like building blocks and which the student of any age pastes together to form a coherent education).

* *The parcelling of human knowledge into predetermined boxes called 'subjects' or 'disciplines'.* Some of this parcelling will occur if only to conserve the time and energy of the learners. Overlaps and interconnections can be more easily accommodated through information technology, and subjects themselves are likely to become hybridized. Much of the sequencing of learning from simple to complex is artificial, and students are capable of travelling by several paths through material, often handling complex matter before the simple emerges.

* *The division of instructional staff by subject specialization.* A lot of the work of a school could, and perhaps should, be done by adults other than teachers. It often does not need a person with a master's degree to handle tasks like materials production, building supervision, computer servicing, financial management or even personal counselling. In any case, if learning is to become nodular and modular, then the educator staff will have to work together in teams, and call in persons (like computer engineers) with different skills from the ones they as teachers possess.

* *The allocation of most school tasks, whatever their make-up or kind, to an all-purpose category of person called 'teacher'.* The educational staff will become more mixed, containing many adults whose skills and expertise complement those of the teacher. It is likely that a category of professional called 'educator' will emerge, much more highly educated and with a more global and theoretical grasp of teaching and learning than the normal teacher, and who will lead a mixed team of instructors and other cognate specialists. Pay scales and places of work will be differentiated accordingly.

- *The assumption that learning takes place in a geographically bound space called school*, and that the student must graze for most of his or her 'learning time' within that fenced paddock. Indeed, the idea of a school isolated on a large piece of real estate and divorced from the community by wide lawns and playing fields is both out-of-date and constitutes a waste of money. The recreational, play and sporting areas which learners use can also be those provided for the whole community.
- *The artificial walls – some real, some symbolic – which barricade school from home and community.* Learning can take place anywhere, and frequently off-campus or in a place not normally defined as a school, especially with computer access and with portable computers (lap-tops and notebooks). It is likely that much greater use can be made of the home as a learning location. Students have easy IT connections with any place called 'school'.
- *The notion of the stand-alone school, relatively isolated from other schools like it even within the same town or suburb.* The constraints over sharing resources and expertise among 'schools' (including the sharing of teaching staff) ought to be removed, and the education provisions within the town are likely to function as an interconnected web of learning sites and resource people.
- *The notion of a 'school system' bounded by a locality or by geography such as a province, state, territory or even country.* Schools can and do make connections with counterparts elsewhere in the country and around the world. The imperative for students to become citizens of the globe, and not parochial, is overwhelming.
- *The limitation of formal schooling to twelve years, and between the ages of 5 and 18.* These traditional starting and ending points are simply accidents of history. In the new suburb, learning is life-long, involves literally everyone in town, and its organization commences at birth and ends at death. Assessments, certificates and credentials are awarded on the strength of what one can do, not on age. 'Tests' are demonstrations by the student that he or she has learnt something.

These features are not new, nor is the list exhaustive, and we have covered them elsewhere in this book. In our new town or suburb, however, we must begin with the proposition that the facilities for learning, especially those for the young, must not be inhibited by designs which incorporate ideas already going out of date. Form follows function; and it is Angelica's future which fashions the function. A bit of foresight might focus the future. So it is prudent to start with what we think the future will be like and backward-map to the point where we can formulate design briefs for the town planners and architects of our new town. We give more details about these techniques in the next chapter.

Some additional design features

If one takes as a basis some of the generally agreed ideas about the future which were addressed in Part One, then several other design features for this town's educational amenities can be added to the list given above:

- Learning is now accepted as life-long. In Senge's (1990) sense, this is a 'learning city', a place in which it is taken for granted that literally every person is engaged in learning of some kind. So the town's educational facilities are for people of all ages, and it is unproductive to have usage stratified by the chronological age of the users.
- Commencing formal schooling at age 5 and concluding it at age 18, wedging twelve formal years between bookends, can be superseded. In short, the educational facilities are not bounded by or limited to year-levels.
- Early childhood and the Years 0–5 are so important that good facilities for all parents to use during this period of their children's growth must be available all over town. The terminology about child-care, child-minding, kindergarten, play-groups, crèches and the like will undergo a change. Young children benefit from places which provide experiences, play equipment and learnings beyond those which any one house or family can provide. So, in our new town, there are constructive and educationally defensible programmes available for all children aged 0–5.
- Equity is essential. The same quality of provisions and the same degree of access, without social stratification, must be available all over town.
- Learning is the objective, not teaching or formal schooling or the creation of 'schools'. It is legitimate to design quite different educational structures and programmes if they will provide formal learnings with more efficient use of resources and with better outcomes than can be obtained with conventional schooling.
- Because of the explosion of knowledge, the new ways in which it is stored and retrieved, and the burgeoning accessibility to it through information technology, it seems best to start the educational planning with the changes information technology is likely to cause to the process of schooling.

Everyone has access to information technology

For our hypothetical new town, which we shall call Neoteric City, then, we can begin with two simple propositions about education. The first is that learning involves a *learner* (of whatever age), a knowledgeable adviser who is already familiar with the pathways into the fields the learner wishes to enter (we usually call this person a *teacher*), and a body of experience, information or knowledge to explore and extend (we have usually called this a *curriculum*). It is the classic simplicity of a learner on one end of a log and Mark Hopkins on the other.

The second proposition is that information technology now gives us the capability to realize the first proposition. So we begin the planning for Neoteric by ensuring universal access to computers, the most obvious new breakthrough for education. But it is technology which turns most of the techniques of education on their heads, and which allows us to get rid of a lot of the administrative, pedagogical and curricular baggage which went with mass schooling predicated on the analogy with manufacturing and production lines.

And obviously more is to come. Denning and Metcalfe (1997) talk of the 'revolution yet to happen' when computers will understand speech, anticipate our needs and will become as common in the home as the electric stove has been. The power of computers to simulate reality and to give vicarious experiences – to create virtual realities – could alter human consciousness. Reality is only what *we* take to be real, and is what we choose to put our belief in (Barnatt, 1997), a situation which changes what we (and especially children) accept as 'knowledge'. Computers also make us global, able to surmount most of the constraints of geography and many of those of cost. For better or for worse, it also introduces markets; for the computer allows its user literally to buy services or educational programmes from a wide range of providers, and, as we have pointed out earlier, may well explode the artificial categorizations of public and private schooling.

Information technology is what gave the Edison Project in the USA its rationale. From the outset, the Edison proposers (1994) worked on the assumption that if they were given the same amount of money which goes into a normal school (it is called 'cashing out' the education dollar), they could redesign the whole schooling process into an enterprise giving predictably effective learning – and still make a profit. So every family associated with an Edison school is given a home computer; and everyone in the education team, including students, has 'access to a personal computer at school'. This is not an unreasonable proposition. By the mid-1990s, Singapore put in place plans to have every classroom in its schools computerized by the turn of the century; and a proposed governmental goal for Hong Kong was 'a computer for every family'. For a twenty-first-century school, then, computers come before bricks-and-mortar buildings.

For Neoteric, the first educational requirement before anything else is that every newly built home is cabled, on line and equipped with computer facilities. The cost of these services is charged as council rates in the same way as households currently are billed for water and electricity. In this way, the local government itself can run at least partially a 'paperless' town, with public notices and business communications piped into every home in town. Just as now it would be inconceivable to consider education without any reference to books or libraries, so in Neoteric it is taken for granted that education will use computers and information technology.

The computer screen and the TV screen are to be merged. Internet connections, e-mail, telephones, television and some home services (like electronic newspapers) use the same cables. Thus education can be retooled to accommodate the learning modes implicit in this emergent information technology.

The central education barn or gateway

Theoretically, then, schooling in Neoteric could take the form of individual students, each advised by a team of educators, accessing a big central facility or gateway connected to the outside world, to other schools and programmes, to libraries, to multimedia sources, and so on. Somewhere in town is a dedicated educational space, a metaphorical aircraft hangar, from which are co-ordinated all the dedicated educational people, places and programmes available to the town. There would need to be an administrative wing attached to the facility whereby the whole network is co-ordinated and the town is kept connected to the educational grid.

It would be an advantage not to regard any educational amenities as stand-alone, or as the preserve of any one group, and to consider them all as essential nodes in the town's interconnected educational facilities. In a literal way, the town will run an 'educational system'.

But a simplistic configuration along those lines would clearly not be acceptable to most parents. No one wants five or six thousand students, either metaphorically or literally, milling around inside an educational supermarket. There needs to be something else more local than the barn, more of human size and more able to satisfy in particular the learning needs of quite young children.

Neighbourhood educational houses

At the least, the very youngest learners – toddlers and children – need some-where in their own (or the next) street where they can physically go to access programmes; to learn with other groups of learners; to interact with their teachers, tutors, counsellors and co-ordinating educator; to access richer learning materials than those which they have on line from their own home; and also to develop an identification with their neighbourhood storage house of learnings. The same holds true of learners of all ages.

The problem which educational authorities have always faced is that when neighbourhood buildings are put up and labelled 'primary school' or 'kinder-garten', their use becomes limited, they are reserved for only some learners, they become identified by age, territoriality sets in, and they are no longer considered a community or common resource. Furthermore, there is no guar-antee in a mobile society that we can predict accurately how permanent they need to be or how many rooms or spaces need to be provided.

It seems far preferable to keep the scheme flexible and to use 'found space' – literally to set aside some houses or a clutch of houses which can be used as educational centres and converted for other use when they are no longer needed as schools. In any case, a schooling facility and the other houses in the neighbourhood ought to be physically in harmony. Providing small 'found space' for education to serve several streets looks desirable. The houses ought to be strategically selected in order to capitalize on open community space for the learners using it – such as parks and playgrounds. Conceiving of schooling in this way, as bedded in community, makes it possible to co-opt any of its people and places for educational purposes.

Intermediate educational precincts

Some of the programmes which students will want to access could not be accommodated in small community houses. Schooling needs to have science laboratories, workshops, libraries, art studios and gymnasia, and these kinds of facilities are not always provided as a matter of course in most towns; sometimes only the conventional schools had them and regularly made use of them. Almost certainly, then, larger accumulations or premises serving several neighbourhoods with increasingly specialist equipment and experts are necessary for schooling. The larger facilities would put on stream what it is beyond the capability of any one neighbourhood house to provide, but would not be as grandiose an accumulation as that which is available in the system barn. In the same way as with the street-houses, the intermediate precincts ought not be allowed to be a-thematic. They must not become a big block of buildings imposing symbolical boundaries on clients and usage.

It could (and will!) be argued that we have merely reinvented neighbourhood primary schools, junior or middle schools, and the large senior secondary school or schools, run by a central bureaucracy. Perhaps it does look like that, and may even need to be, although the network organization runs such a process in a much different way from the bureaucracy. What we have described is the way systems of schools grew up in the first place, at least in North America. There are important differences too. The differentiation of facilities by the age of the learners and the lockstep progression of curricula are missing features here. Nor is there an intention in Neoteric to limit the neighbourhood houses to children, the middle schools to early adolescents, and the senior schools to young adults; for this is a system where the parts (including the instructional and support staff) are co-ordinated and available for use all over town and are not tied to a single school or site. Nor are the programmes. Nor are the students.

Indeed, there is produced a new rationale for the provision of educational space and resources, interconnected by technology, and including without exception every home in town. It is a town-wide system of educational access. The provisions at first blush may look like a conventional set of schools, and early on, as the suburb settles down or attracts dwellers, that sense of stability may be an asset. But the rationale itself, the universality of computer access, the interconnectivity it gives for learning, the flexibility it offers and the fact that all parts are systemically and systematically available make it so radically different that it could liberate education from the fetishes and the inhibitions inherited from the past (Lipnack and Stamps, 1994).

Put simply, education in this new town is provided through a constellation of interconnected and interacting educational sites which are symbiotic with each other and with the communities in which they are found. Site-based, home-based and portable (lap-top) computers put a huge range of learning materials and locations within the ambit of the town's learners. At the least, our new rationale for Neoteric revisions what education is, does and can be.

For 'system', read 'school'

Most readers who are concerned about schooling for the future, however, will be thinking in terms of individual schools, not systems of schools. That is indeed the rub, for to keep putting schooling into the straitjacket of what we have come to regard as schools is inhibiting, it approaches planning from the wrong end of the spectrum, and it closes the mind to the most exciting of prospects for the twenty-first century. The imaginative jump now required is to take our picture for Neoteric (that is, our concept for schooling within a city) and translate it into the shape of a single school (that is, schooling within a localized or smaller zone). Think of your 'local school' as a Neoteric writ small.

To do so immediately transforms your school, away from a tightly meshed control-oriented institution and into a professionally liberated network bonded by the mission of serving a population of learners; away from a geographical island and into an interactive archipelago; away from a set of buildings and into a body of differentially housed learning stations; away from a single school and into a linked system of educational units. It is a profound move to plan the future of your 'school' from this new perspective.

The school effectiveness movement

'Big picture' thinking like this is both helpful and provocative. It helps to create a new idea of what education is and aims to deliver. It also provokes us to think outside the frameworks which constrain existing models for schooling. But it needs more detail if it is to be used to deconstruct some old ideas and to reconstruct new ones. Most of all, we do not want to throw out both baby and bathwater.

We are helped in determining some of that detail by the school effectiveness movement. That genre of research, writing and practice created a climate for thinking about new formats for schooling which are clean breaks with the past by putting the school's focus on outcomes. Effectiveness simply means achieving one's targets; it is impossible to be effective (literally, achieving desired effects or outcomes) without at some prior point naming what those desired effects or goals are. Through the school effectiveness research were isolated the characteristics which make for excellent schooling, and these findings were widely used by policy-makers through the 1990s. Further, the school effectiveness movement put its emphases in the right place – what is producing appropriate learning, what classroom (as distinct from school) actions and what pedagogic methods made for the best learning outcomes. It showed again that effective learning does not mandate a certain kind of organization or a standard set of bricks-and-mortar structures.

One of the ironies of the 1990s was that the school effectiveness movement took place just as planners were talking about a process for schooling which might render the traditional school obsolete. The same discontent which led US President George Bush to call for break-the-mould schools also led to a world movement to improve the schools which we already have. The President's initiative produced the New American Schools corporation and nine radically new school designs for schooling (Stringfield *et al.*, 1996). The concern for school improvement produced the International Congress on School Effectiveness and Improvement (ICSEI) and a spate of international studies and co-operation over designs for better schooling, especially to diagnose the characteristics which seemed to be generally applicable, which were not culture-specific and which would carry across national boundaries.

The school effectiveness movement of the late 1980s and the early 1990s was in many respects a counter-revolution against the 'school effects' research, literature and policies of the 1970s. The Coleman Report of 1966 had thrown up a finding which shocked the educational establishment and which was congruent with the views of the social activists of the time. Coleman showed that *school* inputs had an almost negligible effect on how well a child performs at school. Home environment variables, the social capital which the child brought to school with her, explained most of the variance in achievement levels. Other studies confirmed this view, including Sandy Jencks' studies in the 1970s on the inequalities of educational opportunity. Rutter *et al.* neatly summarized the movement in the first chapter of their 1979 book *Fifteen Thousand Hours*. Put bluntly, we were being told which school a child attends does not make much difference to her academic performance, and it makes *much* less difference than educators think it does. Since the socio-economic status of the parents is the key determinant of a child's school performance, public policies and funding must attack that variable first.

In keeping with the times, there followed a spate of policies and programmes like Headstart, *Sesame Street*, inclusive curricula, examination and assessment reforms (like the GCSE in Britain), positive discrimination for gender and ethnic background, social justice measures, integration by bussing or by open enrolment, and so on, to ensure that the educational providers balanced out any deficits the child inherited from her home background. 'Equality of educational outcomes' became a catchcry, even if it was hard to define, and even though the phrase was open to wild misunderstandings.

There was sure to be a counter-revolution, and it came predictably from those who had most to lose from a destruction of the social and educational order which had put them on top of the tree or which had provided their livelihood. People outside of education, and especially conservatives, were uneasy about the debunking of conventional schooling. As early as 1973, for example, Klitgaard and Hall had proposed that there was a blind spot in the way schools were being considered. Significantly, Klitgaard was an economist with Rand Corporation and Hall a Deputy Assistant Secretary in the Defence Department. They wrote that it must surely be the case that some schools are better than others; indeed it was obvious that parents thought so, for they were prepared to spend a large amount of money to ensure that their child was placed in a superior school. 'Some schools consistently have higher achievement scores, lower dropout rates, more college-bound graduates, wealthier alumni and so forth.' They suggested that research attention should be given to those outliers, the schools which did much better than expected, given the nature of their student intakes. Don't look at the averages, they advised; look at the exceptions.

Several powerful factors fed the movement in the 1980s. One was the spate of reports which were critical of education and which seemed to demonstrate that the school effects policies of the 1970s and the progressive education policies which put emphasis on individual differences and lack of competition had contributed to a decline in standards, especially in basic skills like reading, literacy, number, science learning and languages. The most celebrated of these reports and, in retrospect, probably the most influential was the White-House-sponsored *A Nation at Risk* (National Commission on Excellence in Education, 1983). It signalled that the time had come to reassert the need for tough-minded, traditional schooling.

It so happened that the school effectiveness studies began to impact at the same time as Western societies, those of the so-called developed world, had moved away from dependence on manufacturing industry as the prime employer and wealth creator, and into a high-tech, service-based, brain-powered economy. They were experiencing, in short, that transition from an industrial to a post-industrial economy which was the subject of Chapter 3. The country's ability to make that shift is almost entirely dependent on how well educated its workforce is. Suddenly, it seemed, education and schooling had become economically central and therefore politically crucial.

It is hardly surprising that the school effectiveness movement also coincided with the movement towards school and system restructuring, and towards the introduction of the new managerialism across all areas of government enterprise which came with the same economic transition. Educational policy-making was slipping out of the hands of the providers (schools, teachers and educators), and increasingly was falling into the hands of those on whom the economic transition was impacting, those who understand economics, politics and business.

As we saw earlier, this was the period when the new international economic order became dominant. Countries across the globe found themselves thrust into a new, fiercely competitive, international market for goods and services, which made each nation's own economic survival problematical. So *national* governments almost universally became strongly interventionist in education. In country after country, electorates were confronted by a spate of policies about a national curriculum, national benchmark testing, national certification, national registration of teachers, national standards for teacher education, and so on. In these contexts, the national usurps the personal, the predictable replaces the innovatory, national benchmarks overpower concerns about individual differences, a nationally mandated instrumental curriculum crowds out considerations of a personally emancipating liberal education. Right-wing policies (which are business-oriented, and profit-driven) tend to dominate over left-wing policies (which are union-dominated, or provider-controlled, or concerned with equity in income distribution).

Education and especially schools were not slow to react, and they underwent a spate of innovation. There was a sea change with self-management (Caldwell and Spinks, 1988, 1992; Caldwell and Hayward, 1998), and schools beginning to function like free-standing business enterprises. Self-managing or locally managed schools came into play simultaneously with economically oriented policies which emphasize competition (called 'excellence'); customer (that is, parental) choice; accountability (especially outcomes-oriented funding in a kind of educational version of a fee for service); a market niche (call them magnet schools); quality and customer satisfaction – what Handy (1985: 402–3) calls the 'economics of quality'; employment contracts (which weaken the power of teacher unions); flexibility in style and structure; and management prerogatives.

In this context there has been remarkable synchronicity accompanying school effectiveness policies. A telling factor running through all is that the effective schools movement has tended to reassert the primacy not of schools but of *schooling* as a process. By the 1990s, then, the educational landscape had been reworked. Examples are easy to find. The Australian Schools Commission, which had brought in major innovations since 1972 and was an instrument of progressivism, was abolished in 1987. In Great Britain, the Schools Council (a curriculum reform body) and the Inner London Education Authority (a progressive but left-wing-dominated school system) were both abolished in the late 1980s. In the USA, the state governors began to take firm control of schools and the legislation governing their practices. Also importantly, with the educational achievement of the newer economies like Japan, South Korea, Taiwan, Singapore, the emergence of huge countries like China and Indonesia, and the transformation of Eastern Europe, there were suddenly other huge and significant players who seemed to have developed winning strategies, not least in schooling.

What happened with the new field of school effectiveness was predictable. Educators accepted the new agenda, handed to them through pressures from outside of the educational establishment, and they worked assiduously to make the best educational sense of it. The field quickly became sophisticated. There were hundreds of policy-makers, researchers, scholars and educators across the world involved with policies which went under the various banners of 'good schools', 'excellent schools', 'school improvement' and 'school effectiveness'. 'Quality of outcomes' had replaced 'equality of outcomes'. 'Excellence' had replaced 'equity'. International research was being used to show up which *school* characteristics guarantee effective learnings.

In summary, then, the developments from the effective schools movement and the thrust to develop new school designs (break-the-mould schools) which depart from the patterns of the past presented school planners with a matrix from which to crystallize some creative new plans for the future of schooling, and for particular schools. The time was ripe for the development of educational clades, not clones. And best of all, the effectiveness research had made overt what characteristics need to be built into the new models to guarantee the planned-for outcomes. It is time, then, to ask how an individual educational provider, a 'school' under the old parlance, might set about planning for its future.

8 Choosing what future to have

Principle No. 2   Devise a futures planning strategy for your school to use.

When educators try to refashion their school-as-a-provider and its learning programme to embody the new world-view discussed in Part One, they usually are unable to begin with a new school or a new site, like that of Neoteric as described in Chapter 7. To be practical, educational planners and Principals must start with what they have already got – and generally speaking that will be an existing school. Before the details of any plan can be thought through, those doing the planning need to have in mind some format for planning, a technique which will make their plans materialize.

Every educational leader must now possess planning skills; it is a constant part of their job. When a school building is to be remodelled, or when a new curriculum is to be introduced, or when the activities of the school for the next three years are to be planned, or when a school changes the way it intends to operate, planning skills are called upon. To be involved with these tasks, the educational leader needs to have looked at the future, to understand where the trends are carrying us, and to be capable of devising the strategies which need to be set in place so that the school is creatively abreast of international best practice. The process requires of educational planners and leaders not only clear ideas about what they wish to implement, but also the practical conse- quences of introducing them. It is they who must convert the ideas in Part One into operational realities.

A planning procedure

I have developed a fairly simple, two-part rule of thumb about reading the future. The first part of it goes like this: *The most reliable way to anticipate what the future will be like is to observe the trend lines in the present.* Almost nothing comes by revolution, even revolution itself. The new is always emerging from the womb of the already existent. To know what teaching or education will be like in ten years' time, it seems best to begin by diagnosing what big-picture developments are already on the way (Beare, 1996: 9–14). It is this method which threw up the matters discussed in the first half of this book.

The second part of my rule is that *nothing happens in isolation*. To be technical, there are no closed systems. As we extrapolate current trends into the future, they will be pulled and pummelled by other trends, many of them more powerful and influential than the practical ones we are confronted with at school or system level. We must therefore be perceptive about the way trends vector, one trend pushing others off their known course, and all of them tangling themselves in the process. Some of the skeins become plaited and bonded into what Naisbitt (1982, 1995) called megatrends.

How far ahead is it possible or prudent to plan for, then? As one sage is supposed to have said, 'If you want to be seen as the leader, it is wise not to get more than two city blocks ahead of the parade you are supposed to be leading.' Educators tend to talk in terms of one decade ahead, ten years, but there are problems about that. It is usually too short a period.

- Producing new, conventional, physical premises requires a long lead-time. To design and construct a set of buildings for a new, relatively large school or addition to a school, you are on a relentless six-year conveyor belt. The process – from design brief through the preparation of architectural documentation to the calling of tenders, the letting of contracts and sub-contracts, the preparation of the site, construction work, the fitting out of the shell and the handing over of the completed buildings – takes at least five years.
- A long lead-time is involved in the training of teachers. A new teacher takes four to five years to train and place in a school. At the least, a new primary teacher will now have undertaken a four-year undergraduate bachelor's degree, a secondary teacher will complete a first degree (a B.A., B.Sc. or the like) and then something like a two-year postgraduate Bachelor of Teaching or its equivalent as her pre-service preparation. Deciding on and then preparing the kind of teachers we may want for the twenty-first century puts us on a five- or six-year time-line.
- Devising learning programmes is also time-costly. The conventional process of redesigning the curriculum is a continuous task. By the time programme planners have worked their way through all the key learning areas – usually about eight in number – it is time to start over at the beginning again. The cycle, even at the fast rate of one or two areas (KLAs) a year, will take between four and eight years.

Or look at it another way. The children now in the first grade of their primary schooling will emerge from secondary school in twelve years' time. Because all of them will then need to undertake some post-school study, higher education or occupational training after they leave secondary school, they will not join the labour market until about fourteen years' time. Can we safely predict now what skills and knowledge those students must have? As a test, could we have predicted in 1990 what schooling in the year 2010 would be like?

But we can go further. On known mortality rates, a girl in first grade will still be alive in the year 2070. Is it possible to know what knowledge and skills she will need through her lifetime? It was Elise Boulding (1976) who suggested that our real-time window is probably one hundred years in both directions; we identify with our grandparents, who were probably born around a hundred years ago, and our grandchildren could still be alive a hundred years from now. Would it have been possible in 1901 to imagine what the year 2001 would be like? How far ahead can educators plan for?

So there are problems in *not* looking far enough ahead, of course. Looking into the middle distance is at least prudent before a more precise, formal plan is developed, presumably drawn up against the backdrop of the 'big picture'. But in practical terms, a detailed five-year or three-year plan is about as much as a school can reasonably be expected to handle. Beyond that time zone, so many factors will have intervened that the existing plan will have become obsolete.

No one can predict the future with accuracy, for there are too many unknowns in the equation. Nor is the future set in concrete; believing that is called determinism or fatalism. What happens in the future – which means what happens from tomorrow onwards – is clearly affected at least in part by what you, I and others do today, as well as by what people elsewhere on the planet do. It is therefore unhelpful to talk about 'the future' as though it is a single option. It is better to use the plural 'futures', the many options available.

A framework for thinking about futures

For several decades, those who have systematically studied futures have tended to use the following framework. First, there is an almost infinite range of *possible futures*. We can draw a branching tree of possibilities as the result of events and decisions impacting on other events and decisions. But there are many factors to consider in calculating what is possible, and what we forget or omit can confound even the possibilities we can know about. It is easy to overlook or not to know about a major storm brewing from an unprecedented quarter.

But some simplification is needed. We do this by focusing on an area (a subject, a place, a group of people, a bio-region), and then, selecting the factors which seem to be the significant determinants, we track the interactions which are likely to be important. In short, we draw *a model*, a simplified version of the slice of reality we are giving attention to. Models, though valuable, can also blind us, for they are always framed by our own paradigms and systems of belief, and they can be based on taken-for-granted assumptions which ought to be examined. One must never forget that a model is only a simplified, shorthand version of what we think reality is.

Of the huge list of possible futures, most are unlikely ever to occur – they *could* happen but it would be improbable. It is safer then to ask what are the *probable futures*, given what we already know about the context and the actors in it. These are the futures which have a fairly strong likelihood of coming into existence, judged from known trend lines. Some probabilities can be calculated by the computer, mathematically; others we can judge intuitively. By whatever means, we can be fairly sure that some developments, unless disturbed, will have taken place by certain dates.

But most people will want to intervene to change those trends, especially if they seem to lead to some kind of disaster. We would prefer to work strenuously to prevent many of the developments suggested by the trend lines and many of the probabilities we may *not* like. We can decide as actors to perform in ways which will change the plot, and make some of the probabilities more likely to eventuate than others. Thus there is a third category called *preferable futures*, the futures we really want. Planning deals with those preferable or desirable futures, the futures it is our intention to bring into existence.

Concerning futures

As you plan the future options for school and schooling, keep in mind this framework. There are:

- **Possible futures**
  These are things which could happen.
  Some of them are likely; most of them are unlikely.

- **Probable futures**
  This is a sub-set of 'possible futures'.
  They include the likely futures.
  They are things which probably will happen, unless something occurs to throw them off course.

- **Preferable futures**
  This is a sub-set of 'probable futures'.
  They are things which you prefer to have happen.
  They are things which you will plan to make happen out of the possible and probable futures.

Planning is a timetable for taking deliberate actions to maximize the chance of achieving your preferred futures, a kind of road-map to guide you into a future of your own making.

Two conventional planning techniques – scenarios and trend lines

We begin our planning by asking what would happen if the present trends were left to run without interference. Where would we end up? We may discover that we will arrive at a place or places we did not want to go to. (This is a common awareness when schools are confronted by demographic data about their catchment area.) Two useful planning techniques to clarify the options are trend analysis and scenario-writing.

A trend is literally the path along which something will roll; it comes from an old German word meaning 'to roll' and from which we get the English word 'trundle'. To be precise, the trend line is the path the rolling object has *already* taken, the line it has already left in the sand. More important than the trend line are the *projections* we make from a trend. This is what happens when we draw the trend line into the future in an attempt to show where the ball will roll if nothing is done to deviate it from its path.

A *scenario* is the storyline for a play, giving scene by scene what the characters say and do. It can also be the document which gives the detailed directions for a film, or it can be what is called the 'shooting script'. A scenario is usually written *before* the detailed script of the play or film is written, as an outline to guide the author. The essential thing about a scenario is that it works out the actions and interactions among the characters in order to plot where the storyline is going.

So a fairly conventional (and interesting) way for planning your own future or that of an enterprise (like your school) is the following:

- Select the **factors** which are likely to affect your future options; pare them down to those which are the most significant to you or the school.
- Then study the **trend lines** for those factors, noting especially where they might intertwine and influence each other. Brainstorm about them, if you like, and try not to overlook possible developments which might be really important.
- Choose a **milestone** or milestones, a date for reference, and determine where each of those factors will have trended by those fixed points in time.
- Next, draw a picture of what you want to be (or what you want the school or enterprise to be) by that point in time or points of time. In short, picture (image, literally visualize) your **preferred future**.
- Next, ask what you could or need to do to change or to capitalize on the trend lines. What will help you and which ones will impede you? **Scenarios** composed at this point will show what options you have, who needs to do what and in what sequence, and what actors are involved. Some actors or events may be beyond your control, of course.
- Finally, you plot backwards from your fixed points in the future to the present, laying out – step by step, actor by actor – a plan of actions which will maximize the probability of achieving what you want. It will include detailed timelines. This action is called **backward mapping**. A **master plan** results.

Backward mapping into the future: a process for planning

In summary, then, you can 'plan your preferred future' with the following procedure.

Step 1   Select the **significant factors** which are likely to affect your future.

Step 2   Study the **trend lines in those factors**, to determine what is likely to happen if they continue undisturbed.

Step 3   Choose a **time in the future as a reference point**, and try to depict what will have occurred by then, given the known trend lines.

Step 4   Knowing what you know, what is your **preferred future** at that reference point? Draw a detailed portrait, preferably in living colour.

Step 5   Compose a story or two about how you might act to revise some of the trend lines, or to build coalitions, and so on, to achieve the preferred future you have decided upon. In short, compose some **scenarios**. Commit yourself to one of them.

Step 6   Devise a detailed road-map of how to get from here to there. By **backward mapping**, come up with a **master plan**.

The purposes of schooling

Planning, whatever its methodology, must be based upon a purpose or purposes, upon what is the set of core objectives for which the organization exists. We have alluded to these purposes in Part One, but it is possible to simplify them as follows. Wherever schools or schooling processes are found in the world, they have three general purposes, namely:

• acculturation of young people into society;
• preparation for the world of work;
• personal formation.

These three purposes overlap, and all aspects of schooling make contributions to all three purposes. This is, of course, the same set of purposes outlined in Chapter 6; there we applied them to the issue of the funding of education, developing the split-level model. Here we apply the same three purposes to the particular aims of your school-as-a-provider. They also need to be applied to the curriculum, to the learning programme the school offers. Emphases vary and those who pay for schooling (particularly taxpayers, governments and parents) put different weights on each purpose. Governments around the world, for example, are now tending to be quite prescriptive about what aspects of schooling or a school's work they will fund and what they will not – a trend line to be noted.

Acculturation into society

As was pointed out in previous chapters, every tribe, community or nation since the dawn of civilization has made some of its members responsible for introducing the young into the patterns of behaviour and the essential knowledge needed to become a full, participating member of the community. Every human group has its rites of passage which formally mark the progression from birth into full citizenship. There are some essential skills to acquire, some knowledge to be learnt, social conventions and political and governmental arrangements to understand, some behaviours to learn, some taboos to be respected, and laws to be observed. You might call all of this a core curriculum.

In the past, acculturation was a responsibility usually given to elders or tribal priests, but in modern societies schools have largely inherited this role of educating and initiating the young. For this reason, the state (however defined) requires attendance of every learning child up to an age deemed to be the entry point to full citizenship. The state approves a curriculum which embodies those essential knowings, and requires that they be taught. And the state pays for, or at least subsidizes, the education which is deemed to be 'in the public interest'.

Education for employment

Schooling is also preparation for the world of 'work' or, more precisely, for an occupation. Traditionally, not all the roles taken on by members of society have been paid employment, but it is assumed that every member of society will acquire the skills to use his or her time productively and for the good of society. Everyone, then, is expected to have an occupation. In modern societies where there is huge differentiation in roles and specializations, it is now almost impossible to have an occupation (of any kind, including parenting) without some prior formal training.

Because education for employment is so crucial to the economic well-being of the society or nation-state, governments (especially national governments) have been prepared to finance that part of education which contributes to the country's wealth creation and economic performance. They have also been prepared to prescribe and regulate what levels of competency, knowledge and intellectual skills are required in a person before he or she is permitted to operate in areas which are of critical importance to the economy. The process is often called registration or accreditation.

Personal formation

Schooling is also the means whereby an individual cultivates his or her own unique set of skills, temperament, potentialities and physical attributes so that over time each will develop into his or her 'best self'. Personal formation includes an individual's self-image, system of beliefs, codes of behaviour, physical fitness and social relationships as well as intellectual, emotional and spiritual well-being. These areas were addressed in Chapter 4.

Many of the expressive arts (like music, literature and drama), physical education, sport and extracurricular activities tend to be viewed in terms of personal formation. Certainly a curriculum pruned of these offerings makes for stunted education, but the subjects can just as easily contribute to the other two objectives of schooling. Many artists, actors, musicians, professional sportspersons and film producers, for example, have well-paid and sometimes lucrative occupations.

Governments are unlikely to give high priority – and therefore funds – to an individual's personal formation (unless it is seen as investment in human capital), but those close to the learner (such as parents) may put it as their highest priority and will outlay their own personal funds and efforts to promote it.

In summary, then, a master plan for schooling or for a school-as-a-provider or for a learning programme must give attention to each of the three major purposes of schooling listed above, as well as any prescriptions or formulae laid down by those who are stakeholders in the process of schooling. It will also need to acknowledge that no one client is likely to give full funding for each of the three purposes of schooling, but only insofar as it feeds the prime interest that client has in the schooling process.

In planning a balanced schooling programme for the future, it is prudent to ask what each activity and programme contributes to meeting each of the three general objectives.

Dimensions of a schooling programme

Every aspect of a school's activities is likely to contribute something to the following three general purposes of schooling, prompting one to ask the following questions of each activity at every level of the enterprise.

1 **Acculturation**
   In what way does this activity contribute to the skills, knowledge, competencies and attitudes the student needs in order to become a fully functioning citizen in this society? Does this enterprise or activity formally provide for the conventional rites of passage which successively induct the learner into membership of the society?

2 **Preparation for the 'world of work'**
   In what respects does this activity help to prepare the student for satisfying, life-long, productive work, suited to this student's particular skills and abilities?

3 **Personal formation**
   In what way does this activity contribute to the formation of a well-rounded, balanced, creative, altruistic and personally secure human being?

The new approaches to change

All of the above sounds logical, rational, tidy and do-able. The fact is, however, that planned change never works out like this! The processes of planned change have been researched and theorized about for over forty years. By the 1960s so much had been written about the field that scholars were trying to synthesize what were the writers' collective findings (Bennis *et al.*, 1970; Thomas and Bennis, 1972; Bennis *et al.*, 1976; Carver and Sergiovanni, 1969; Culver and Hoban, 1973; Baldridge and Deal, 1975).

By the 1990s many of the change processes were no longer relevant. The earlier writings were being supplanted by works like Peters' *Thriving on Chaos* (1987), his *Liberation Management* (1992) with its revealing subtitle *Necessary Disorganization for the Nanosecond Nineties*, and Mackay's *Swim With the Sharks Without Being Eaten Alive* (1988). The essential message in the new approaches was that we no longer have the luxury of adapting quietly and systematically to planned change. We cannot take our time, for time is not a commodity available in unlimited supply. Time is an expense which must be treated as though it is money, and like all good currency it has to be invested wisely, used sparingly and not squandered.

Further, what we knew about planned change with its neat flow-charts and lead-times, its phased introductions, its consultative frameworks and its coherence proved to be too simple. We may still use the techniques, but with scepticism, knowing that most plans will have to be modified. By and large, crash-through tactics have replaced those approaches, largely because legislators, politicians, national leaders and chief executives cannot allow us as much time as we think we need, for *they* do not have time on their side either. Unless they act quickly, their enterprise goes out of business or bankrupt, is bought out or taken over, they lose office or are replaced, or some other country or agent secures an inside advantage. The change imperative waits for no one.

On tactical and strategic planning

If that is the case, what ideas and tactics about change are likely to work now? Mintzberg, an assiduous analyst of organizations since the 1970s, in his provocatively titled *The Rise and Fall of Strategic Planning* (1994), suggests that strategic, long-range planning has by and large failed. Rapidly changing events unpick long-term plans. Furthermore, to conceive of planning as a separable, detached exercise in trying to make things happen, and especially when it is devolved to people outside of the mainstream, is wrong-headed. Unless planning is embedded in everyday action, in the daily life of the organization, it is merely cosmetic. Mintzberg (1994: 10) quotes George (1972), 'Every managerial act, mental or physical, is inexorably intertwined with planning. It is as much a part of every managerial act as breathing is to the living human.'

Strategy is vision, a picture – created in the imagination and held constantly in the mind – of what the manager wants to bring into existence. Plans are simply the vehicle to carry that vision into reality. Plans, then, are essentially means to an end, never an iron rule or a straitjacket for behaviour. Mintzberg (1994: 111) explains:

> Companies plan when they *have* intended strategies, not in order to get them. In other words, one plans not a strategy but the consequences of it. Planning gives order to vision, and puts form on it .... One can say that planning operationalizes strategy.

As the result of years of investigation and experience, Mintzberg (1994: 155) identified the 'ten most important pitfalls' which stultify the ability to implement change. Put another way, these are the ten most important things a manager must observe if he or she wants to be on top of change. It is a kind of planner's Ten Commandments.

1 *You* are the planner. Do not delegate the planning function, and certainly not to a so-called expert or specialist planner.
2 Avoid becoming so engrossed in current problems that the planning process is overlooked, accorded low priority or discredited.
3 *You* must develop the company goals which are the basis for formulating long-range plans.
4 Major line-personnel, that is, all senior staff, must be involved in the planning process.
5 The plans should be used as standards for measuring managerial performance.
6 You must create in the organization the climate which is congenial to planning and which does not inhibit it.
7 Corporate, comprehensive planning is part and parcel of the entire management process. Everyone in the organization is part of the process; no one misses out.
8 You must avoid injecting so much formality into the planned system that it lacks flexibility, looseness, simplicity and creativity.
9 You should review with departmental and divisional heads the long-term plans which they have developed.
10 You need to be vigilant lest you make intuitive decisions which conflict with the formal plans and which thereby weaken the credibility of the formal planning mechanisms.

What emerges from Mintzberg's list, then, is that the leaders or managers can live with turbulent change and with overload only if their sense of direction is right, if they have conceived a clear map of where they are driving the enterprise. It is called 'vision' advisedly, for it is a picture, formed by the imagination, carried in the head, often visited, and which forms a template of the way they want things to be. If they do not have such a vision as an educational manager – as any kind of manager – they are in no position to take charge of change.

All of the above Mintzberg calls 'strategy'. A plan merely actualizes it. But the plan is a road-map, with many possible side-roads and detours; it is not a set of orders, to be followed slavishly and to the letter. So, Mintzberg concludes, the manager needs to be a strategic *thinker* rather more than a strategic planner. He has an evocative way, using the metaphor about gardening, to describe how strategic thinking works.

> Strategies grow initially like weeds in a garden, they are not cultivated like tomatoes in a hothouse .... These strategies can take root in all kinds of places, virtually anywhere people have the capacity to learn and the resources to support that capacity .... Such strategies become organizational when they become collective, that is, when the patterns proliferate [and begin] to pervade the behavior of the organization at large .... The processes of proliferation may be conscious but need not be; likewise they may be managed but need not be .... Put more simply, organizations, like gardens, may accept the biblical maxim of a time to sow and a time to reap (even though they can sometimes reap what they did not mean to sow).

> To manage in this context is to create the climate within which a wide variety of strategies can grow ... and then to watch what does in fact come up .... Management must know when to resist change for the sake of internal consistency [that is, when to do some weeding] and when to promote it [that is, when to do some manuring] .... [Managers] must sense when to exploit an established crop of strategies and when to encourage new strains to displace them. It is the excesses of either – the failure to focus (running blind) or failure to change (bureaucratic momentum) – that most harms organization.

> (Mintzberg, 1994: 287–9)

This, then, is not a set of change processes, not a set of coping skills, but rather the creation of a kind of organization, not so much the development of a collection of functions as the nurturing of a livingness, of something organic.

This view has been expressed well by Senge in *The Fifth Discipline: The Art and Practice of the Learning Organization* (1990). 'Forget your tired old ideas about leadership,' he counsels. 'The organizations that will truly excel in the future will be [those] that discover how to tap people's ... capacity to learn at *all* levels in an organization.' As the book's title suggests, there are five qualities, competencies or 'disciplines' which characterize the enterprise which thrives on change and yet still achieves its purposes. They are qualities which should be found in all its members and most importantly among its senior team.

- *Systems thinking* The ability to understand the whole and to know how things interconnect.
- *Personal mastery* The discipline of continually clarifying and deepening one's personal vision, and of focusing energy. It is assumed that everyone

in the organization is committed to improving himself or herself, always learning, life-long, and never resting.

- *Mental models* These are deeply ingrained assumptions, generalizations, or even pictures or images that influence how we understand the world and how we take action. In short, everyone in the organization acquires the technique to uncover the pictures about the world which are bedded deep in the mind, how to bring them into the light, scrutinize them and refine them.
- *Shared vision* The shared vision occurs when the group has genuinely brought their pictures of the future together and as a team harmonized. The organization is bonded by a common sense of destiny.
- *Team learning* The team learns collectively, interlocks its skills, tries out new strategies and deliberately sponsors each other's development.

Not surprisingly, this set of prescriptions from Senge is remarkably in keeping with the image of the living system enunciated in Chapter 5; metaphors beget compatible metaphors. Here it is the enterprise which is colligative, a living system consisting of interacting parts which have harmonized their thinking and acting. Such an organization keeps learning because it is dynamic and alive.

Schools differ: developing an appropriate model

In setting up the school-as-a-provider and in determining the learning programmes which it will commit itself to foster, it is important not to let second-order considerations overrule prime purposes. And while there may be a commonality of purpose among schools and other educational providers, idiosyncratic and distinctive characteristics about this particular provider (or school) ought to be preserved; some will result from the size of the enterprise, the location and the nature of the population (or set of students) it has chosen to serve.

Regardless of any school's size and the governance system it works within, Principals generally now have sufficient autonomy and freedom to use a flatter, collegial, multi-skilled operating structure which puts emphasis on having flexible work teams. An educational provider (a school) arrives at its modes of operating in the same way that most other enterprises do, through a cyclic process of (1) determining the organization's vision, (2) converting the vision into operationalized objectives, (3) which are then translated into annual action plans, (4) which try to be specific about both intended outcomes and priorities, and (5) which are implemented through a series of school-based decisions and procedures, (6) evaluated regularly in a systematic way and then (7) reviewed and refined ahead of a new cycle commencing.

All of these factors about the operation of a schooling enterprise, about the way it carries on its business, about its measured outcomes, about its evident quality, are certain to vary according to how big it is. To use a practical example, consider the function of the supervision and appraisal of the people in the enterprise, a function which always begins with the organization's chief executive.

Small schools

In very small enterprises or schooling providers, there may be very few personnel (teachers and other staff) to be reviewed and evaluated. In this situation, Principals may have to invent ways of involving more than themselves in the process. Where a number of schools are geographically close, Principals can build into their routines opportunities to visit and be visited by Principals from neighbouring schools and, where possible, to release teachers to do the same. Principals concerned about the problems of objectivity may need to explore ways of providing 'buddies' for the people working in their own school, or to find external mentors for each of their teachers, or to form appraisal teams involving staff from another school.

Larger single-site schools

While they may have more teachers to review and evaluate, Principals in larger single-site schools (whether primary or secondary) have greater flexibility over staffing configurations. It is therefore easier to involve others in the processes of collecting and evaluating teacher-performance evidence. Many of the suggestions for small schools are also appropriate for larger schools, but it is likely that a mix of approaches emerges. Principals may take advice from panels they have formed for each teacher to be reviewed and evaluated, although such an approach can produce role conflicts and may use up too much teacher time.

Multi-campus schools

Potentially these schools face the greatest challenges. Schools which operate in several locations are really mini-systems, and will find that they have to function like a small education authority. They therefore require system-like structures to run effectively.

To summarize, then, every educational provider needs to be concerned about its own and its students' futures, and needs a formal plan to guide its operations and to prepare it for the future. But a plan is a strategic document, not an inflexible set of orders. This chapter proposed a framework for thinking about the future which includes considering the possible, probable and preferable (or desirable) futures, and then the device of backward mapping to help decide on the deliberate interventions to which the schooling enterprise and all its members commit themselves. Ideally, a test of relevance prevails; every detail of every plan has to be interrogated to determine that it does in fact enhance the achievement of the enterprise's core purposes.

Approaches to systematic and planned change have themselves changed in recent years, in the face of political imperatives and the demand for speed. What is needed, therefore, is not so much a strategic plan as strategic thinking, exercised by every key member of the staff. Effective strategic thinking grows out of a common vision, foresight and the possession of both tactical and strategic skills.

There is no single approach or structure which suits all schools-as-providers. Size, for example, is a critical factor. A small school operates in a manner different from that of a large, single-campus school. A multi-site school is really an interconnected set of operating units and operates like a mini-system; it therefore needs systemic structures to make it effective and function well.

This chapter has addressed the planning imperatives for a twenty-first-century school, and has suggested a methodology to keep such a school future-oriented. As providing for the schooling process becomes inevitably more complex and diverse, so there will be a need for the enterprise to retain its focus, to be collectively professional and not to allow its activities to become scattered, dispersed or unsystematic. The greater the uncertainties in the operating environment, the greater the need for a focus on the enterprise's basic purposes. In the past decade, the need for the educational provider called a school to maintain purpose, to plan ahead, to be recognizably distinctive and to be disciplined in its operation has produced the phenomenon of the school charter and of charter schools, and to that topic we turn in the next chapter.

Note

I am grateful for the assistance of Mr John Gelling in researching the materials for this chapter.

9 Building a manifesto for the school as a provider

Principle No. 3 Make your own and the school's objectives explicit, simple, and crystal clear.

In this book, we have been considering the nature of schooling appropriate for a student like Angelica as she prepares to become a committed, contributing, contented and confident citizen of the world in the twenty-first century. The first part of the book addressed the big-ticket items which are affecting and changing her world and especially her world-view, and the second part has concentrated on what might be done with the schooling process, in particular with the local providers called schools, to ensure that their operations are also forward-looking, appropriate for Angelica, and consistent with the extant world-views which have superseded those held in the twentieth century. Chapter 7 was therefore a discussion of what a schooling provider (a school, a set of schools, or a configuration for a learning programme) might be like if we had the option of planning from scratch on a greenfields site. Most existing schools will have to consider how they would reconstruct themselves to resemble those kinds of schooling provision. Chapter 8 dealt with some planning strategies which a schooling provider may find helpful for that process.

The next chapters will deal with fundamental issues any educational provider or school must confront, namely

1 how to organize the enterprise to ensure that it achieves its core goals – a **management** consideration;
2 how the school is to convince its audience that it has achieved its purposes – an **accountability** consideration;
3 how the learning programme for the user-clients is put together to ensure that it is both relevant and of the highest quality – essentially what happens with the **curriculum**; and
4 how to think of the staff and the way they are deployed, especially as the teaching service becomes both professionalized and diversified – essentially a consideration about **teachers and the teaching functions** of the enterprise.

In this chapter, we turn to the first of these issues, the management of the educational firm in a way which will guarantee the achievement of its core purposes.

When self-management was granted to state schools in Victoria, Australia, after 1992, it was assumed that they could be given a one-line budget and left alone both to devise and then to carry out their educational programmes. But there was one dominant proviso. Each school had to negotiate with the Minister of Education a charter which defined the areas, literal and metaphorical, in which it would operate, what its educational goals were, and the learning outcomes on which it was prepared to be judged. Education Victoria (1992) determined that there were six essential goal areas which had to be covered in that agreement or charter.

- The school's current *profile*, and its underlying guiding philosophy about education and schooling.
- The school's *curriculum and learning programme* (including what learnings it intended to provide and the targets it would set itself in each of the key learning areas).
- The school's *learning environment*, including the relationships among students (such as a discipline and attendance code), the characteristics of the learning climate it would foster, the safety of the school, and the quality of its physical fabric.
- An *accountability* profile, which included its statutory and legal responsibilities, and the publics (the plural noun is deliberate) to which it must justify its quality.
- The school's *management*, including its internal structures, its human resources and how they are to be deployed, and its governance patterns.
- The school's *resources*, including its finances, and the management of its physical facilities.

The charter, then, assembled the tiles for a wall mosaic which pictured what the school was aspiring to be, gathering into one document what the school is now like, what it stands for as an educational institution, what its priorities are, how and on what criteria it agrees to be assessed, and how each of its functioning parts are to be made to conform with its vision statement.

In other places (such as in New South Wales), terms like 'strategic plan' were used for a document of this kind, but in all cases they implied that every well-managed school needs formally to deliberate on how to plan, cohere and carry out its purposes.

It is useful to ask why the word 'charter' has come into the currency of education at all. According to the dictionary, a charter is an official document which grants certain rights – to a town, a company, a university. In another sense, a charter contains the founding principles and articles of incorporation for a duly constituted body, officially confirming that the company is qualified to practise, and laying down its legal jurisdiction, within which it has great freedom to operate but outside which it is debarred from practice. It can also be said that a school is 'chartered' in the same sense as one would charter a bus; the school is a company hired to do a job or to deliver a service. The funds provided to the school, by government no less than by a paying client, are in effect a fee for service, and those paying for the service have a right to demand the quality and level of service formally assented to in the contract or charter document. Whenever the term 'charter' has been used around the world in connection with schools, then, it has been used to define the freedoms which the school may (and may not) exercise, to empower the school to operate without undue interference, but to arrive at a contractual arrangement whereby the school must deliver a quality product (learning) of a kind specified by that agreed foundation document.

Drawing up a charter for a school, therefore, makes some things explicit which before may have been only implicit, it helps to clarify the school's educational purposes, and it should confront the school council, the Principal, the staff and the students with the responsibilities they must carry if the school collectively is expected to discharge the charter arrangements. To come to terms with these matters, then, the school's management and its operators would have to consider questions like the following:

- In the light of the charter, what role is a school-site council required to fulfil for the government or its sponsor or the supplier of its operating funds; for the community; and for the school?
- In the light of the charter, what precisely do the school's sponsors require of the school?
- What powers and freedoms may the school exercise in the light of the agreement embodied in the charter?
- What services and functions *must* the school deliver and to whom, in the light of the charter?
- How will the school prove that those services have been delivered, and that they are of an acceptable quality? Who precisely has to be convinced by the proof? And what are the consequences of non-delivery, or of lower-than-required quality?

The charter school movement

Charter schools began to appear in North America at about the same time as the grant-maintained schools (GMS) did in the United Kingdom; these latter were schools which during the Thatcher and Major Governments had opted out from control by the local education authorities and were operating with funds disbursed to them directly from central government. In New Zealand, following the Picot Review reforms in 1988, it was also required that every school draw up its own charter. And in New South Wales, the reforms following the Scott Reports (1990) drew on the NZ experience and brought in a kind of charter at every school. The Victorian developments with the Schools of the Future programme

(Education Victoria, 1992) drew on and then developed further these international practices.

International practice therefore seems to suggest that a foundational document like a charter makes a school specific about its intentions, resource efficient, more educationally effective, and more accountable for its learning outcomes. Because what is put in the charter is binding and must be honoured, there are serious consequences if its dicta do not become part of the life and management of the school. Every member of staff and every parent is expected to understand that.

Implicit in all the writings about school charters is an outcomes-based approach. According to Bierlein and Mulholland (1993: 4), the proponents of a charter school in the USA were universally required to develop a proposal outlining 'how they would operate [the] school and what specific outcomes they would achieve'. The New Zealand Picot Report (1988: 45) said that a charter 'described the purposes of the institution and the intended outcomes for students'. So the charter embodies a fairly precise profile of the school, especially (1) what the school is and what it is not; (2) what the school hopes to achieve, especially as learning outcomes for its students, within a certain timeframe; and (3) how it intends to organize and use its resources to achieve those outcomes.

Once these three things are agreed to and contained in the wording of the charter, there is effectively a 'suspension of standing orders' from an external authority, releasing the school from undue external controls and allowing it to get on with the job of running itself in the way agreed to in the charter. So, Bierlein and Mulholland explain,

> Decentralization would be achieved by granting full control over the entire school budget as well as management and personnel decisions to school-based councils. Removal of most state and local regulations (other than those to ensure safety, nondiscrimination, and high educational outcomes) … provide opportunities to be innovative and eliminate the ability to lay blame for poor achievement elsewhere.
>
> (Bierlein and Mulholland, 1993: 4)

The concept of charter schools had been under lively consideration in America since the mid-1980s. The title of Ray Budde's pivotal book on the issue, *Education by Charter: Restructuring School Districts* (1988), is significant in its emphasis on districts. From the early 1980s, schools in the Western world experienced wave after wave of reform effort which left educators, parents, the public, industry and politicians unsatisfied and the schools largely unchanged. By the early 1990s, American reformers began to turn their attention on the school *systems* in the belief that schools might work better if there were fewer formal constraints on how they were required to operate. During this period, there was a strong movement internationally towards self-managing schools (Caldwell and Spinks, 1988, 1992); New Zealand, for example, put through reforms which gave each school its own Board of Trustees, and in Great Britain the trend to local management of schools (LMS) was pushed to the extent of allowing some government schools to become free-standing, quasi-independent, grant-maintained schools (GMS).

In the United States people like Albert Shanker (1988) of the American Federation of Teachers argued that teachers should be encouraged to put forward proposals about how to make better use of the resources in the school and at the same time to achieve better learning outcomes. Thereafter, Philadelphia developed a programme to run 'schools within schools' – separate chartered academies set up inside large high schools. Detroit's Public Schools Empowerment Plan proposed to give 92 per cent of the school's operating budget directly to the school, to free the school from district regulations, to allow it to enter into contracts for the supply of the services it needed, and to require it to draw up its own learning programme in which its performance targets were clearly specified.

In short, charters were an attempt to reorient conventional schooling. The device would sponsor open enrolment, encourage wider choice among schools, offer a better approach than school vouchers, and concentrate on the learning outcomes achieved by schools rather than on how the school used its inputs. Both the Bush and the Clinton administrations developed national statements of aims for America's schools compatible with the charters approach, acknowledging how fundamental to their country's future is effective schooling (Pipho, 1993: 102). By the early 1990s the interest in charter schools, Amsler reported, had begun to gain momentum across the country, providing 'a new vision of schools and the educational services they offer', and allowing the group organizing the school to build a contract with its sponsors and its public based on 'what the educational plan for the school is, what the educational outcomes will be and how they will be measured. In exchange for this agreement of accountability, the school receives autonomy' (Amsler, 1992: 1, 6).

The view was emerging that a school which had worked its way through the process of drawing up a charter is different in kind from a conventional school. Charters made possible for schools modes of operating unlikely to be achievable under a centralized administration where there are tight, day-to-day, conformist, bureaucratic controls. But to fulfil such a promise, those charged with the management of such schools were expected to jump the tracks and to capitalize on what this innovation was designed to bring about. The act of formulating a charter would force the school to consider what makes it different and distinctive from other schools, implying that it is a difference to be welcomed, celebrated and enthusiastically advertised abroad. So the charter became essentially a process rather than a document, a style of operating rather than a piece of paper. It became a framework for thinking coherently about the school and what it aims to achieve, approaching the school's work from the service-delivery end (the outputs) rather than from the tradesperson's entrance (the inputs).

By the beginning of the 1993/94 school year, eight states in America had enacted legislation to allow for some form of charter schools. Minnesota led the way in 1991, with California following in 1992; Colorado, Georgia, Massachusetts, Missouri, New Mexico and Wisconsin came on stream in 1993; in the same year several other states (including Alaska, Connecticut, Florida, New Jersey, North Carolina, Oregon, Pennsylvania, Tennessee and Washington) were considering such legislation. Indiana, Iowa and Ohio had bills waiving current school regulations for break-the-mould schools who agreed to rewrite their missions (Sautter, 1993: 16).

In contrast with the New Zealand and Australian contexts, schools in the United States are owned and governed by local school districts through elected school boards. The United States is a federation of states like Australia, and in both countries the constitutional power over education resides with the states. The difference in the USA is that while the states may pass the legislation which sets the framework for schooling, it is the fifteen thousand local school districts of varying sizes which control, indeed *own*, the schools. In the US, therefore, a charter allows the school to step outside the jurisdiction of one of those local school districts and to function on its own. The charter school arrangement in the USA, then, like the provision for the grant-maintained schools (GMS) in Great Britain before the Blair Government came to power, was a means whereby a public school could become a single, non-aligned, independent entity. The state charter schools legislation had the effect of incorporating the school as a company, with the charter containing its articles of incorporation.

Because the conditions in one country never exactly parallel those in another, it is wise to be circumspect about making applications from what prevails elsewhere. The *ideas* can be borrowed, but the practices will take a shape determined by the particular conditions in a particular country. Even so, it is important to note that the charter school movement, in whatever way it manifested itself in several countries, did signal a new framework for public schooling based upon service delivery, quality enforced by market conditions, and the downplaying of both central and external control of day-to-day management.

The school and its stakeholders

The charter process forces the school to consider constructively its relationship with its stakeholders. Because the charter embodies an agreement about the way the school will operate and what its objectives will be, it has almost always led to the setting up of a formal school-site council or (where one already exists) to a redefinition of its role. Among other functions, the school-site council becomes both the charter's public custodian and the body which ensures that its implementation is honoured.

New Zealand pioneered much of the thinking about stakeholders following the 1988 Picot Report and the government's implementation document *Tomorrow's Schools* (1988), initiatives which pre-dated the similar reforms of North America. The intention in New Zealand was to treat schools as mature institutions, capable of running their own affairs without much control from the national office and freed from the oversight of regional boards. When the school received its operating funds from the national government, it was clear that, although the school must serve the local community, the local community did not own it. Hence the terms of the NZ charters were negotiated with government, and every school was required to have a council called a Board of Trustees, a term which defined the relationship with government accurately. Even while the Trustees were drawn from among those interested in the well-being of a particular school, they had to be people whom those funding the school (in this case, the government) trusted. They were to hold the school's money 'in trust', and guarantee – through a mandatory reporting-back to government – that the money was being put to appropriate uses. The New Zealand government therefore required a regular (annual) report from the Trustees, and also a regular audit, both financial and in terms of service delivery (along the lines of any public organization).

Just as appropriately, the government could lay down what areas were to be included in each charter, since the signatories were the school and its sponsor, the Education Minister. Early in the implementation period, the NZ government's Department of Education issued a model charter which could be adapted school by school, but which contained the essential functions and characteristics which the school's owner (the government) could legitimately enforce. The same situation prevailed in Australia when the state of Victoria took up the idea of charters.

The common characteristics in this new approach for *public* schooling were summarized well by Sautter (1993: 16) and Amsler (1992: 3):

- Public, charter schools are *not independent schools*. That is, they were not to charge fees for instruction, and must operate within the normal funding parameters laid down for other public schools. They could not choose to be discriminatory on the basis of religion, race, gender or intellectual ability.
- Charter schools are nevertheless *free from the regulations* which govern the way other schools operate. The charter set the schools up 'as if they were school districts' in their own right (Amsler, 1992: 3) – as if each school was a public mini-system or sub-system. 'In the true spirit of decentralization,' wrote Amsler (1992: 2), 'charter schools make all their own instructional and administrative decisions. Site-based management eliminates the problems districts encounter as they grapple with giving schools the decision-making responsibilities while remaining legally liable for decisions made.'
- The *charter is quasi-legal*, even when it is not actually legal (although in some places it is covered by a state law).
- A charter school is not to be regarded as *a magnet school*, serving only students with special skills. The school could of course have an organizing theme or a particular philosophy to shape the learning programme, but the charter did not permit it to be exclusive or elitist. So the admissions policies of a chartered school had to be non-discriminatory.
- Concerning *funding*, the students tend to attract 'average per pupil' funds

when they enrol at a charter school. The school therefore tended to be driven by the number of students served, a kind of customer-orientation in the way it is financed.

• It was an explicit intention of the charter to *free schools so that they can make more efficient usage of their resources,* encouraging what in other contexts would be called micro-economic reform.

• The *quality of learning outcomes* ranked above every other consideration. Sautter (1993: 10, 16) put the view succinctly. The charter law (he is quoting the case of California here) is designed to 'improve student learning', by using 'different and innovative teaching methods', by increasing the 'professional opportunities for teachers', by expanding educational choice, and by 'holding schools accountable for meeting measurable outcomes'. He went on: 'Outcomes-based means that students must demonstrate what they have learned and know, before they move forward in their diverse studies. The goal is to prove active student competence and knowledge ... rather than merely [to] record attendance and effort at learning.'

The new movement, then, focused schools on their core task, learning; it encouraged each school to be different, distinctive and innovative; it freed the school to 'do it their way'; made overt the school's accountabilities; and created space for its teachers to become professionally diverse (Amsler, 1992: 3). Put simply, the charter process was designed to produce a resource-efficient, outcomes-based, professionally oriented, accountable school in which improved student learning is the prime focus and objective.

It is therefore appropriate to return to the details normally included in a charter and to consider what a school as a broker for learning needs to do to reorient its approaches along these lines and away from those of the conventional schooling associated with an industrially based society.

On profiles and vision statements

The first (and relatively simple) step is to draw a profile of the school as it is at present, which would include:

• the nature of its student population and the home backgrounds from which they come;
• its enrolment levels and catchment area and whether the population of the school is rising, declining or has plateau-ed (for the school's size must be predictable to enable accurate planning);
• the nature of the community which the school serves or from which it draws its students;
• the school's geographical location;
• the facilities which the school has at its disposal.

Mapping what the school is should be a straightforward exercise. It requires good data and hard-nosed honesty, but it is simple description, a portrait rather than a prognosis.

The school then might draw up two lists. One contains the characteristics which the school's stakeholders most value in the school and which attract its enrolments. Experience suggests that there are likely to be about ten to fifteen such characteristics on the list. The second is a list of the features about the school which need improvement or which the stakeholders would like to change. From such an analysis emerges a picture of what the school currently *is* and what the school *aspires to be*.

The terms 'vision' and 'mission' tend to have been bled of their potency by being overworked. Even so, every person has ambitions and a relatively coherent web of beliefs within which she plans and runs her life; a credo is a set of such principles, usually arrived at by deliberate choice. Each Principal, senior educator and council member has a personal sub-set of principles which embody their aspirations about education, about schooling, about this partic-ular school. Until this credo has been committed to paper (even if no one else will ever read it), it will probably lack power because it lacks definition. If the statements in the credo are in sharp focus, in clear, pungent, crisp prose, if they have been pondered and refined, then they concentrate energy. A credo is the sort of thing you print out and paste behind your cupboard door, or frame and put above your desk in the way Rotary members do.

A 'personal charter', a 'vision', an 'educational platform', a 'mission state-ment' (all those terms have been used) is best written as a set of dot points. It is unlikely to run to more than ten or fifteen terse sentences. Someone observed that a mission statement is ineffective if it contains more than twenty-five words. That may be too restrictive a limit, but it serves to emphasize that the statement must be short. You must be able to memorize it, in fact. Further, avoid all jargon words in stating the set of principles. Use your own fruity, down-to-earth, emotive, picturesque language. Use metaphors and picture-language. Capture your own fervour in the few words you choose. As Starratt (1993: 23) has pointed out, drawing on Block, if your mission statement sounds like a combination of motherhood and apple pie and is somewhat embar-rassing, you are on the right track!

The *school* (especially when it is envisioned as a learning provider and broker) needs a mission statement too, a manifesto of what it stands for. Most of the new school designs around the world and all of those included under the New American Schools (NAS) have been based upon a clearly stated set of principles (Stringfield *et al.*, 1996). A vision statement or educational credo ought to be composed for the school and included in its charter or strategic plan. Devising that credo or mission statement is best done by trying to pool the dot-point principles of all those who are daily involved in its management and operation. This exercise is often done in a day-long or residential retreat; but whatever the venue, it needs to be done. The school's statement may not incorporate everything which every member of the team believes, and in the end it will inevitably be a compromise. It needs also to be terse, pungent, memorable and something to which every member of the staff team feels a strong commitment. It needs to be nailed to a mast somewhere, literally.

If there is discordance between the school's credo and the personal credos of those on its staff, then the school has a fundamental problem which simply must be addressed, and some changes need to be made. In extreme cases of incompatibility, it may mean that some of the staff ought to leave and find a school where they feel congruence with its purposes. This is exactly the reason behind local selection of staff, matching people with a climate where they will thrive.

The school's objectives, its priorities and especially its budget must be brought into conformity with this credo; and this leads to an important negative point. The school community and governments have priorities of their own, and it is usually incumbent on the school to meet those aspirations. When the community's expectations are not consistent with the principles in the staff's or the school's credos, then the school has a serious blind spot; for neither educators nor individual parents can safely ignore what the school's stakeholders collectively require of the school. The very existence of a school-site council is a safeguard here; and assigning someone senior in the school with the job of acting as the school's conscience over the credo is probably a prudent administrative act.

The process of building a profile and a credo can be illustrated from two particular cases.

The example of Fitzroy North Primary School (Australia)

This excellent school is situated in a Melbourne suburb close to the city's central business district and it has been attracting enrolments through a reputation spread by word of mouth. As part of its triennial review, the school needed to know exactly what features of the school were attracting attention, if only to make its enrolments for the next triennium explicable. It resolved therefore to incorporate these attracting characteristics in the new charter's profile. The list included characteristics like the following (but not in order of importance):

1   The historic nature of the school (it was over a hundred years old).
2   The school's remarkable record in academic performance, especially in language and mathematics.
3   The school's strong commitment to social justice and to public education.
4   The gender modelling, particularly with women in the Principal and senior staff roles.
5   The locality, it being a school with a sense of openness (literally as well as metaphorically).
6   The school's culture, exemplified by practices like the way the school's students hosted visitors to the school and contributed to the school's style.
7   The strong and creative after-school-hours child-care programme.

8   The programme in arts and music, and its public visibility through performances.
9   Its physical attractiveness as a school, located opposite a large urban park.
10 Its inclusive, non-aggressive and humane approach in making its programmes accessible to all its students.

This is not an exhaustive list, but the renegotiation of its charter (which was part of the review protocol) allowed the school an opportunity deliberately to add, subtract or highlight characteristics in its profile. It also helped the school's planning and day-to-day operations to have this list made explicit, agreed to by staff and council, included in the charter's preamble, and thereafter used wherever appropriate both in the body of the charter and in the general operations of the school.

The previous charter, it was discovered, had implicit in it the agreed educational principles which underlie the school's activities and which gave rise to these characteristics. Those assumptions were obviously inherent in the way the school operated, and were taken seriously. The school realized that it would give pungency to the new charter if those guiding principles were made explicit, listed as dot-points, and tested out with both staff and council to verify that they were indeed accurate, had the strong concurrence of every member of staff and council, and were already taken for granted in everything the school, its staff and its parents did in the name of the school.

As a starting point, then, the set of assumptions from the previous charter were set out as follows:

1   At Fitzroy North Primary School, students are encouraged to achieve high educational outcomes, to grow in self-esteem and self-confidence, to learn to work co-operatively in groups, to take pride in their school and their community, and to be responsible for their own learning.
2   Fitzroy North is a caring school with a community focus.
3   The school puts emphasis on the participation of students, parents, community members and staff in all aspects of the school. Parents participate in classrooms, curriculum, policy and review.
4   Students are encouraged to play an integral part in the school's decision-making.
5   The school is strongly committed to the principles of social justice and equal opportunity, and endeavours to reflect these qualities in every aspect of the school's activity.
6   The school is committed to full consultation, open communication and democratic decision-making, especially among students, staff and parents.
7   The school takes a systematic and whole-of-school approach to planning and evaluation.
8   The staff have a strong commitment to professionalism, working in co-operative teams and putting high priority on continuing professional development.

9   The school provides a learning environment which is challenging and stimulating, where a range of learning styles is developed, and where students are safe to explore interesting topics and programmes of learning.

With definition of this kind and a wise documentation of the school's culture, this school was in good shape to lay out a detailed, year-by-year action plan to carry it through its next triennium.

The example of Oak Ridge School (Canada)

A second example is that of Oak Ridge School, which adopted a quite simple but profound approach to the way its students dealt with the curriculum. The mission of the school, it was decided, was to teach its students 'to use your mind well', and it encouraged its students to develop habits of mind based on five questions which were to be asked of any and every matter under investigation in the learning programme:

1   How do I know what I know about this matter?
2   From what perspective is this matter being considered?
3   How are things related or connected?
4   What if things had been different?
5   Why am I studying this matter? Why is it important?

Converting vision statements into objectives and action plans

The profile of the school as it is and the statement of the foundation principles on which its activities are based become the starting point from which the school can draw up its objectives. Those fundamental principles have to be translated first into operational terms and then expressed in a practical plan of action.

At this point it is best for the school to do the obvious and to compose an aim or objective for each of the major aspects of the school's functions. Especially for a school conceived of as a provider and broker for learning, it is almost certain to address these areas of schooling:

•   the school's operating style and its profile;
•   the curriculum or learning programme;
•   the school's learning environment, including the physical facilities which it uses;
•   its governance, organization and management;
•   its resource usage, including its financial management, and how it ensures that its priorities are truly reflected in its budget, and that items in its core business are given precedence over anything else;
•   its expectations concerning its students and its stakeholders.

A school will generally have between eight and twelve such objectives, no more.

In the case of each objective, the school will then lay down a set of year-by-year implementation strategies, with intermediate (probably annual or half-yearly) targets to be aimed for, and, for each dimension, a set of performance indicators which give unbiased and consistent data as evidence of progress. The indicators need to be carefully chosen, especially bearing in mind the ease of data collection, and they must minimize any disruption to a concentration on the school's core business. Two indicators per dimension is about as many as a school is likely to be able to handle well.

Just as it is helpful to think of the increasing degree of specificity involved as the planning team moves from statement of principles to implementation, so it is prudent in this connection to revisit the distinction between strategic and tactical planning. 'Strategic' and 'tactical' are military terms. Strategy concerns the whole war, the kind of decision-making which falls to field commanders, chiefs-of-staff and war cabinets. Tactics relate to particular battles, to manoeuvres on the field, to what individual soldiers or platoons do to gain an advantage in a skirmish. The responsibility for working out winning tactics has to be entrusted to staff or to sections within the enterprise, but what any one of them does in the field should be imbued with winning the skirmish, the battle and the war. In short, it should be consistent with the overall strategy. Although teachers and parents tend to be uncomfortable when the war metaphor is applied to education, it does explain the difference between strategic and tactical planning. The charter movement is itself a reaction to the impression (whether true or false) that schools have been good at tactics (the details) but not so good at strategy (the big picture items).

The military analogy also implies a chain of command and a top-down, imposed discipline which fits uneasily in a profession, which is inappropriate in a post-industrial organization, and which the charters themselves are designed to supersede. It grates in the same way as traditional bureaucracy, an outgrowth of the factory metaphor, does. Even so, because the terms have been so widely used, everyone in the team needs to know what is involved in strategic and tactical planning.

As was explained in an earlier chapter, planning implies that there is a blueprint, a set of builder's charts for what is being constructed. 'Backward mapping' is a well-used planning technique which lends itself well to the charter process. We determine where we want to be, what we want to have achieved, at a specified time in the future; then we track backwards, plotting where we need to be at intermediate points along the way in order to achieve that ultimate objective. The plan starts from where you want to arrive at, and then plots a route backwards in time to where you are at present.

Of course, some actions depend on the completion of others, and there is often a set of branching actions or sub-actions which have to come together at a certain time. The Programme Evaluation and Review Technique (PERT), its PERT chart and critical path analysis, has traditionally been used for this kind of planning. The important point is that progress towards the achievement of a planned goal needs to be paced, and there must be review points along the way to ensure that the plan is still on target. At each of these signposts, the clutch of indicators or measuring gauges should be able to give an accurate reading of the extent of the progress being made and whether that progress is satisfactory.

In summary, then, a charter and a set of guiding principles are the foundation on which good, achievable, well-articulated plans can be drawn up, with increasing degrees of specificity, by a school which has become both a supplier and a broker for learning. Further, the document should ensure that everything, small and large, done in and by the school conforms both with the overarching vision, with its operational objectives, and also with its detailed planning. By separating the detail of implementation from the statement of principle, the charter or plan guarantees that first things are kept first, and that what falls outside the agreed goals and priorities of the school should not be fed any energy or resources.

There is a well-established convention which has operated for years under the Westminster system of government, which legislators, politicians, senior administrators and policy-makers take for granted, and which may be usefully applied to the process of implementing a school charter. It concerns the relationship between an Act of Parliament (the law, or legislation), the Regulations under the Act, and the working rules used in implementation.

When a bill is introduced into Parliament, its sponsor is expected in the Second Reading speech to discuss the ideas underlying the legislation and to explain how the bill embodies those ideas in a form which can be implemented in the state or nation. So the bill sets a framework, but does not necessarily go into the fine detail of its administration. Once passed, the legislation is then referred to a ministerial or executive portfolio where it is broken down into its component pieces, and where departmental officers draft Regulations which spell out in greater detail the procedures for putting the bill into practice. Regulations are formal, and are usually submitted to the legislature for comment; they have the force of law (since they represent the outworking of what was in the original bill), but they can be more easily changed than a law. Once the Regulations – the practical ramifications of the legislation – have been assented to, the departments which are to implement the legislation may, and usually do, draw up their own internal documents (policies, working rules, guidelines, handbooks) which lay down the *modus operandi* for those who will be involved with the daily administration of the law. The point is that details of administration ought not to be put into the enabling legislation; it is better to have the law as a framework, and to put the details of management into subsidiary documents.

The same principle should apply with the charter. Like a law, it is an overarching document, a road-map which gives a bird's eye view of the territory to be traversed, which states the direction for the ensuing journey of three years and the destination, and which gives indicative routes to reach there. As with a piece of legislation, the charter's implementation then needs to be parcelled out to the appropriate units and departments within the school or enterprise, who in turn draw up their own procedures. They will almost certainly produce something in writing so that all the team members responsible for the implementation of that section of the charter have common understandings and know what to do in an emergency – such as when a key team member is absent. These working rules are analogous to the Regulations which accompany an Act. There will also be formal, informal or ad hoc actions and papers which emanate from the implementation of the charter.

In short, when you liken the charter to a piece of legislation, there is a model to give body to its implementation, to parcel out to groups, units or members of staff the responsibilities which flow from it, to ensure that no part of it is overlooked, and to make action based on the charter a normal part of the life of the school. At the least, treating the charter like this will affect the organizational structure of the school, and will influence how the school's functions are rationally allocated. The charter becomes everyone's business.

Note

I acknowledge the assistance of Shirley Francis, Gina Morra and Peter O'Connell in the research and literature survey for this chapter.

10 On reporting outcomes

Principle No. 4 Collect – systematically and routinely – credible evidence which documents your achievements.

The idea of 'trading flexibility for accountability' ran strongly through the early advocacy for school charters in the USA (Sautter, 1993: 14), for the charter process invited the school to make explicit the terms on which it is confident to have itself judged. There is not much poetry in the word 'accountability', and it is often applied in ways which do not provoke much enthusiasm, joy or excitement. If you had to assign a colour to it, it would be a dull, steely grey – cold, unimaginative, a trifle threatening, routine, mechanical and unfeeling. Unless, of course, accountability is deliberately painted green! The issue of accountability can be made into something living and interesting by asking the question, 'When we are successful, whom should we tell about it?' A second question follows naturally: 'How can we make the telling not only interesting but full of meaning, and a good public performance?'

If reporting about good things being achieved is a cause for such a celebration, it is easy to include in the report a comment about the aspects of the stage performance where you would like to improve, where to finetune the script, or to recruit another lead actor, or to rework the scenario in a way which will increase the applause and make it more spontaneous. Accountability is the process you adopt in order to report improvements, and especially those which you have deliberately planned to make and enunciated publicly. Accountability means that you *are* able to give an account of yourself.

But who is listening; who wants to hear? Whom *must* the school tell about its performance, and especially its success? Four sets of people come readily to mind as audiences.

- First, whatever their age, the school needs to tell its **students** some things, systematically and regularly, for they are the client-learners, and the encouragement of learning is the task which transcends everything else the school does. The school needs to arrange its affairs (and usually does) in such a way that the students being served by the school receive constant, understandable, helpful feedback about how well they are progressing. There may be other things about the life and health of the school on which the students need feedback also.

- Second, the school needs to give a similar kind of account to its **parents**. The feedback to them will differ from what the students receive. To be frank, what the students get will be more detailed, more frequent, even more sophisticated, because students are daily involved with learning and understand the nature of the studies they are undertaking. The parents want feedback which is more general, but in a form which answers their serious questions and which gives them reliable information. Parents are likely to want some statistics about the school's, the students' and their own child's academic performance. Among other things, and in the overwhelming number of cases, the parents are likely to use that information to help both their child and the school which she or he attends.

- Third, the **community served by the school** has a right to receive carefully constructed feedback. This kind of accountability is usually met through an annual report from the school council. A wise school will first poll the opinions of its supporting community to discover exactly what it is about the school on which they want to have regular information. It will then negotiate what systematically accumulated data or information the school can supply to prove that it is achieving what the community wants it to achieve. In short, the criteria, the indicators and the form of the reports can be sensibly negotiated with the client community. The report then becomes a formal documentation of what they have asked to see.

- Fourth, the school is accountable to those who sponsor or fund the school. In the case of government, state, provincial, local or denominational systems, the school is partly regulated and has systemic as well as local responsibilities. Its operating funds are often supplied directly by government from taxpayers' contributions which have to be audited, and those governments themselves have to be responsive to the people who elected them. So **the school's or system's financiers** will need to be given evidence of a particular and detailed kind. Those data and the format of reporting will have to be negotiated too.

In terms of accountability, these people and groups are audiences. But *what* they must be told will differ for each audience. Students will be interested in data about their own learnings, but are not likely to be much concerned about how the school's finances are spent. The funding authority, on the other hand, will be concerned with the husbandry of money, but will look to have student achievement reported in ways quite different from what an individual student will need. The school, then, will be forced systematically to collect basic information about its core activities, yet it will have to use that information to give an account of itself in different ways and in different settings and formats according to whichever audience it happens to be addressing. In short, it will have to think in terms of providing several kinds of 'reports'.

Thus the school will find itself having to assemble data about its students' achievement levels; about the school's health and style; about how it is implementing policies like those relating to curriculum frameworks; about the behaviour patterns among its student body; about its management routines; about its plans for the future; and so on. It could be a long list, and later we return to consider how to cope with it, including how to shorten the list. There could be a great amount of similarity about the way these data are used in the reports to the different client groups. To ensure speed, simplicity, validity and there are advantages in having guidelines and agreed formats for reporting.

In summary, then, there are at least four sets of significant stakeholders to whom the school must give accounts of progress, but it cannot speak to them all in the same way, nor will it need to report the same things to each set. It will have to use different language for each audience. But it is useful to have agreed ways, times and formats in which to give feedback, and agreement about what subjects and items should be covered.

System accountability

Every school which is part of a larger system owes it to the system to garner the information which the system itself needs to show that it is performing well. There is, and always has been, a great amount of flexibility within these kinds of systemic guidelines. The items to be reported on, the nature of the data to be supplied, the format in which they are to be supplied and the frequency of the reporting are malleable and are usually arrived at through consultation among all involved. The information required by the system usually needs to be collected and relayed in a parallel way from each school so that it can be easily collated and so that on the basis of those data it is possible to speak authoritatively about the collectivity of schools which make up the system. Every school gains if those documented claims can be made. Increasingly now, data about the academic performance of students, suitably norm-referenced, are being asked for.

Reporting to the community served by the school

Generally speaking, each school should give an account in a way which is meaningful and helpful to its client-community. There is no need for all those individual reports from schools to their publics to be identical; indeed, not only would it be surprising if they were, but absolute uniformity across schools may well indicate that the local feelings and wishes of the community are not being treated seriously. On the other hand, it would also be surprising if schools did not report about similar facets of their operation. So uniformity is not usually asked for, but it does help to have similar, broad structures for giving an account to each set of stakeholders.

Even if left to their own devices, then, most school communities would choose similar things to make comment upon, and the data used to report accountably to its governors would also be used, suitably adapted and presented, in the report to the community. It is probably helpful for schools to follow similar procedures over compiling their information. Furthermore, there are survey instruments, data analysis devices and computer programs which, by being shared among schools, will save a lot of time.

Longitudinal data

A single photograph can tell you what a person looks like at one point in his or her lifetime, but several snapshots taken at regular periods will indicate how that person has grown and changed. The most useful longitudinal data are those collected at carefully chosen points of time and using exactly the same collection instrument so that the data can be compared. If it keeps nothing else, any school would be prudent to collect, store, analyse and use data like these *which relate to its core purpose or mission*, namely, how well its students are learning.

Supplementary data

Further, the school must be ready to proffer supplementary information whenever the need arises among any of the groups to which it feels a responsibility to give an account of itself. The school staff therefore needs to anticipate, to be forewarned and forearmed. It should give careful consideration to what information it will systematically collect and store, and every member of the staff needs to be party to that process and to co-operate in the data collection. The school does not need this consistency on everything, but it certainly does on the matters which are really crucial to the school's health and well-being.

'KISS: Keep it simple, stupid!'

This is the advice Peters and Waterman (*In Search of Excellence,* 1982) gave to enterprises which want to remain excellent. Don't be too complicated, tell what you need to tell simply and directly, and stick to the fundamentals, they advise. Already it will be obvious that the school could spend a lot of its staff's valuable time in compiling reports and collecting materials. Writing reports which are never read (for whatever reasons) is a waste of resources. Short, sharp, selective, targeted reporting is needed. You target your audience, use that audience's language, select exactly what that audience wants to know, and then supply the details succinctly and with transparent honesty. You report only as often as they want it, no more, no less. It is on the basis of *which* audience you are addressing that you choose what items you deal with, which performance indicators you quote, the format the report takes, and the language you use.

So how does a school-as-a-provider do it?

Information about student learning

Schools have always collected information about their students' academic progress. Sometimes the data have been less precise and focused than they could be, and often they have been idiosyncratic to particular teachers and classrooms. Sometimes the teacher keeps the material only to herself, to help her in adapting her classroom methods. Just because of the way classes have been organized in the past, teachers have tended to act independently and have not always co-operated among themselves in a strategy to collect and record their feedback data consistently across the whole school. It is neither hard nor a big step to do just that. A school (and by implication each of its teachers) is vulnerable unless it can give an account of its whole-school performance, especially in terms of its core mission.

Although teachers are used to accumulating data about learning, these data are often meaningful only to teachers but not to others outside the profession; in short, it is diagnostic material, expressed in teacher language. It cannot be reported to others in that form without being misunderstood. A report suited to one group will not necessarily be satisfactory for another, but that is not a great problem providing teachers are aware of it; they have to be selective and (in a metaphorical sense) multilingual.

It is a good policy anyway to compile one formal report each year, addressed to the most significant of the audiences, and in a format which makes it a semi-permanent record. But it is easy to go overboard, to make it too long, and even to produce something that is almost unreadable. If the report (*any* report) exceeds about twenty pages, very few people (in any of the audiences) will take – or have – the time to read it. Most people read only the executive summaries of long, public reports. Compiling an annual report should not be a burden, therefore, especially if it is kept readable, attractive, fairly short, well documented, and tells the important things surely, honestly and convincingly.

Like the charter itself, reporting is a process too. There is a routine cycle of review which produces the best reports. 'They look before and after', backwards over recent achievement, forwards over business still to be tackled. It is helpful if a natural cycle is built into the charter process – from charter to detailed plans, to reviews of progress, to formal reporting, to revision of plans, to reporting progress, and ultimately to revision of the charter, to its formal assent and signing, and to the beginning of a new cycle. If the school does not have a routine annual cycle built into its operations, then the Principal and senior staff might be wise to institute one.

What follows here is a well-proven, logical method to tackle the accountability cycle, including the means to keep it to a size which can be easily handled, and to invest it with some intellectual zest.

On performance indicators

There is a well-established rational framework which has been in use for more than three decades and which was first laid out by the international scholar of policy processes, Yehezkel Dror, in his *Public Policy Re-Examined* (1973). He built his model after analysing dozens of examples from around the world of how policies are arrived at and implemented. What follows is an adaptation from Dror's model. Knowing this basic and well-tried schema will help a school to handle some of the unknowns in the accountability area.

Step 1   Name your categories

The first step is to list the aspects, categories or areas which encapsulate what the school does, and where you intend to monitor and assess your performance. This is not a particularly difficult act of definition because the charter process will have enunciated them. The list can quickly become very long; and the school will not have the time, resources, people or energy to collect useable data on them all. The school *must* of course include those aspects which relate to the essential mission of the enterprise and its credo. Unless other enterprises and businesses do that, they quickly go out of existence!

Each of the goal areas for a school (curriculum, including academic outcomes; school environment; management; accountability; resources) can be broken into sub-categories to cover all the activities which go on in a normal working week in a school. Once the categories are known, the school will then select the ones where it is quite essential that it monitor progress or performance. Immediately three clusters of items stand out to be asterisked.

- The *first set* are those legal, statutory, financial or systemic areas where it is simply essential to keep records and document what happens. For example, if the law requires that children between certain ages must attend school, then the school is bound to record whether the law is being kept. The system itself may lay on all (or some) of its schools certain requirements, and not only must those requirements be met but the school has to accumulate the evidence which proves it has met them.
- The *second set* are the result of the school's own priorities, the special areas where the school has decided to concentrate attention over the next year or so. It will obviously need to assemble information to satisfy itself that it is making the progress it intended to make.
- The *third set* contains those areas where it is prudent to accumulate convincing evidence because one of the school's audiences is at some time likely to ask for it.

There may be other aspects of the school's life and performance which the school may want to document, tracking through with evidence. The topics may relate to the school as a whole, to particular parts or faculties, to the performance of learning groups or individual students, to teacher or parent reactions or behaviours, to the role of the Principal and senior staff, or to some other aspects of the school's work. The focus will not always be on the whole school. By whatever methods of choice are suitable, then, there needs to be a deliberate, strategic, calculated selection of the categories, areas of activity or aspects of the school's performance on which it will systematically accumulate indicative data.

Step 2   List your audiences, category by category

It is wise at this point to draw up a grid with the categories as the vertical axis and as the horizontal axis the several audiences (including teaching staff, students, parents, the community and the governors). It is then possible to go through the categories one by one, ticking in the appropriate box which audiences will have an interest in receiving accountability evidence on the category items selected in Step 1 (see Figure 10.1).

You will no doubt discover that you must now add to your listing a category or two which one of your audiences would choose, but which you did not. If you are really accountable to them, then you must consider their interests in this way and include items they want to have on the list. Of course, it is wise to consult them in some way, and not just to guess. You might also ask what kind of evidence would satisfy them for each item.

This surveying of the field from the perspective of the different audiences being addressed will guide the data collection and also suggest what the school should do with the data once they are collected. But *what* data can you collect, and *how* do you collect them? Those questions lead us to Step 3.

Step 3   Select your indicators, category by category

On each of the items which appear on the selected list, it is necessary to ask, 'What kind of data or materials could we systematically and regularly collect to show whether we are meeting the targets, deadlines or expectations in this category?' This is a search for appropriate indicators, and at least one and probably two are required for each of the listed categories. Having *only* one indicator is usually insufficient.

On some items, it is obvious what data need to be collected. If it is required that the school give an account of the extent of suspensions and expulsions for the year, then recording the statistics is all the school needs to do, and then to report them. Those measuring devices are called *primary (or direct) indicators*.

On many items, however, especially those dealing with areas where it is quite difficult to define exactly what the objectives and the outcomes are – and educational objectives are a classic case – the school will not have primary indicators, and will therefore need to invent *secondary (or indirect) indicators*. Let us take an example.

> *Employee commitment*   A company was concerned about raising the commitment of its employees to the mission of the firm. The company managers could have used primary (direct) indicators like a regularly administered questionnaire or a regular series of interviews with a random sample of the people in the firm. Collecting these data and then analysing them is time-consuming, costly and intrusive. Instead, the company chose a secondary (indirect) indicator. The managers reasoned that if people are enthusiastic about the place they work in, are motivated about its aims, are doing work which interests them, and not only like but feel a responsibility to

Figure 10.1 The several audiences for feedback and reporting

AUDIENCES	Curriculum	Environment	Management	Resources	
Students	What do students need to be told about a) the curriculum? a) the school's targets and achievement levels? b) their own targets and achievement levels?				→ **Report**
Staff					→ **Report**
Parents	What do parents need to be told about a) the curriculum details? b) targets and achievement levels for all students? c) the targets and achievement levels of their own child?				→ **Report**
Community			What does the community need to know about the school's management?		→ **Report**
Trustees				What do trustees need to know about the allocation and use of resources?	→ **Report**

1. How many formal reports are needed?

2. What does each audience want included in their report?

3. What language and terms are appropriate for this audience?

4. How long should this report be?

5. How frequently is a report needed for this particular audience?

the people they work with, then that commitment is likely to show up in the rate of absenteeism (excluding normal holiday leave) among the employees. So the company used the pattern of worker absenteeism, tracked over time, as an indirect indicator of employee commitment to the firm

This example throws into relief some of the important considerations about secondary indicators. An indicator has to be credible. The association between the prime quality which one is wanting to measure and the indirect indicator ought to be strong and obvious. But it will also be partial, and it is prudent to be aware of what the secondary indicator by its very nature is going to miss. It may also need some explanation when it is proffered as evidence. Indeed, that is the very reason why teachers have been so sensitive about literacy and numeracy tests. They are good diagnostic devices, but they test only certain facets of skills from which the educator can extrapolate some other information. They are secondary indicators. When they are used in public as though they are *primary* indicators, some quite wrong conclusions can be drawn from the evidence.

Thus where it is impossible to measure something because it is intangible, multi-faceted, intensely personal or very hard to define exactly, one is always forced into inventing secondary indicators. Teachers do it all the time. So do parents. For example, in Britain and its former colonies, whether a school enforces the wearing of a school uniform has for decades been taken by parents as an indirect indicator of whether the school has good discipline. It may not be a very good indicator, but it has been used nonetheless. Are there better indicators a school can invent to give evidence of good behaviour patterns among the student population? How could the school demonstrate unequivocally that good behaviour was on the rise? Or that good is good enough? That is Step 4.

Before proceeding to that step, however, let us be clear that the evidence the school accumulates does not have to be only *statistical* (although some of it must be, of course). To show that much of the best evidence is *not* numerical, let us cite the example of the Coalition of Essential Schools in the United States.

The Coalition was formed in 1984, following Professor Ted Sizer's five-year national research study of the American high school. Sizer came to the conclusion that schools had over time been loaded with a multiplicity of social and cultural functions designed to remedy community problems, and that schools now needed to be refocused on what were their essential tasks, those which are learning-related. So the Coalition drew up a list of 'nine common principles' which schools must commit themselves to if they wished to join the Coalition.

One of the principles is 'that the governing metaphor of the school should be student as worker' and not that of 'the teacher as deliverer of instructional services'. So a Coalition school sets out to help the student to be a self-starting learner, someone who can teach herself. And this principle leads naturally to another; it is the *student's* responsibility to demonstrate that she has learnt. A certificate should be awarded when the student has successfully proved that she has acquired the mastery of what the certificate testifies to. In other words, the student must exhibit evidence of her learning. Because the diploma (or certificate) is awarded when earned, the onus is on the student to demonstrate that she can do important things. This is an outcomes-based approach, but it is the student who has to present the evidence which exhibits that the outcome has been achieved.

Numbers of schools, using this approach, now ask the students (whatever their age) to build up a portfolio of the materials which demonstrate their success as learners – a particularly good essay, a piece of art work, a project which involved original research, the marks from some kind of test. Teachers also collect other student work to be used as a benchmark against which a child can compare her own performance. And when the school comes to address the individual parent-audience to give an account of how well her child Angelica is progressing, Angelica herself can produce her portfolio and tell her mother what she can do, showing the exhibits in her file. Further, she can produce another student's exhibit as a standard against which her mother can assess how well Angelica is progressing. And none of this evidence needs to be statistical; indeed, it could be less effective if it were.

And finally for this step, Dror lists several general ways in which people use secondary (indirect) indicators to signal hard-to-measure achievement in an associated area. First, some operators, unable to demonstrate empirically that the outcomes of the organization are satisfactory, will argue that because the internal *procedures* are efficient, the organization is bound to be good. Second, an organization is deemed to be in good heart when its *structures* are good. The operators argue that if everyone has clearly defined functions, that the modes of interaction are clearly laid down, that there is good co-ordination, that the files are well kept and accessible, that the communication is good, then the outputs are bound to be good – an argument from the secondary indicators of structure. Third, there is the argument from *inputs*. Because we can show that money has been allocated to the area, or certain new equipment has been bought, or a new facility has been provided, then we make the assumption that that area must be in good shape and the programmes must have been enhanced or improved by means of the new inputs. For years, schools used the secondary indicator of the number of new books added to the library and the ratio of books to student population as secondary indicators to show that the library was effective.

Of course, the most important as well as the most sensitive area over which to cite outcomes data is that relating to student achievement, the area of the school's prime mission. Nothing will be considered satisfactory if these data are withheld; and a lot of other things will be overlooked by an audience if these data are good. The problem for the school staff is to select professionally defensible indicators, and then to interpret them to the appropriate audiences in a manner and language which are clear and honest.

In summary, then, the school needs at least one indicator, primary (direct) or secondary (indirect), and preferably two, for each of the categories where progress is to be monitored. It is also prudent to negotiate with each of the audiences to which the school must give an account of itself what indicators, direct or indirect, they are happy with and what evidence they would like to see produced by means of them.

Step 4   Setting a standard, or benchmarking

Now we must determine whether 'good' also means 'good enough'. With what can we compare the evidence thrown up by the indicators? What is an appropriate or satisfactory standard, indicator by indicator? Put another way, how do we calibrate the measuring stick?

There are seven conventional ways of setting a standard whereby to judge the adequacy of a performance or an outcome, and teachers, long experienced as student performance assessors, use them all. The school will need to set a standard for every one of the indicators it is using, both primary (direct) and secondary (indirect). These are the usual ways it is done.

- *Past practice*
  How does the quality or the outcome achieved now compare with what was achieved by this group last year, or the year before? How much have this group improved? We frequently compare trend lines across years like this, to arrive at the typical 'learning curve'.
- *Similar cohort*
  How does the performance or quality compare with that of a similar group or population somewhere else? For this reason, educators often use standardized tests so that a learner's performance can be compared against the mean of the whole population of the same age: against their peers, in short. In a school, it is possible to compare the performance of one class group with that of a similar class group, or of one child against the performance of her age cohort.
- *Professional standard*
  Would a professional colleague in the same field give the same value to this level of performance? Sometimes a professional association sets agreed or desired standards, based upon the collective wisdom of their professional experience. Sometimes an expert can be called in to give a second opinion. Sometimes expert opinions from last year can be compared with the expert opinion given this year. School Inspectors' reports on schools were for decades used like this as the basis for accountability within the school systems of Great Britain, New Zealand and Australia. When a school asks consultants or key teachers from another school to give expert advice on its work or practices, it is in effect using the method of 'professional standards' to calibrate the outcomes or indicators for its work.

- *Survival levels*

  This is the argument of minimum standards. Above what level must the person or the group or the school perform in order to survive? Obviously, anything below that level is unsatisfactory; it might even be lethal, literally or metaphorically! Some skill development activities (such as in driver education or in workshop practice) are judged under this standard. So are considerations of functional literacy and numeracy.

- *Demand levels*

  Is the standard achieved satisfactory to those who have a right to require a level of performance? Does it come up to expectations – of ourselves, or of significant others? In short, what standard are we *required* to meet?

- *Planned levels*

  It is possible to specify ahead of time the target level of quality which we will aim to meet, and by what time. It then becomes possible to plan a timeline and a sequence of actions to plot the path to the level we plan to reach. When the data are collected through our indicators, we can ascertain whether we are meeting or are likely to meet our planned levels of performance. Final examinations at school and summative evaluations normally use this method as the basis for setting a performance standard.

- *Optimal level*

  Finally, we might ask, 'What is the *best* we could achieve in these circumstances, or with this activity, or with this group, or with this person?' In this case, it is usually something more than a survival level, more than an expectation level or even a planned level. It is taking the best that we know of as a marker, and then scaling the performance data against that standard (see Figure 10.2).

With these methods of setting a standard and calibrating the measuring stick, a school or enterprise can arrive at a means of interpreting the data which emerge from each of its chosen indicators (both primary and secondary) set up to assess performance in those categories where accountability is required. In each case and category, of course, the outcomes will have to be expressed in the language and format which are favoured and understood by the particular audience to which the report is addressed.

Step 5   Sub-optimizing

Although the logic is clear for devising the categories, setting priorities, selecting wisely from among many possibilities, choosing at least one performance indicator for each category or area, calibrating the measuring instrument by which to judge the data, and setting up the system to regularize data storage and retrieval, it is now looking a large, formidable and time-consuming exercise, and it must *not* become that. If it is too cumbersome, too complicated and takes too much time, the system will collapse! The accountability process must be simple, direct, accessible to the users and supremely *do-able*. So there is a last step to use to keep your

Figure 10.2   Calibrating the measuring stick

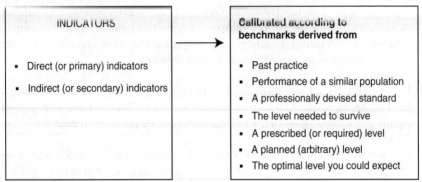

CATEGORY BEING ASSESSED: ....

INDICATORS	Calibrated according to benchmarks derived from
• Direct (or primary) indicators • Indirect (or secondary) indicators	• Past practice • Performance of a similar population • A professionally devised standard • The level needed to survive • A prescribed (or required) level • A planned (arbitrary) level • The optimal level you could expect

system on track, namely sub-optimizing. This means that you limit the collection to what you are able to handle. You choose what you *can* do, since you cannot do everything.

Each individual teacher learns to sub-optimize over the evaluation of her students and over the information she stores about them. Teachers have no choice about whether they keep such data or not; it is a part of their professional duties which they cannot sidestep. Testing, assessing and evaluating are not add-ons but essential functions which come with the teaching and learning role. But they can sub-optimize, select, sample, spot-check. In the same way, the school must keep aggregated data, gleaned from all its teachers and staff, about the way the school is working. But the school also can, indeed probably must, sub-optimize, select, sample and spot-check.

There are three common ways to sub-optimize:

- *By time*   The data are harvested only at determined times. For example, the school may choose to track how well its students are progressing with their reading skill acquisition. The staff could, if they so chose, test every child every week across all levels of the school – and might end up with an unworkable evaluation programme and heaps of unusable outcomes data. Teachers are more likely to sub-optimize; they will decide to collect the feedback data once a term, and in a designated week so that the data are parallel and comparable. That is sub-optimizing by time.
- *By population*   Testing the whole school may be unwieldy. The staff might therefore decide that if they tested only the first, third and sixth year levels for their reading skills, the school could extrapolate from those data what was likely to be occurring in the years not included in the tests. The teachers would limit their data collection, in other words, to only a part of the population they are dealing with. They test a sample of the population, not the whole universe.
- *By task*   There are many factors and skills involved in reading – comprehension, spelling, vocabulary, difficulty of text, eye movements, and so on.

It was the overwhelming complexity of itemizing those sub-skills which brought to grief most of the legislated competency-based education (CBE) policies in the early 1980s in the United States. Faced with the size of the task, teachers are inclined to sub-optimize by choosing only one or two sub-tasks. By testing the reading skill of comprehension only, they might then extrapolate from those test results what the levels of attainment are across the whole range of reading skills. The same approach can be used in the management and other areas of the school's operation.

As with all sampling or sub-optimizing, you will need to satisfy yourself that your results are valid, that they tell an authentic story even though limited in scope, and that you have a sufficient range and depth of systematically gathered material to give a convincing report about yourself. (See Figure 10.3.)

Planning for accountability is an essential part of school management and it involves the entire staff. Just as the functions of the school are broken down into parts and allocated as responsibilities to the members of the staff, to groups or to units, so the implementation of what is in the charter or strategic plan and the accountabilities which flow from them need to be parcelled out among the school. It needs to be routine, not burdensome, but is almost certain to require careful initial planning.

All of this may seem a long and formidable task, but it should not be. It will be bigger the first time than the second time, and then fairly routine and

Figure 10.3   An outcomes-reporting protocol

CATEGORY BEING ASSESSED: ....

INDICATORS	Calibrated according to benchmarks derived from
• Direct (or primary) indicators • Indirect (or secondary) indicators	• Past practice • Performance of a similar population • A professionally devised standard • The level needed to survive • A prescribed (or required) level • A planned (arbitrary) level • The optimal level you could expect

A SAMPLE IS A
SUBSET
DETERMINED BY:

- Time
- Population
- Task

straightforward thereafter. Storing data on computer files simplifies the process, and also gives staff access to multiple ways of analysing the data, and very quickly. Soon, as the data accumulate into a longitudinal set, the analyses, trends and timelines can become a powerful tool for both staff and learners and can also contribute to impressive, even breathtaking, feedback to the school's several audiences. The only major hurdle is setting up the system in the first place for data collection, storage and retrieval.

So decide on a planning day. Get agreement about the categories which need attention. Agree as a school about the indicators and how they are to be systematically used. Agree about the reporting procedures. And then, like Nike, 'just do it'.

The accountability task

In this chapter, we have worked through the logic of setting up a system which will allow the school regularly to harvest the evidence it needs to have available in order to give an account of itself. Since there will always be limits on how much it can collect and analyse, it is important to be prudent and selective, and not to miss out on the most persuasive evidence from the most significant categories of activity. It is silly to collect unnecessary data, and worse still to collect material which is invalid or which no one believes in or which is not used. It is better to have a bit more than you need rather than too little. It is better to have something than nothing. Ensuring that those essential recordings are systematically kept is part of the managerial role. But, most of all, it is foolish to invent a system so demanding that it deflects the school from its prime task as a learning institution.

And at certain stages, there is a formal reporting, an 'accountability episode', it might be called. I prefer to call it a performance, a song-and-dance routine with memorable melodies and exquisite footwork; it should demonstrate an expertly professional cast, dextrous stage management and direction, remarkable control of technology, superb stage business and teamwork, and a bravura masterpiece by the performers showing depth of passion and awesome skill. It is a production which brings the house down. The applause is thunderous ....

But is it as loud and prolonged as the applause last year? Was it a full house? Which sections of the audience cheered the loudest? Did anyone boo? The indicators are never ending! But the school needs to know how well its reporting is being received. Education Victoria produced an excellent booklet, *What Do Parents Think?*, explaining how to monitor parent opinion about the school, and including a decibel counter to measure the strength of the applause. For many years, the Edmonton school system in Canada has had a protocol to collect the data which indicate the level of public and parent satisfaction with the school and the system.

This kind of accountability can be green, a living thing. The charter process was designed as a powerfully positive aspect in the life of the school, leading to a strong, new partnership among the school's stakeholders, giving coherence to its management, and involving all its members.

The approach can be an instrument for school improvement, freeing the school to make the best use of its resources, putting in place an outcomes-based approach to schooling (especially to student learning), and giving the school the means to show that it is not only distinctive but demonstrably successful as well. If such a device did not exist before, then a modern school would surely have to invent one like it.

The student-learner also reports

All of which brings us to the most important and illuminating point of all in this discussion, namely that what we have discussed in relation to the work of the school ideally *ought to apply to the learning programme of each individual student*. Indeed, each student needs to be taught the routine of devising their own learning programme for each year (or term; choosing an appropriate time-zone is part of the learning). Each student can handle the sequence above, namely:

- giving focus to the big picture they have for their learning;
- choosing their areas for study;
- making their objectives crystal clear for each of those areas;
- setting targets (proximate, medium-term, longer-term) for each of the objectives;
- selecting indicators (direct and indirect) for each of the targets; and determining a way to collect consistent performance data on each indicator;
- calibrating the indicators so that performances are benchmarked in some way;
- determining the nature of the accountability episode, when it will occur, and the audience (or audiences) to whom the summative report will be addressed.

Being aware that it is the student herself who is responsible for the shape of the learning programme and for her own progress through it is perhaps the single most significant thing which establishes the school as a provider and a broker. Allowing the student to work through the process listed in this chapter puts the correct perspective on what are the proper roles of both the school and the schooling process itself.

11 Reworking the curriculum within a new mindset

Principle No. 5 Everything in the school focuses on the learning programme, and every learning programme itself has focus.

While people can imagine how schools, school systems, governance arrangements and organizations might be reformed, they find it harder to visualize any fundamental change to the curriculum, to what is to be 'taught'. They even balk at the possibility that subjects, just the notion that there are subjects, and the sequencing of material from elementary to complex could undergo a really deep or radical transformation. Gates came to the conclusion that the 'change in mind-set and culture' (Gates, 1999: xviii) occurring at the turn of the century was not superficial or shallow change, not a tinkering at the edges which leaves things substantially in the same framework. Why should it be different with learning programmes? Furthermore, the changes seem to sneak up on us without our noticing. He wrote: 'We always overestimate the change that will occur in the next two years and underestimate the change that will occur in the next ten' (*ibid.*: 69).

In Part One of this book we dealt with those deep-seated changes which have developed almost a life of their own and which are building into a new way of looking at and interpreting reality. The movement from a factory-dominated society to one in which knowledge workers shape our societal patterns, the widespread replacement of bureaucratic organizations with small, interlinked, autonomous network organizations, the replacement of machine-metaphor explanations of why the world is as it is, and the displacement in learning organizations from acquiring knowledge into inventing knowledge – these are inexorable megatrends which impact on curriculum no less than on other aspects of schooling.

Part Two of this book has therefore dealt with some of the practical implications of those matters. We have considered the need for schooling to discard much of the physical baggage which hampers good futures planning. We proposed a new way of viewing education as an industry. We looked at a planning format which enables a school to choose what it intends to be in the future; and then, drawing on the experience gained with the school charters movement, we considered a realistic procedure for a school to cohere its efforts and its planning. The previous chapter has laid out the logic for assessing outcomes and for accountability, reporting and review. The final chapters arrive at the two most fundamental questions for schooling: What will happen to the curriculum, to the way students learn, and to the nature and format of the school's learning programmes (the topic for the present chapter)? And how will teachers and teaching change (the topic for the next chapter)?

The transitions are already well advanced, of course, and children are picking up the implications and skills for an information society far more quickly than adults are doing. The fundamental change in world-view driving the transitions is so well established across the world that individual schools have no choice but to confront its implications and in such a creative, imaginative way that they enhance the future possibilities for the learners for which they are responsible. The most obvious new component in the twenty-first-century world-view is the place of information technologies in it.

Information technology and the knowledge society

Gates' thesis is that information technology is not only revolutionizing our lives, but fast. In the space of the twenty years 1978–1998, he has pointed out, the microprocessor's capability grew ten thousandfold. If the production of cars and breakfast cereals had followed the same development pattern, 'a mid-size car would [now] cost $27 and a box of cereal a penny [or one cent]' (Gates, 1999: 143). That is the difference between an information or knowledge economy and the industrial or manufacturing economy which it is replacing. Does it also indicate the difference between the learning programmes of the twentieth century and those of the twenty-first? It is easy to illustrate the extent of the information revolution, but in doing so we must be aware that every element referred to below influences the content of the learning curriculum and how learning is delivered.

Access to information data-bases

When I was a young married teacher with three children in primary school, a salesman appeared at our door one afternoon trying to persuade me to purchase a twenty-five volume set of the latest edition of the *Encyclopaedia Britannica*. Not only would it be very valuable for me as a teacher, he said, but it came with a research kit and methodology by means of which a child or teenager could study almost any topic under the sun by tracking through a cross-referencing trail through the entries in this huge compendium of knowledge. We would have on call in our own home, I was being told, a complete research library. No one with a computer linked to the Internet would consider buying a print version of the encyclopaedia now. It is available on a single CD-ROM, the equivalent of the twenty-five volumes can be carried by a child as easily as a pencil, the text is regularly updated, and the disk gives international access to it. The consequences of having just that one disk for a child's learning programme are profound.

The production of information is now exponential, and the skill of accessing the data-bases has become more important than the rote-learning of basic information. Indeed, very little has to be learnt by heart now. Learning information like that can be inert learning. Active learning now involves the essential skills of being able to sift material, to test it for reliability, to synthesize it into meaningful chunks, to link it with other learnings, to apply and to extend it in other contexts, not least to solve problems or to analyse issues. As a professor in a medical faculty remarked to me, all that a doctor needs to learn in five years at medical school could now be fitted on to one CD-ROM.

Video and film

There has been an enormous increase in the amount of material in the print medium, much of it presented as charts, diagrams and photographs, and through linear text. Now, however, the amount of material, both documentary and story, available through video, television and film presentation is astonishing. In some parts of the globe, a person can access more than a hundred TV channels, for example. It is possible to replay online, as often as one likes or needs to do so, significant demonstrations, lectures, talks and teaching episodes, and to access them from around the world. These are visual and contextual presentations, of course, which use a whole-of-frame, image-based, presentational format quite different from that of linear text. A new kind of reading and decoding derives from whole-of-screen presentations.

Virtual reality

These techniques and others using three-dimensional methodologies make possible experiences which transcend the time and place where the observer is located, in formats described as virtual reality. The potential for in-school programmes is enormous. Virtual reality presentations can take a learner back in time, or to another geographical setting, or into simulated experiences difficult to have in another format. It can parallel much of the learning which students have until now had to acquire by visits or by organized excursions.

The e-book

Print materials like books are costly and heavy to carry about – ask any academic who has collected documents from overseas, or any secondary school student who has to carry a haversack each day to transport her textbooks to, from and around school. Just as all of those textbooks can be placed on one small disk, so it is possible to buy on disk the text of a book such as a novel and to load it into a lap-top computer. Better still, the text can be paid for and then downloaded into an e-book from which it can be read anywhere; since the screen is backlit, the text can be read without the need for external lighting. So, for example, one can buy a novel in digital form from the book store at an airport, download it on-site into one's e-book, and board one's flight unencumbered by heavy print versions of inflight reading material. In effect, these are 'go anywhere' books. It is certain that schools will make extensive use of e-books.

Transportable computers

The production of notebook computers and lap-tops has made possible the creation of a work-station anywhere, including a school-learning station. The one portable machine has wide possibilities. PINS, one's personal telephone (voice-mail) number, e-mail addresses, mobile phone and fax machine can be included on one machine. It is due to have a single, personalized universal number; it will need no power outlet, for its energy is transmitted by light (usually sunlight). It can combine (or be compatible with) the amenities of a smartcard (for accessing a line of credit with a bank, for tracking investment accounts, for transactions in lieu of cheques or credit cards) and to hold in its memory one's driver's licence and passport, all secure through a secret pass-word. With this facility, a student can be on call, at call or on line from anywhere. She does not need to be anchored to one geographical setting, to one set of school premises, in order to pursue her official learning programme.

Computers, then, are as commonplace in the new patterns of schooling as paper, pen and pencils were in the conventional schooling of the twentieth century. Since they are enhanced by use in 'smart buildings', schools are likely to favour using rented plant which the owner agrees to adapt to the changing needs of the school as technology develops new capacities. It may be a liability for a school to be burdened with ownership and upkeep of obsolescent school buildings which do not easily suit the new formats for learning.

The wired or cabled city

Linking the world to home, office and school by networked systems enormously expands the power and versatility of learning programmes. IT links the home to an array of services delivered down-line where once they required physical delivery or a shopping excursion. The same facilities put academic and personal advice on tap twenty-four hours of the day, connect parent and school, allow e-mail and web-page communication, and provide a powerful network from which serendipitous extensions to schooling can develop.

Both print and digital skills

None of the new information and learning technologies wipe out the need for a student to master the skills of print – in other words, reading and writing conventional printed text. It simply means that 'literacy' becomes a more expansive term, covering both print and digital skills. Every student must now acquire a greater range of skills, rather than one set substituting the need for the other.

A new kind of schooling

The implications of these inventions are enormous and wide-ranging. New learning technology releases a student from the need for physical, full-time attendance at a place called school. It releases her from sole reliance on textbooks and printed materials. It requires of her literacy in digital as well as print materials. It affords routine access to an awesome array of people, places and databases, and it changes the role of the teacher-as-purveyor-of-knowledge. It makes possible a range of learning media and styles, and puts on stream vicarious experiences like virtual reality. It enhances learning through imagery as well as words. It puts new emphasis on skill development and knowledge production.

And it frees her from an education which is parochial and narrowly local. The Internet is what the word implies; it is an international network. Regardless of what the school and its teachers may want or plan, when students can join the international highway of knowledge transmission, their curriculum is automatically internationalized. The consequences may not be entirely desirable, but they are inevitable. Further, students are able to find information which their teachers do not know about, a situation which alters their role from that of expert and authority to that of mentor, adviser, fellow learner and wise friend.

What schools must do to accommodate to the knowledge society

It is already clear how schools are changing in order to be compatible with the new information-rich, wired and interconnected society which is replacing the society based on an economy dependent on manufacturing and factory production. The following is a synthesis of what planners from across the globe have been advocating as the obvious components which a school must acquire in order to be abreast of the Knowledge Revolution. They appear in documents like that of Education Victoria's *Learning Technologies in Victorian Schools 1998–2001*.

- Computers are found in all classrooms and are used routinely and daily for learning projects, group work, written composition and information access in all subject areas. Computers are a learning aid, not a subject. As Bill Gates (1999: 402) observes, 'Computer labs are a lousy place for computers.' The classroom uses computer graphics for oral and written presentations, and does some desk-top publishing of its own.
- Classrooms have been physically reconfigured to allow appropriate usage of the computers by teachers and students during lesson time. Part of the room space has been converted into learning alcoves and made suitable for group-based round-table sessions.

- The whole school and every classroom in it can connect to the Internet and the intranet, and can use e-mail.
- The school and its classrooms are connected to the whole community and especially its resources like libraries, museums and government offices and their homepages. The school accesses some elements of its learning programme from interstate or overseas.
- As well as books and other printed materials, the school's library has extensive digital materials, including CD-ROMs.
- The school can supply the child's entire textbooks for the year on CDs.
- The school is wired for large-scale instruction or demonstrations, and has 'great lecture' or 'key lessons' available online. As a result, the school can capitalize on its pedagogic range to enable some students to receive one-on-one instruction from a teacher, and to progress at their own rate.
- Consistent and comparable data on every student's academic progress is collected by every teacher in every key learning area and routinely stored in the school's information system or data-base. Every teacher can access that data-base at any time. The school regularly reports to its parents about the trend lines in this body of consolidated data.
- Because some examinations and tests are conducted on and marked by computer, there is a growing tendency for students to take their tests when they are ready to do so.
- There is a whole-of-school approach to management through computerization.
- The school has its finances, budgets and the student management system on a school-wide data-base.
- The school uses computerization for internal communication and information-giving; it is in part a 'paperless site'.
- There is a school-wide information technology plan, including a long-term programme for updating software, for systematically replacing obsolete machines, for training and retraining of staff and students, for inducting new staff and students into the school's technology resources, and for familiarizing parents with the school's technology capacity and how they can make productive use of it.
- Every teacher has a computer, preferably a lap-top, whose software is compatible with the school's.
- Every teacher has an e-mail address, provided through the school.
- Teachers network regularly with professional colleagues in-school and across schools.
- The school uses its website or homepage to keep parents informed with details about the school's learning programme, including what assignments, assessments, home study and projects have been set for their children.
- The school has its own site-based experts and peer support personnel available. In particular, it has a staff member (not necessarily a teacher) appointed to advise on information technology, including giving at-call technical advice on computers.

- Every teacher keeps up with developments in learning technologies through release-time to undertake professional development activity in IT.

These are the standard adaptations which schools need to have made in order to be abreast of the information revolution. The list is not exceptional, for many schools around the world are already operating like this.

Rebuilding the approach to curriculum

It would be surprising if a reformation about learning as fundamental as that produced by the information revolution did not also produce a deep-seated revision to the way educators and students think about the curriculum. The most likely manifestation is a reconceptualizing of the learning programme through the use of new and more appropriate metaphors. In undertaking such a task of redefinition, one needs to be aware how deeply entrenched are the old metaphors and the way they channel thinking about curriculum and learning programmes. What are the frameworks which are outmoded and which schools need to break out of?

For decades schooling (especially learning and the curriculum) has been depicted as climbing stairs ('grade' is from a Latin word for 'a step'). So the student is promoted (literally 'moved forward') through 'grade levels' until he or she 'graduates', even proceeding to 'higher' education, where the student will be granted a 'degree' (a word whose prime meaning, the Oxford Dictionary tells us, is 'one of a flight of steps, a rung of a ladder'). Or again, the student undertakes 'courses', a word (derived from the Latin verb 'to run') which implies that every learner is an athlete in a race around a single track (the same track for everyone), that some run faster than others, and that a few come first, are designated winners and are in some way rewarded with privilege or prizes. The very word 'curriculum' (which in Latin is a small running track) is part of this cluster of metaphors about steps, stages and winners.

The problem is that these analogies (they are effectively one extended metaphor) represent learning too simplistically. Even so and as a result of that thinking, the traditional curriculum or learning programme has been viewed in the following way. It is seen as:

- *linear* There is a set of graded exercises for each subject area, and the student proceeds from simple to more complex ideas in one logical progression. Indeed, the grades are not only typecast but it is usually assumed that there is a single best track upward through those stages.
- *age-related* It is as though certain skills belong with certain age groups. Such an assumption poses artificial problems for adult learning, and for deciding how studies are labelled. When a graduate student undertakes initial learning in a foreign language, why is it called tertiary study for her when it is almost identical with what a student undertakes in second language studies at an elementary school?

- *disconnected into discrete subjects*   Those official and acceptable subjects are now being called key learning areas, but they still line up with what are the official disciplines in tertiary education. From experience with the policies around the globe concerning a national curriculum, we know what happens when subject categories are varied, for there are many vested interests, not least in the universities, to patrol the boundaries of the academic disciplines. The curriculum (and especially senior secondary and higher education) has met great trouble when it is made interdisciplinary, or when it passes beyond content into skill development. The curriculum is deemed to become illegitimate when it does.

The above is an education programme modelled on the same tidy hierarchies and divisions which characterized bureaucracy, the mode of the industrial economy. Skills and knowledge were set in orders of status, importance and difficulty. A student worked her way up the pyramid of skill and a select few made it to the 'top of their professions'. The less able fell away, or occupied a lesser status of learning, qualification and work. It was a bureaucratic and hierarchical way to explain both learning and knowledge.

As was pointed out in a previous chapter, mass-produced education (education for everyone, universal primary and secondary education) came into existence concurrently with the mass production of manufacturing. It was carried out in buildings which somewhat resembled factories; the curriculum became divided into specialist subjects with sequenced processes, on the rationale of large-scale production lines; and teachers were assigned tasks and statuses like the operatives in factories. The same terms were applied to schooling, the same imagery, the same framework of analogies and metaphors.

These factory metaphors need to be discarded, for both the imagery and the expectations which go with it constrict the nature of schooling. The 'school reform movement' of the 1980s and 1990s is a symptom of a change in mindset, but it is now generally accepted that the piecemeal adaptation of schooling which characterized that reform movement has been ineffective; it does not work. It left the basic structures and assumptions unchallenged. But schools are not alone in this discovery; Hammer (in *Beyond Reengineering*, 1996: 3) has said that 'the revolution that has destroyed the traditional corporation began with efforts to improve it'. For schools and school systems, then, the changes will need to be deep, different, across-the-board and probably radical. Many of the entrenched assumptions underlying schooling for the past ninety years will have to be superseded. Perelman (1996: 20) therefore concludes: 'The nations that stop trying to "reform" their education and training institutions and choose instead to totally replace them with a brand-new, high-tech learning system will be the economic powerhouses through the twenty-first century.' Those which cannot adapt or remodel themselves will simply be overrun, or fall behind, or perhaps even be destroyed.

In recent years, the curriculum has been subject to re-imaging processes, often by forces outside education. Because many of the new ideas about learning have been built on market or business analogies, the extent to which schooling is depicted as utilitarian, as serving economic purposes, should not surprise us. Educational discourse has moved away from concerns about students and towards concerns about curriculum content. For example, we do not hear a great deal about individual differences (except when it concerns education of the able and the gifted, who are viewed as national resources worth investing in), or about the processes of learning, or about individual fulfilment and self-actualization. Parents and teachers may talk this way, but not policy-makers. In fact, the 'progressive education' based on Deweyan principles was maligned in the early 1980s, labelled as passé, and regarded as something aberrant and wrong. On the other hand, a great deal was said about standards, about general levels of achievement, about certificates and credentials, and about core curricula. What is to be learnt has occupied more attention than the nature of the learner. Education was being depicted as concerned with tradable skills and workplace components, no longer couched in terms of individual fulfilment but rather in terms of standard learning, conformities, being useful. In a sense, the curriculum was commodified by use of a market analogy. There must be a more embracing and ennobling set of metaphors than this available.

Transferring to a new world-view therefore imposes two imperatives. The first is to get rid of the vocabulary which is obsolete and unhelpful. In short, stop using that language! The second is to find a set of descriptors – perhaps a new extended metaphor – which is compatible with the new world-view and which explains schooling's processes more adequately.

If the curriculum has been set in the metaphor derived from the industrial organization, why cannot it be transcribed into the imagery used to describe the post-industrial organization? Knowledge production and information manipulation are enormously expanded by the Internet; and that medium is radically international and widely used. Small, knowledge-based, niche-driven enterprises are replacing the large and ponderous ones. Radically different in shape and style of operation, they are small, resilient, well-connected, non-hierarchical and strategy-driven, and the people in them run their careers on fundamentally different lines. Leveraging knowledge is the essential aspect which gives them competitive edge, achieves results and assures them of employment, not loyalty to their company, to which they will owe about as much allegiance as we give to our local delicatessen (*Management Today*, 1999: 10–11).

Put another way, the network metaphor is becoming a more appropriate descriptor for the curriculum. People now think of a 'curriculum' not as a single running track but as 'pathways', of several alternative routes through a plurality of learning programmes. The curriculum has become 'modularized' (like modern car parts) for multiple usage, and can be assembled into optional packages. There are now 'generic' (general) and 'specific' (occupation-determined) skills and knowledge, a kind of branching tree of competencies rather than a single concrete path. It is now less usual to advance a cohort of students in lockstep through years of instruction of fixed duration. There is a tendency to talk of 'learning groups' rather than 'classes'. There is a lot of discussion about 'credit transfers', about joint degrees and certificates, about educational consortia which provide components for credentials across institutions, and which reconcile the multiple offerings from a variety of providers in a clear working out of the educational ramifications of networking.

These are beginnings, but the development of the cluster or network organization is sure to impact more deeply on education. Many of the world's companies survive by breaking themselves up into smaller component parts. An organization is often more efficient and attracts lower costs not by doing the job itself, but by leasing out a production or function to another firm which already has the expertise to do it; and also by buying in competencies from elsewhere. When firms interlock their specialist skills in this way, they are called strategic alliances. They co-operate, buy selectively from the market-place, and travel light. Can the curriculum be thought of in the same way?

The final justification for any practice, any reform, any new explanatory system of any kind anywhere in the school is whether it contributes to the prime function of the school, namely that of assisting student learning. Does it *sponsor appropriate learning at an appropriate pace for every student formally enrolled?* It is helpful to use this principle as the final test of anything done in the curriculum. For our purposes here, we will first study the ramifications of using the organizational rationale of networking to illuminate the curriculum provided in a twenty-first-century school. Then we will endeavour to put the pieces together to show what that curriculum would look like in more practical terms.

The metaphors of networks and student-as-knowledge-worker

The patterns of the Information Society (and of the curriculum compatible with it) and the new logic on which that society is being built are propelled by the information technology revolution, by the way national borders (and economies) are being made permeable, and by the rise of professionally educated knowledge workers and how they do business. This has produced a new rationale for the activities of government, and new approaches, some of them radical, to the provision of public services like education, health and welfare.

The global economy has produced an international market-place in which large and small companies operate in ways which surmount national borders (Reich, 1992; Ohmae, 1990, 1995a), buying, selling, leasing and franchising component parts and services across the globe, virtually disregarding national boundaries and national governments. The very idea of a national economy, then, is becoming meaningless, asserts Reich (1992: 8). So too, perhaps, is the idea of a 'national curriculum'. No one country any longer owns the inter-linked businesses which are involved with car manufacturing or footwear and textile production, the computer industry or food processing. The same border-lessness is now appearing in education.

> What is traded between nations is less often finished products than specialized problem-solving (research, product design, fabrication), problem-identifying (marketing, advertising, customer consulting), and brokerage (financing, searching, contracting) services, as well as certain routine components and services, all of which are combined to create value.
>
> (Reich, 1992: 113)

In these circumstance it is better for a firm not to carry expensive overheads. So Reich (1992: 90) comments:

> Office space, factories, warehouses can be rented; standard equipment can be leased; standard components can be bought wholesale from cheap providers (many of them overseas); secretaries, routine data processors, bookkeepers, and routine production workers can be hired temporarily. In fact relatively few people actually work for the high-value enterprise in the traditional sense of having steady jobs with fixed salaries.

If we draw a parallel with the newly conceptualized curriculum, then, there will be an emphasis on seeking out and then buying, hiring or leasing the best modules of learning for each student. Rather than trying to manufacture the learning modules on campus, the school (acting as a learning broker) will search for and then supervise the use of the best exponents wherever they are available. The curriculum will dwell on skills rather than on content, and emphasize the progressive deepening of skill in identifying and analysing a problem or issue, in devising ways to solve or handle the problem, and then in the application of the findings both to this problem and in other areas of knowledge and skill.

The problems and issues considered in the curriculum will also be increasingly borderless and transnational, for this is an information-rich society and accessing the sources both of the storage and generation of knowledge is not only possible but relatively easy and routine. Thus what is to be 'learnt by heart' in the curriculum will shrink to a core of knowings essential to negotiating one's way around the global community of knowledge. Learning how and where to access knowledge and how to handle it may be a more productive use of a learner's time than rote-learning a great number of facts.

If we use the past as an indicator of what will happen in schooling, then the negotiation of a programme of learning will resemble the way a person operates in the internationalized, professionalized, information-rich organizations which emerged in the 1990s (Handy, 1989: ch. 2), with a high emphasis on cerebral rather than manual skills, on learning how as much as on learning what, on understanding underlying principles, on working jointly with others in a team, on joint problem-solving as much as on individual learning.

And this raises an important issue for educators. Conventional schooling has been built around the individual (and comparatively isolated) learner. Each student is given learning assignments, she is assessed and given individual marks, her individual progress is monitored, and she is promoted or graduated on her own performances. Borrowing the work of another has been considered cheating. Indeed, a fellow student is in many respects a competitor whom the student must out-perform. So how does the educator award 'marks' for joint achievement, for joint performance, for a team effort? Learning team skills and how both to rely upon and to use the contributions of others are now essential skills to be acquired through schooling.

The new generation of students also understand almost intuitively that learning is neither linear nor even. It comes in intensive chunks. There is often a long lead-up in which material is gleaned and assembled, there can be periods of white heat while the gathered material is internalized, massaged, combined and brought to a focus, and there can often be a plateau for systematic and painstaking application to details. It is like the intensive working life of knowledge workers, as Handy (1989: 36) describes it:

> The next generation of full-time core workers ... be they professionals, managers, technicians or skilled workers, can expect to start their full-time careers later – and to leave them earlier .... The core worker will have a harder but shorter job, with more people leaving full-time employment in their late forties or early fifties, partly because they no longer want the pressure that such jobs will increasingly entail, but mainly because there will be younger, more qualified and more energetic people available for these core jobs.

When these people step out of their intensive period of employment, they will be ready for a series of intellectually demanding assignments, but they will do them in their own time and on their own terms, said Handy (1989: 39). Are schools geared up to handle the chunkiness, the peaks and troughs, of a student's learning path?

For students who are virtual 'knowledge workers', 'class-work' and 'school assignments' will less and less resemble conventional jobs – a regular set of work, regular time in class or as a class, regular hours of the day committed to a subject, and a fixed place in which the work is done. The biggest propellant out of that mindset is the computer and information networking, which will make the segments of the learning programme differently organized, managed, accessed and assessed, and then used. Students are likely to put the same number of working hours into their schooling, but it will be done in intensive chunks of time interspersed with lean time as the work-flows dictate (Handy, 1989: ch. 4). They will see themselves as acquiring expert skills in a networked curriculum applied through effective learning teams and alliances. Their learnings may not be acquired through one particular school. Rather, they will see their home school as the facilitating base which enables them to access the learnings appropriate to them at their stage of development. The best home schools will be the networked and connected ones.

Students who pattern their work-programme on that of knowledge workers will think of themselves as pursuing a set of assignments and projects individually tailored to fit their own learning interests and needs and pitched at an appropriate level of sophistication. These students will understand that, to be successful, they must remain learners for the whole of their lives, always reading, always questioning, always intermeshing work and learning. For such students, schooling means acquiring deeper and deeper knowledge, skill, and experience.

The student, operating like a knowledge worker, will understand that she (and not the school, or the teacher) is responsible for her own learning career, and for her own progress. She knows that she is judged on outcomes; and graduation or promotion is dependent on whether she is able to give detailed evidence about her levels of performance, and about whether those levels conform with the best standards being achieved elsewhere in the country and the world. At least in the later stages of her schooling, many of her educational programmes and services could be generated overseas or come from offshore locations.

We have known about the pressure to remodel the curriculum along these lines. Many things about the way schools teach and what they teach are due for remodelling (Gardner, 1999), and they include the following:

- It is only partly correct to associate certain learnings with certain ages. We need to determine which learnings they are, and then for the rest of the time free the curriculum of unnecessary or artificial straitjacketing. When the learning programme for children and adolescents is fed by technology, it involves a lot of spontaneous search and is partly serendipitous, yet at the end it must still be systematic, coherent, and cover key areas which all young learners should be introduced to or become proficient in.
- The linear curriculum with its apparent one-best-way approach and which sequences 'knowledge' into step-by-step gradations will be overtaken by a curriculum which is *nodular* (that is, consisting of chunks of learning, the various components of which will have to unpacked, probably with the help of a teacher or tutor) and *modular* (that is, packages of intense learning which are like building blocks and which the student pastes together to form a coherent education).
- Some parcelling of human knowledge into predetermined 'subjects' or 'disciplines' will occur if only to conserve the time and energy of the learners, but overlaps and interconnections will become regular through learning technology, and the subjects themselves will become hybridized. Students are capable of travelling by several paths through material, often handling complex matter before the simple emerges.
- The educator staff will perforce work together in teams, and call in persons (like computer engineers) with different skills from the ones they as teachers possess. So the educational staff will become more mixed, containing many adults whose skills and expertise complement those of the 'teacher'.

- Because of extensive computerization, international access, the need for time flexibility and for after-hours access to equipment like computers, the school day will have to be reworked. Any good educational facility, especially one housing sophisticated equipment and amenities, ought to be available on a round-the-clock basis, certainly after normal working hours and into the evening, and again early in the morning. It should not be closed up for extended holiday periods either, except for maintenance purposes. More staff are needed for an extended day, and most of them would work in shifts.
- The assumption that learning takes place in a geographically bound space called school and classroom, and that the student must graze for most of his or her 'learning time' within that fenced paddock is disappearing. Learning can take place anywhere, and frequently off-campus or in a place not normally defined as a school, especially with computer access and with portable computers (lap-tops and notebooks). Education will function through an interconnected web of learning sites and resource people.

The heart of the curriculum will shrink to a core of knowings essential to negotiating one's way around the global community of knowledge; it has been called 'scaffolding knowledge' (Vygotsky, 1978; Berk and Winsler, 1995; Hill and Russell, 1999). There will be high emphasis in the curriculum on learning *how* as much as on learning *what*, on learning how and where to access knowledge and how to handle it.

The assessments, certificates and credentials which result from the process of schooling are awarded on the strength of what one can do, not on age. 'Tests' are demonstrations by the student that he or she has learnt something.

These developments do not seem startling to those schools which have already confronted the future and planned their routes ahead. To them these patterns are not futuristic; they are already being adopted. Nor are the developments iconoclastic, for teachers are practical idealists; they do not throw away what is valuable to make room for the untried and speculative. Teachers and educators around the world have their own maps of the learning terrain, in the form of syllabuses, core curricula or essential knowings, curriculum frameworks, the skills and knowledge expected of the normal child at specified stages of his or her growth. They carry with them a grid or matrix with subjects to be covered (or 'key learning areas', or what might be called scaffolding knowledge and skill) on one axis and expected level of year-by-year attainments (skills and knowledge) on the other axis. As part of their professional craft, teachers can place every student in their care within that matrix, and identify what they have learned and where gaps exist.

What will become standard, then, is this. Educators as a group will find themselves responsible for mentoring a group of learners, directing them sequentially into projects or modules of activities, and keeping track of progress and outcomes. It is obvious that a project about volcanoes, for example, can simultaneously result in deepening reading skills, learning some physics or mathematics, and acquiring some knowledge about geography and geology. It is probably silly, if not impossible, to label such a project language or science, maths or geography.

It will fall to the educator-mentors, together with the student or students involved, to assess at the end what skills have been acquired and what contributions have been made to the scaffolding on which the whole learning regimen rests. It requires professional skill to make summative assessments like this, but it is after all part of the learning technologies landscape which a professional educator knows about.

It will produce some brilliant learning in the hands of emancipated tutors, as was the case when in the 1870s Oxford's Professor of Art, John Ruskin, took his students physically out of doors to repair roads. It may have started as an exercise in the practical application of art, but imagine the provocative questions evoked: What causes a pothole anyway? Can we predict where the next one will occur and what shape it will have? Why is this road potholed whereas the next one over is not? Why has this road been allowed to deteriorate whereas another was preferentially repaired? Can the repairs be made in ways which are at one and the same time effectively useful, environmentally friendly and aesthetically pleasing? Who pays for the aesthetics, and do they cost more (or less) than a merely functional repair? This kind of learning has been called a 'thinking curriculum' (Hill and Russell, 1999).

Learning in and about community

There are two important considerations which must be visited before we can end a discussion of the curriculum for twenty-first-century schools. The first was one which featured in the second chapter of this book, namely enculturation – the induction of the novitiate into the community, the development of a set of enabling personal beliefs, and the rites of passage into the culture which one is joining. These are not so much separable subjects to be included in the curriculum, but rather are factors which interpenetrate the whole of learning, aspects which must not be forgotten no matter what subject or issue is the topic of the day's learning programme. We need therefore to construct a kind of mental edifice which will allow us to check not only that enculturation is being kept to the forefront of the learner's and mentor's thinking, but that it is also being treated in a balanced and focused way.

There are at least four specific curriculum implications which flow from the premise of education for community membership. The first is that *schooling requires learning about the community* in which one lives. Every citizen, to be fully functioning, must have a working knowledge about how his and her own society works – the country's geography; its political system and the responsibilities of citizenship; its social patterns and values; its history; and so on. It need not be training in accepting those patterns, and certainly not in subservience, for questioning, analysing and critiquing those characteristics are healthy activities in that to do so requires understanding the community creatively and at some depth. All citizens must include somewhere in their education a common set of learnings about community.

Second, *schooling conducts the learner through the rites of passage into community membership.* Every society on earth, be it tribe or metropolis, requires the formal, ceremonial induction into the ages and stages of growing up in it. That role has now in large measure been entrusted to schooling. This aspect of learning will cover: the introduction into formal education; what the society values as knowledge; the passage through childhood, puberty, adolescence and into adulthood, with some understanding of the physical, sexual, mental, and social implications of each stage; the introduction to the world of work or of productive employment (with or without payment); the meaning of family, marriage, parenthood; and so on.

Third, *schooling provides the survival skills for planetary citizenship*, including what is involved in being a citizen of the world and a steward of the planet's ecosystem. Every learner needs to know something about the planet, its political and geographical boundaries, about life forms, science, and so on. Language skills and number skills also come under this heading of survival skills.

And fourth, *schooling involves an apprenticeship in being a fully functioning individual in society.* It involves more than 'content' knowledge, but what are considered the acceptable frameworks for knowing, and for inheriting the wisdom of the elders. Unless society ensures that each of its members is educated in this respect, it will incur considerable costs, literally and metaphorically, in terms of law and order, crime prevention, welfare, health, and even defence and international relations. In this dimension each person's education is person-specific and idiosyncratic as well as general. It contains some learnings quite particular to each individual, but it also includes factors one needs to know about being human and about living harmoniously with others.

From this perspective of enculturation, then, the learning programme for every citizen is therefore likely to include the following:

- Some *common learnings*, materials or areas which must be included in everyone's schooling programme, regardless of innate skill, latent abilities or family background. These elements may be described as a core curriculum, as key learning areas, as basic skills, or as compulsory subjects. There is no stereotyped way of describing what the common learnings are, how the programmes in them should be put together, how they should be structured or sequenced, or at what stages of growth a young person is ready to learn some things.
- Some *cultural and ceremonial learnings at periods of personal transition*. These are concentrations of learning at or near key points of development in one's life. We are used to these periods being included in a religious, cultural or tribal upbringing. In traditional societies some of the most socially and individually important ceremonies occur at birth, at weaning, at puberty, at marriage and at death.
- Some studies or learnings or experiences which are *specifically for the individual's own development*.
- Some *sequenced and programmed learning*, which may include parts of the above categories. For example, subjects and disciplines are simply formalized knowledge arranged in systematic order, and usually taught in a

sequence. The sequencing is often logical rather than psychological, taught for intellectual coherence rather than because the student is at an age when he or she is ready for such learning. The sequence itself is a human invention, and there may be many ways in which the subject matter can be traversed with coherence. This learning programme consists not simply of information (facts or a syllabus), but also includes skills and some basic and developed competencies which interpenetrate, and are enhanced by, other learnings.

- If schooling is the prime means to induct the learner into society as a fully functioning citizen, it seems important not only to educate *for* community but also – as far as is possible – to educate the learner *in* community. So the atmosphere and sense of belonging within the school itself are important, and so is its connectedness to the community at large, where the school should try to locate some of its programmes.

The curricular and instructional implications of the above should now make it obvious that it is no longer possible to depict the learning programme as linear, unidimensional, divided up simply into subjects, or as information passed from teacher to taught. Those simplicities are a thing of the past. From the enculturation perspective alone, we could depict the curriculum's elements on a three-dimensional grid along the lines of the following.

- One dimension concerns *self and community development*. On this axis are placed aspects like developing one's own identity and abilities; valuing oneself (self-esteem); developing a value system and set of beliefs; understanding society and how it operates, the world community and the planet's ecology; and negotiating the rites of passage.
- A second dimension concerns the skills one needs to be a fully functioning citizen. Thus a substantial part of one's learning is gained from tackling real problems thrown up within the community, analysing what the problem is, determining what information and skills one must acquire to confront the problem, getting access to that knowledge and skill, and drawing up or planning a project for taking some effective action about the problem. These are not problems invented for the purpose of schooling (as many school projects in the past have been). Engaging what is happening within one's own community and taking constructive responsibility for it is an endemic aspect of becoming educated.
- A third dimension is what in the past has been called *disciplinary studies* or the knowledge curriculum. Over millennia, some human knowledge has been consistently systematized and it is unwise (it may also be inefficient) not to avail ourselves of its categorizations. It seems almost inevitable that at some time during her education the learner will undertake some disciplined learning in some of the traditional fields of knowledge. Some of these areas are regarded as core studies and probably will always be – like number, literacy and science. There are other areas common by reason of our being human, like art, drama, sport and music.

The important thing about these dimensions to the curriculum is that they are not self-contained or exclusive domains. They can be separable characteristics, but they are usually of equal concern, they are interactive and combinable, and the same materials can be used to further an understanding of any of the three dimensions. In short, they are effectively the axes of a three-dimensional grid, shown below as Figure 11.1; and almost any learnings one can think of – it can be a single project, a week's work, a formal subject, a set of assignments – can be

Figure 11.1 A three-dimensional grid to consider how a learning task contributes to cognitive (X axis), cultural (Y axis) and personal (Z axis) development

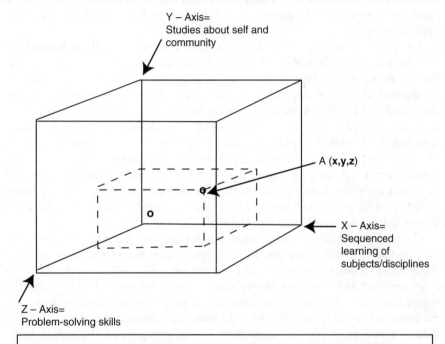

- Some studies are single-dimensioned, sitting on lines o–x, o–y, or o–z.

- Some studies appear to be two-dimensional in intent

    On x–y plane, the subject/disciplines are used to explain issues about one's self, the community, relationships, and politics.

    On x–z plane, the subject/disciplines are applied to problems (such as in laboratory work).

    On y–z plane, people-oriented studies confront issues and use problem-solving skills.

- In a three-dimensional sense, in the Project A (x, y, z)

    x = the degree to which the project develops 'knowledge'.

    y = the degree to which the project develops the ability to confront and solve problems.

    z = the degree to which the project develops self-understanding.

positioned spatially in this framework. Very, very few will occupy a position on a plane (that is, affecting only two dimensions), and almost none could appear on a single line or axis (that is, it is single-dimensioned or linear learning).

Looked at from the perspective of a three-dimensional grid like this one, any learning task can be positioned somewhere within the grid and with three co-ordinates. Any learning task can be assessed on the degree to which it contributes to each of the three dimensions – and probably should. Further, an individual's education is stunted to the degree to which any of the three dimensions are underplayed, overlooked or not capitalized upon, or if there is a skewing which shows that any one of the dimensions is consistently under-valued. A curriculum which is linear, or which can be placed in a single plane (there are three possible planes available here), will be an inadequate and impoverished one.

The grid is of course simplistic, but at least it forces us to think beyond the obsolescent, linear curriculum of the traditional school. Let us use an example. Rather than approaching a learning programme always from a subject's perspective, it is often preferable to pick a real problem or issue within the community or the world society, and then to release the learner or learners on to it, encouraging them to assemble all the knowledge, information, under-standings and support needed to address the issue. Such an approach throws the learners back on systematically compiled information (that is, on the subject areas), but they will engage it as problem-solvers and appliers. They will no doubt later also have to address the disciplinary complexities in the mate-rials they have assembled and tried to use, a context which will make them keener, better-motivated and more fulfilled learners!

If the three curricular dimensions which make up the grid are constantly balanced against each other, any learning programme will progressively develop the ability to identify problems, and to search for viable solutions; the ability to build a project and to carry it through; the capacity for model building, and the exploration of possibilities; the capacity to make choices, and to make the material and social trade-offs which go with such choices; the ability to nego-tiate, in a variety of situations and from several perspectives; the skill to make knowledge active, not inert (to use Whitehead's distinction); the orientation consistently to ask why one thing is to be believed above another. In short, an adequate curriculum endemically leads to the development of the skills (from physical and social through to the intellectual and transpersonal) and the acquisition of competencies (including occupational ones) which are now part and parcel of living and working in a modern and international community. Furthermore, an adequate curriculum must not marginalize these things, as a content-based or subjects-driven curriculum frequently has done in the past.

In fact, an effective curricular approach assumes a person-by-person moni-toring of their learnings, an expectation not only reasonable but now almost mandatory. After all, the technology exists to enable such monitoring to be carried out, both by teachers and by the learners themselves. An effective curriculum puts the documentation of learning increments at the heart of the

process, and probably dispenses (for ever, one hopes) with a school being organized around classes formed on the basis of age.

The teaching staff need to be professionally skilled to work in this kind of
curriculum setting. First and foremost, they must be able to 'model community'. Their style of operating, individually and collectively, must be collegial
and not hierarchical, collaborative rather than in isolation. The teachers are not
controllers so much as connectors and interactors. In a cultural sense, they act
like tribal elders who are able to harness the wisdom within the community.
What disappears – comprehensively – is the school as a place of domination, of
conformity, of intellectual straitjacketing.

Second, the teaching staff must work as a team, since – in spite of their
specializations and qualifications – it must be possible for them to work across
disciplines and across age-groups. Training in team skills will become indis-
pensable for these teachers. As well, each of them needs to be credible – which
probably means respected – within the community, persons who are so well
educated themselves that they are capable of breaking knowledge boundaries,
and so self-assured that they are not threatened by the unusual. This is a
curriculum context where teachers have obligations and mutual responsibility
to each other, and in which teachers are forced to interact and interconnect.
Classroom isolated they can never be, ever again.

Third, every teacher and staff member must aim to make students active
and responsible agents in their own learning, and must be able to monitor
progress, to evaluate their own teaching inputs, and to assess accurately their
students' learning. They will be the kind of people who can vigorously engage
students in purposeful interaction with each other, with various data sources,
and with other adults. So the pedagogical skills of teachers will inevitably
become more, not less, sophisticated in these circumstances.

One further effect has to be noted. Internationalized materials and individualized learning programmes inevitably push both learners and their mentors
into using cross-national, cross-cultural data where they confront value
conflicts, religious dissonances, prejudices and social choices. The variety and
range of such materials makes it impossible to pre-programme minutely and
to control a student's learning pathway. Teachers cannot expect to be on top
of all the materials either, and they will have to become active learners themselves.

The characteristics of effective schooling

The second important consideration to address before we leave this discussion of
the curriculum is this. Over the past two decades, a great amount of international research has been done into school effectiveness, into what makes for
effective learning. Learning can of course be individual, by an isolated learner
devising his or her own programme. The more usual format has been that a
school-as-provider is involved; there is an educational institution or agency,
usually a school, which sets up the means for systematic study, which services

many client-learners, and whose internal dynamics and structures impact on what, how and how well the learners learn. As the curriculum becomes more complicated in the twenty-first-century school, it would be prudent to preserve in the school as provider and in the school as learning broker those character istics which we know contribute to effective schooling.

There is a rich literature to call upon, but there are several syntheses of it which can help us. Reynolds and Cuttance (1992) and then Reynolds *et al.* (1994), for example, have assembled the outcomes of international work in this field. Later, Scheerens and Bosker (1997) have made an insightful coalescence drawing on the formative syntheses of Levine and Lezotte (1990), Sammons *et al.* (1995) and Cotton (1995); they then take the 'effectiveness-enhancing conditions' about which the experts agree and break them down into what those characteristics look like when converted into action within schools and class-rooms (Scheerens and Bosker, 1997: 112–59). Here, then, we need to ask what characteristics the school-as-provider-and-broker should safeguard in its operation in order to ensure that its learning programmes will be effective. To ensure that we read this list in the new and not the old paradigm about schooling, we must think not in terms of buildings or physical premises, not in terms of class-rooms and teachers, and not about the institutional school. Instead think first about the *school as an enterprise* whose prime function is to arrange for the learning of the students who have enrolled with it. These, then, are the conditions which enhance effective learning.

1   *Shared vision*   The learning enterprise has a productive climate and culture, and there is a shared vision about its goals.
2   *Focus on learning*   The enterprise is focused on learning as its prime mission. There is school-wide emphasis on the centrality of learning and on acquiring skills.
3   *Regular monitoring and assessment*   Each student's progress is monitored and assessed through an appropriate, school-wide, regular reporting regimen, to which every teacher consistently contributes. The students are given positive and clear feedback.
4   *Climate for learning*   There is an attractive, orderly working environment which stimulates one to learn and in which it is safe to learn, which encourages experimentation and open-ended search, which allows risks to be taken and where one learns from mistakes as well as from successes.
5   *Purposeful teaching*   When and where teaching is required, there are effective teaching arrangements, appropriate pacing and alignment, a range of pedagogical techniques used, a clarity of purpose, easy availability of materials, and structured lessons.
6   *High expectations*   It is expected that every student can learn well, and will learn; that students will take responsibility for their own progress, and that they will not be satisfied with make-do performance. There is school-wide emphasis on recognizing and celebrating positive performance.

7 *Professional leadership* The leader and leadership team(s) give highest priority to the professional purpose of the school, personally and frequently monitor the learning programmes, put time and energy into schooling improvement, give support to the staff involved with learning programmes, put tangible emphasis on instructional leadership, and understand their sense-making role.

8 *Home/school partnership* The enterprise puts value on the contributions which parents and home make to the progress of the learner; it involves parents in policy decisions relating to the learning programmes, and keeps parents informed. Parents are regarded as partners in the learning process.

9 *A learning organization* The enterprise assumes that all persons associated with it are active learners, and it has a formal, vigorous and planned approach to the ongoing professional development (PD) of its staff. PD is practice-oriented, is collegial and is based on the skills to which the enterprise needs access, not merely on the benefits which accrue to the individual teacher. Site-based or on-site PD is favoured. The enterprise is analytical about itself, about professional knowledge, and favours inquiry-driven approaches to its work.

10 *Student rights and responsibilities* The enterprise is specific about its expectations of its own students, they know their rights and responsibilities, and they feel both empowered by and involved in the enterprise's processes.

These are universal findings from the school effectiveness movement. They apply even when the school is re-imaged to be both a provider and a broker for learning of the students who are formally enrolled with it. In fact, the ten characteristics become even more salient once the school is disentangled from the constriction of its being considered as a set of buildings and grounds, or as an institution, as site-bound and organization-dominated.

Keeping track

It will also be apparent from the above that devising and co-ordinating learning programmes (and curricula) is a complex job which calls for the creation of expert roles within the education profession. Indeed, the specialist in this domain may warrant high remuneration and may serve more than one school or set of clients, just as specialists in other professions do. But a diversification of roles along these lines is what we should expect from a field like education which is emerging into full professionalization. To that issue we turn for our penultimate chapter.

12 Teachers for the school of the future

Principle No. 6 Deploy the educational staff both professionally and wisely; they are a costly resource.

Principle No. 7 When employing professional teachers, think in terms of bundles of educational functions suited to the skills of each one, not in terms of a standardized package for all.

How will the teachers of the future differ from the teachers we have now? Teaching and the teaching service have metamorphosed so radically over recent decades that the days of the all-purpose teacher might well be numbered. Consider how the in-built cost and complexity of providing professionally trained teachers has climbed in recent years. Some decades ago, it was possible to enter a teacher training course from Year 10 of secondary school, the shortest course was of six months' duration, some secondary teachers were two-year trained, and some had no teacher education at all. In the intervening years, admission to teacher education courses rose to university-entry level, and became selective. The pre-service courses were extended in length to at least four years of higher education, and those courses, once provided in a teachers' college run by the employing authority, were located in autonomous universities. Within the space of about three decades in most developed countries, teaching became a graduate profession. These new graduates sought and were paid salaries commensurate with their graduate status. Now regarded as professionals, they expect when they enter their school to have around them a range of paraprofessional and support staff to do the work which falls outside what is deemed professional.

Further, teachers require sophisticated equipment and materials now. Many of them are employed full-time in materials and curriculum construction, and in advising those working in classrooms. They work in buildings far more expensive to provide, equip and maintain than were the school premises even of a decade ago. And they expect to be involved with many fewer students than was the case with teachers even a decade or two ago. Class sizes have come down, pupil:teacher ratios have fallen, the quantum of face-to-face teaching has dropped, the number of lessons taught per teacher has gone down, and the requirement to undertake staff development exercises has become more widespread.

Thus the pre-service education of teachers is longer, is conducted in the most expensive sector of the system (universities), teachers are more highly qualified and as a result more highly paid, they are bringing into existence other salaried personnel, they need more expensive equipment and better buildings, and *they are each dealing with comparatively fewer students* than teachers did a quarter of a century ago. Hughes (1991: 55–6) has pointed out, using Australian statistics, that at the turn of the twentieth century, about one person in every 800 was a teacher and about 5 per cent of the population was at school. By the 1950s, the proportion of teachers to the total population had come down to 1:300; and by the 1980s about one in every 70 persons was now a teacher! More pertinently, one worker out of 34 teaches. It is a very large occupational group, approximately ten times the size of the lawyer group or of the group of general practitioners. What is more, society was trying to provide one teacher for about every 12 students in primary and secondary school.

There comes a point in this escalation, then, when teachers will price themselves out of the market if present conventions continue, and when serious consideration has to be given to remodelling how teachers are thought of and used. What seems inevitable when the new paradigm or world-view begins to operate worldwide is that the whole teaching service has to be reconceptualized, and practices inherited from the past – for this occupational group, that means the relatively near past – have to be discarded before they become thoroughly dysfunctional. The evidence is all around us that the process of redefinition has already begun in earnest. The roles and functions carried out by teachers are being regrouped, there is much wider separation within the profession, some new creations, like the advanced skills teacher or the master teacher, and some new paraprofessional roles have emerged. And some schools are operating with a suite of people configured in ways consistent with those of the network organizations elsewhere in society, especially as schools are given global budgets over which they have discretion, as they acquire the power to draw up their own duty statements for positions, and as local selection of staff becomes established.

Teachers have always tended to change their work practices as the result of four factors: (1) the changes in schooling patterns; (2) the nature of the organizations they work in, for schools have always copied the best organizational structures used in private enterprise; (3) the occupational behaviours of the professions they admire and aspire to be like; and (4) the career patterns and occupational styles of executives and knowledge workers elsewhere in society. Thus the changes being effected in other organizations will give us a lead about the operating framework within which teachers, given the option, will choose to work.

Further, in the post-industrial information society several occupational groups are moving out of the skilled trade or artisan mode and into the professional mode of operating. Teaching is one such occupation. Nursing is another. The pattern for deploying and using the skills of teachers will change as a consequence of their being acknowledged as a profession and as they begin to act in a professional mode. The employment patterns resulting from an industrialized economy which drew not only its wealth but also its social conventions from manufacturing industry are no longer appropriate for an international, inter-linked economy where wealth is dependent on knowledge workers and information technology. There are important consequences here for the careers of educators, for teachers are obviously knowledge workers. Looking at factors like these enables us to assemble a picture of what the teacher of the future will be like.

Disaggregating and re-assembling the teaching roles[1]

We must start at the beginning, however, and examine what the functions of teachers are now. There has been a tendency to regard teachers in a stereotypical way – a teacher is a teacher is a teacher. That view may have been valid when schooling was simple and linear, when teaching was externally programmed and prescribed, when there was a set, agreed syllabus from which the teacher could not deviate, when all students were set in class groups which simultaneously studied identical material, and when most learning was regarded as rote learning. Teaching is far more complex than that.

Wherever one looks in both practice and the professional/research literature, there is agreement that teachers have five common areas or dimensions in which they are expected to be competent. Further, the teacher must function well in *all five* in order to be regarded as satisfactory. Those dimensions are as follows:

1   *Curriculum*
    The teacher is expected to have 'content knowledge' about the courses she is teaching (sometimes referred to as 'subject specialization') and she is expected to keep herself up to date in it. She is expected to know how to devise programmes of learning, how a curriculum is divided up and taught, the learning theory which provides the framework for a curriculum, and what constitutes the school's or the system's official policy relating to the curriculum currently in use.

2   *Pedagogy*
    The teacher must know how to teach, must know about classroom manage-ment, about modes of student learning and the teaching methods which are appropriate to those modes, and about appropriate teaching technologies. The teacher is expected to have mastered a range of teaching strategies.

3   *Assessment*
    The teacher is expected to know how to evaluate student work, how to assess students' progress, how to report that progress constructively to students and to parents, how to keep cumulative records of progress in learning, and how to benchmark that progress. Every teacher is expected to have in place a programme of regular assessment for every student.

4   *Contribution to the life of the school*
    As a member of the staff of a learning institution, each teacher is expected to contribute constructively to the wider life of the school, both formally by accepting responsibility for certain school-wide functions, and also infor-mally by being concerned about the school's tone and culture, the well-being

of its students, its reputation and community standing, and especially its relations with parents and the wider community.

5 *Contributions to the profession*

Each teacher is expected to be actively engaged with the teaching profession by participating in professional development, by being active in professional societies, by contributing to the development of the profession's knowledge and its craft base, and by being available to and assisting the growth of professional colleagues. The teacher is expected to think and behave like a professional, including being jealous of the validity of teaching's theory base and being earnest about extending it.

Although teachers have been concerned to build up competence in all five dimensions, it is unlikely that any teacher feels equally competent across all those dimensions. Attempts have been made around the world to break down each of the dimensions listed above into the sets of skills or competencies which contribute to that area of a teacher's activity. The advantage in doing so is to make explicit what constitutes satisfactory performance of her duties, and to create a basis on which she can be judged and rewarded. Being specific about a teacher's functions in any school seems to warrant following a process akin to that of setting the school's own objectives. Here it can be represented in five steps:

- *Step One*   The five teaching dimensions are broken down into their *essential components*. These have been alluded to in the descriptions of the categories above.
- *Step Two*   The level of importance and the expected baseline of performance for each of those essential components (they could be called *performance standards*) are spelt out for the five dimensions of teaching.
- *Step Three*   These essential components are then converted into *operational terms* by asking the question, 'In what ways would the teacher need to be operating within her classroom and in this school in order to embody this performance standard?'
- *Step Four*   Then, consistent with the outcomes-based approach, both the school and the teacher determine what *systematically gathered evidence* needs to be accumulated to prove or demonstrate that the teacher is discharging, or has discharged, the function at the operationally expressed standard.
- *Step Five*   Both the teacher and the school then draw up a timetable for target-setting, for formal periodic reviews which includes agreement on the shape of the reporting event, and for a summative assessment of performance.

As a footnote to the above, it should be said that specifying functions, converting them into their component parts, and then determining performance standards, indicators or measures and a review protocol, needs to be as simple a process as possible and endemic to the normal functioning of the school. No school, Principal or teacher can afford the time to assemble exhaustive detail on all the operations implied in the five steps, and even less so if it distracts a teacher's attention from

the prime task of educating. So a selection has to be made, chiefly of what operations will be monitored and of what evidence, illustrative or longitudinal,
statistical or qualitative, the teacher will need to collect throughout the year. It is
best if the selections are deliberately made, are overtly agreed upon by both the
teacher and the school management, that the selections are decided on early in the
year, that the operations to be monitored are ordinary to the classroom rather
than exceptional practices, and that the evidence grows out of the normal life of
the school and would be collected anyway. Indeed, it is desirable that any scheme
for setting and assessing functions should piggy-back for its evidence on data
routinely collected by the school or the teacher. The scheme should be low-key,
simple and ordinary. The most effective forms of performance assessment do not
cause the enterprise any dislocation, are unremarkable, relate to but do not
intrude unnecessarily on the enterprise's core purpose, and do not place additional burdens on its key staff.

Assessing performance is normal practice these days; few organizations can
afford to do without it and survive. Especially in the case of stand-alone or
relatively autonomous institutions which have a fair degree of freedom in their
decision-making, assessment is necessary for accountability purposes, for efficiency, and for explaining and keeping track of how resources are used – and
teacher-time costs real money. Performance assessment, then, is now part of
the normal machinery of doing business, and without it the organization's
management lacks the power to be flexible, to identify strengths and to arrange
resources to get the best value from them. Without it, the enterprise must function by formulae, not by dynamic co-ordinated teamwork which recognizes
individual flair. In addition, any enterprise is at pains now to ensure that every
part of its venture is consistent with its vision, culture and style, dovetails into
its administrative structures, and enhances its essential functions.

There are some necessary concomitants to a review process, however.
Monitoring the activity of the enterprise and of those who contribute to its
health needs to be formal, just and open, for the principles of merit (rewarding
demonstrated good quality), equity (being fair to everyone) and objectivity
(eliminating bias) can take some odd and deceitful forms. Those involved with
personnel assessment learn quickly to be on the lookout for stereotyping,
unquestioned assumptions, undocumented impressions, premature conclusions,
halo effects, projection, subjectivities parading as objectivity, and cloning. It is
prudent for any enterprise to have its checks and balances, and for having
grievance processes in place even though they may be used only rarely.

Performance appraisal is a sophistication which has come with modern organization, the kind which has supplanted bureaucracy which operated predictably by
being based on Toffler's code of standardization. It is also a signal. It
semaphores the fact that functions can now be individually negotiated, and
that there may be better, even individualistic, ways of assembling the roles of
one's staff which build on the particular strengths each can contribute to
achieving the purposes of the enterprise.

As the process of schooling becomes more complicated; as curricula become differentiated; as student learning paths become branching and individualistic but nevertheless must still be monitored and made coherent; as the range of teaching methods and learning technologies expands; as schools shop around for good programmes, borrowing and buying components rather than developing them all on campus; and as teachers themselves become professionalized and therefore more widely specialized and across an expanding field of specializations, the stereotypical teacher will become a figure of the past. Those functions which we have discussed above will still be performed within the learning enterprise but not necessarily all of them will be carried out by all teachers. The functions will be disaggregated and rearranged into new bundles of compatible functions, from which new role-sets will emerge, parcelled out in different ways or put into packages for educators who each negotiate the functions he or she will perform for a contractual period (such as a year). The professionalization of teaching, the complexification of learning systems, and the complications of managing the intricate business of schooling are demolishing the simplicities of past practices and are leading to wholesale diversification, not least in the way educators operate.

A school which has therefore not faced the assignment of making specific what is expected of each teacher or staff member, what particular functions each individual teacher is to perform, and how good performance will be judged and measured is not really in a good posture to meet the conditions which schools will meet as the new world-view takes hold. Nor will teachers be happy to work with the obsolete formats where bureaucracy and standardization reigned.

It is already evident that teachers are eschewing the kind of organizational formats where one of bureaucracy's main characteristics, hierarchy, dominates. Instead of relating to their team members according to status, they have invented work units which are collegial and non-hierarchical. Instead of supervision (where a person of higher status oversees the work of another) and because one can be easily self-deceived about one's own competencies, there has been growing use of mentors and buddy systems in professionally based organizations. Sawatski (1991) describes a mentor as someone who is more experienced than the individual he or she is advising but is not in a line-management relationship to them (Sawatski deliberately using here a bureaucratic term). Most often the mentor is a professional colleague outside the individual's work area, but who is able to act as a reflective listener, ideas giver, positive role model, coach, opener of doors, and sponsor. A 'buddy' is typically someone of the same status as the individual concerned and who operates in the same unit or who is able to see the person fairly regularly in the workplace. A buddy, sometimes described as a critical friend, has a key role to play in observing, giving feedback and acting as a sounding board. A buddy can sometimes act for you, be your advocate or serve as a referee. It is part of the collegiality which goes with being a professional rather than the supervision (oversight by a superior) which goes with being an employee.

From trade to professionalism

Teachers make up one of world's largest skilled occupational groups with about sixty million members worldwide (depending on who qualifies to be counted among them). At least in the developed world, teaching is moving away from the patterns which characterized a trade and is taking up the patterns of a professionalized occupation. One of the remarkable achievements of the teaching service has been that, in a relatively small space of time, it has lifted itself from being merely a certificated to being a graduate service. A new appointee now usually requires a four-year undergraduate degree before being given the licence to practise. Compared with other professional groups, a large proportion of the teacher group holds two degrees, or a higher degree, or a postgraduate diploma, and a large number of teachers are actively and continuously involved in formal, ongoing, professional development programmes, many for academic credit. The working qualifications required in teachers are well beyond those expected of a trade. To put it bluntly, few other occupational groups – the professions included – are as well credentialled as teachers now are.

The comparative decline in *trade* union membership has almost nothing to do with whether trade unions have been or are successful organizations. Rather it is because technology, new production methods, the emergence of a more highly educated workforce and the internationalization of the economy have combined to diminish the proportion of the workforce employed in factory-related work, to decrease the number of artisans and technicians needed in the economy, to force changes to apprenticeship systems around the world, and to escalate dramatically the educational requirements for securing a job of any kind. The 'tradesman's ticket' (the term is appropriately gender-laden) is being displaced now by university degrees and diplomas from technological institutes as the prerequisites for guaranteed, long-term, satisfying employment. In short, the proportion of blue-collar workers in the workforce is in decline. It is probably no longer prudent for teachers to be identified with the kinds of work practices which have pertained in that sector of the workforce.

What is the difference about being a profession?

In the scholarly literature, there is a clear distinction between a trade and a profession (although both terms are becoming dated). There is in fact a logic about professionalism (Beare, 1992, 1997; Marles, 1992). The condition is reached by evolution, and is focused on the knowledge and skill basis which it is necessary for persons to possess before they are given the responsibility to practise. It is a status conferred by the public rather than by the occupational group on itself; it is a status which comes from being earned and deserved. Drawing a mind-map about professionalism lays bare that logic (Buzan, 1993).

But first, it needs to be acknowledged that professionalism only ever arises in an occupation which has some pivotal importance for the public and for particular clients. Because of that importance, it is in the interests of the public good that the community be protected from charlatanism, quackery or inade-quate practice in this area. So the key occupational questions to ask are these:

- What *prior knowledge or learning* do we expect the practitioner to have in this area before it is safe to let that person practise; and
- What *skills and level of competency* in those skills must this person have before it is safe to let her practise?

For some occupations, the prerequisite knowledge and skills can be system-atized, defined or codificd, and a licensing or accrediting board can issue certificates of competence as the right of entry to the occupation. Having such a 'ticket' to practise awarded by an official licensing authority has been a stan-dard feature in the trades for decades; and it ensures both safety for the person receiving the service and quality of delivery on the part of its provider. It was assumed also that the prior training to secure the certificate was all you needed in order to hold your place in the guild. It was a linear concept – train first, join the guild, practise thereafter; no further formal learning was required.

With the emerging professions, their operational core (sometimes called the craft knowledge of the occupation) has expanded to the point where the knowl-edge is so complicated and the skills so complex that it needs *long, pre-service preparation* to acquire them. Further, it is assumed that the practitioner must have acquired *sophisticated theoretical understandings* in that preparation programme. Not only does that theory base give the new practitioner an under-standing of why the profession's practices are the way they are and how they might be safely modified, but it is the foundation from which the professional is able to keep abreast of the field's expanding knowledge, technologies and skills.

The preparation programmes for professions, then, are usually located in the *higher education* sector, and a *degree or diploma* becomes the base-line qualifi-cation for admission to practice. For the newly emerging professions (like teaching and nursing), the pre-service training tends to grow longer, and then is moved from colleges and institutes and into universities.

When the theory base for the profession has become so specialized and sophisticated, it is only members of that profession – those who have a similar training – who are in a position to judge whether the neophyte is fit and equipped to join the profession. So a *profession-based registration* mechanism is forced into existence, and the occupational group has little choice but to become *self-regulating*.

When an occupational group becomes a *graduate profession*, its *salary costs* or its *fees for service* rise commensurate with the esoteric nature of the practi-tioner's skills. This development means that we must pay more highly for each of the professional services, but that we can have relatively fewer of those professionals who are capable of dispensing the service. It is a point many teachers do not readily comprehend. It is also a factor, cost-related, causing upheavals in the public provision of medical and legal services. See Figure 12.1.

By their very nature the profession's knowledge and skills will continue to

Figure 12.1 The professional mind-map Part 1

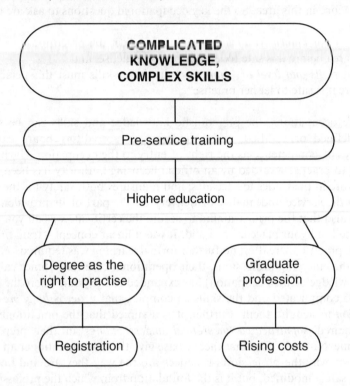

escalate, constantly expanded by *research* and by experience gained through *clinical practice and enquiry*. Wherever a real profession operates, its work is characterized by *theory-based service* which is *inquiry-driven*. Put simply, what a professional practitioner needs to know and be able to do will be constantly developing throughout his or her professional career. As a result, *formal professional development* activity is an essential part of the life of the professional, going on for as long as the person belongs to the profession. No professional would expect the pre-service preparation programme to be sufficient to cover all the gradations and experiences which he or she will encounter during the course of a professional career.

Research and an expanding knowledge base inevitably lead to *specializations* within a profession. While every member of the profession must understand its general theoretical base, there will be parts of it so complicated and specialized that a professional will be forced to defer selectively to the skills of the known specialists within the profession's ranks. For the same reason, in intricate cases or to deliver some professional services of high complexity, the need will arise for *professional teams* whose members must interlock their specialist skills to be in a position to deliver the required service. Inherent in a sophisticated profession, therefore, is the willingness to seek *a second opinion*, to call on and use the skills of others, and to be at all times *open to peer appraisal*. See Figure 12.2.

Figure 12.2 The professional mind-map Part 2

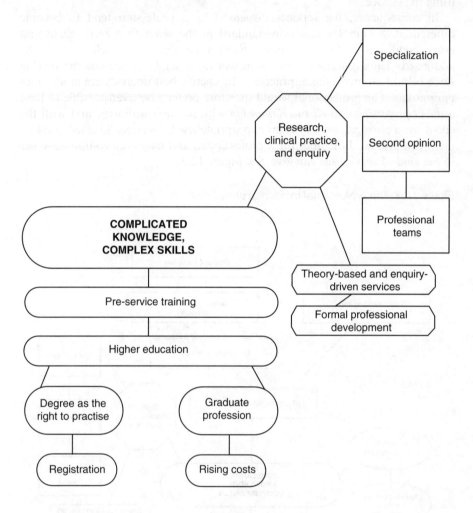

The more complicated the professional area becomes, the less likely it is that the services being dispensed are standard or can be policed, at least by the public or even a public instrumentality. It becomes practically impossible for a public board to oversee all practice or to formalize all professional procedures. So how is *the public interest* guaranteed? In the first instance, the profession has to be jealous about *its public standing and reputation*. It will be forced to develop a tight internal discipline about what is accepted as '*good practice*', usually crystallized as a *code of professional practice* enunciating the behaviours which can be taken for granted in all members of the profession. The code is often accompanied by a *discipline procedure* which allows the profession to remove from its number any person who violates the code, brings the profession into disrepute or endangers the client using the service.

In consequence, the services dispensed by a profession tend to become differentiated, complex and non-standard in the sense that every client and every condition is likely to have its own peculiarities which have to be addressed. Thus *concern for the individual client* tends to become the driving force behind all professional practice. The client's best interests are at all times paramount. The professional would therefore prefer whenever possible to have a *direct professional-to-client relationship* with no intermediaries, and with the client (or a surrogate) charged an appropriate *fee for service*. Salaried employment can present difficulties for a professional, and may even compromise her in the kind of service she can give. See Figure 12.3.

Figure 12.3 The professional mind-map completed

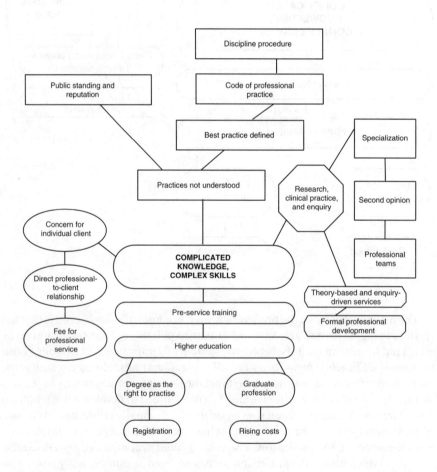

Beyond 'trade practices'

With this mind-map made explicit, it is possible to list the occupational changes and work practices which accompany the shift from a trade to a profession.

1   There is a movement away from standardized practices and towards personalized, individualized services which acknowledge the peculiar needs of each client. The professional group therefore tends to dispense with – indeed supersede – the paraphernalia of awards, standard conditions of work and a set number of hours for the working day. Professionals require the flexibility to make special provisions for the uniqueness of their clients and their professional service delivery.

2   They expect the greater financial rewards which come with an esoteric service, their remuneration proportional to the degree of complication of the work they do. Indeed, they are able to itemize the elements of professional tasks and put a price on the worth of each operation. It would simply not be possible to devise one standard equalized pay package to cover all professional operations.

3   For this reason, there is a tendency for a professionalized occupational group to move away from salaried employment and into contracts. Professionals expect the financial rewards which flow from delivering a service uniquely tailored to particular clients.

4   The educational requirements for the professional service also escalate. Certificates are displaced by university degrees and diplomas from technological institutes as the prerequisites for guaranteed long-term employment.

5   Active and continuous involvement in formal professional development programmes is an essential part of exercising one's profession. It is mandatory, and not merely an option. So professions tend to have members continually studying for academic credit, for higher degrees or postgraduate diplomas, and involved in on-the-job research. There is also an easy interchange between those who practise the profession and those who research and teach its postgraduate courses. There is no gap between theory and practice, for professional practice is interpenetrated by theory.

6   The profession tends to set up its own councils to prosecute best practice and its own acceptable levels of performance. The 'registration and certification' which is compatible with a trade's approach to work practices is replaced by a 'code of professional qualification and practice' which is compatible with the operation of a profession.

7   A profession tends to become differentiated, splitting into specializations each with its own differential remuneration structures. If teaching is fully a profession', then no longer is it the case that a 'teacher is a teacher is a teacher', and no longer can teachers expect to be remunerated in a standard way.

Some of the transitions can be represented as follows:

Transition from trade to profession

From	→	To
1 Standardized practice	→ 1	Personalized, non-standard service
2 Awards and conditions	→ 2	Professional flexibility
3 Wages and salaries	→ 3	Fee for professional service
4 Certificated; tradesman's ticket	→ 4	Degree
5 Technical-college-trained	→ 5	University-educated
6 Only pre-service training mandatory	→ 6	Career-long, professional development
7 'Competencies' base	→ 7	Ongoing research moves skills base
8 Skill-driven	→ 8	Theory-driven
9 Registration	→ 9	Professional codes of practice
10 Technical gradations	→ 10	Professional specializations
11 'Full-time employment'	→ 11	Contracts and projects; 'portfolio careers'
12 Employer/employee paradigm	→ 12	Loyalty to one's professional field
13 Government regulation	→ 13	Self-regulation and international transferability

With the arrival of teacher professionalism, and since salaries are the biggest item on any education budget, it will probably be necessary for educators to modify their practices so that they are less labour-intensive, and to rearrange the school's tasks so that sub-sets of teachers may be paid very high salaries as 'educators' rather than as 'teachers' (a category which may need redefinition if it continues to exist). We are already seeing a demand for some instruction (as distinct from teaching) to be delivered by means of sophisticated technology or by instructors, for more students to be taught, for higher performance levels but not necessarily through 'classroom teaching', for a longer school day and a longer school year. None of this implies more of the same, or that teachers must add to their already heavy loads. The call is rather for schools-as-providers-and-brokers to operate smarter, and to make better use of their amenities, including the use of their educators and instructors.

The new school model

What we have said thus far about teachers is compatible with the new model for schooling described throughout this book, the kind of enterprise with increased legal and professional responsibilities in the form of a global budget, wide discretion over funding, the responsibility to select its own staff as well as to fill its promotion positions from the Principal down, the management and upkeep of its physical plant, and so on. Individual schools have the power to go into the market-place and buy any specialist services which are required to supplement the work of their own teachers and staff. Autonomous schools may share their expertise, pool their resources, contract-in services, or contribute to the cost of a specialist consultancy. They may set up their own school support centres to take on the role of broker for a set of schools, owned and managed by a cluster of schools.

In the systemic re-engineering which was described in an earlier chapter, schools lose their allies at head office, their support in terms of curriculum and professional services, a range of free professional advice, and protection from political winds. As a result, a host of private agencies, consultants and professional firms have filled the gaps left by the dissolution of the services which were once provided free by the system itself. The new service agencies are in competition for custom; and the schools are in a position to require quality, school-specific and thoroughly professional services (for which they pay). The new agencies often operate across provincial, state and national boundaries and recruit into their firms some of the very best teachers out of schools. Individual schools are also earning additional revenue by selling the skills of their own staff and the learning materials generated from that school base. In short, new kinds of career prospects are opening up for able educators.

Many educational services have been privatized, corporatized or commercialized. In 1991, for example, the British government translated the HMIs into OFSTED (the Office for Standards in Education) to bring in a new scheme whereby school inspections and reviews were to be contracted out to private companies. In the same way, some Year 12 certification and high school graduation accreditation schemes have become free-standing, as they are in effect in the UK. It then falls to each school to decide which set of examinations, assessments and certification it will submit itself to, and which examining authority it will negotiate with. In such a privatized model, the examining authorities operate within guidelines determined by government, are franchised to award national or state certificates, and are funded from the public purse according to how many students each one services. The worldwide network for the International Baccalaureate is an example.

It is clear that alternative modes of providing services and the schooling process have become necessary, for the old frameworks are costly, cannot cope and are out of favour. Consider the example of London in the early 1990s. Prior to the abolition of the Inner London Education Authority (ILEA), the Thatcher Government asked the Inner London Education Advisory Committee (ILEAC, set up in 1988) to resolve 'cross-borough issues' including the transfer of services from the ILEA to the thirteen inner London boroughs. For the forty-one education centres listed in their report, ILEAC proposed that some would be handed to a lead-borough which would run the centre for itself and for other boroughs who would contribute on-demand payment for services. Some centres would be located in higher education institutions; the ILEA's reference library and its research arm went to the London Institute of Education. The English and Media Centre became a charity, virtually a privatized, non-profit organization. ILEA's impressive and interrelated set of school-support services – teachers' centres, libraries and reader services, a life studies centre associated with the London Zoo, a film and drama costume collection, and its internationally renowned science centres north and south of the Thames – tended to languish when the system which created them folded up. They became nobody's business. When services in the boroughs had to be cut in 1991/92, among the first to go in the majority of the boroughs included adult education; the Youth Service; careers education; and further or post-school education. Pre-school education survived largely unscathed (there would have been an angry reaction from working mothers if this area had been affected, so it was preserved for business as much as for educational reasons). Schools diminished excursions and school visits (especially those involving overnight stays); music tuition; the use of theatre groups and the like; the use of off-site swimming pools and sports grounds; and after-school and latch-key programmes. The boroughs 'varied the provision downwards' (to use the euphemism) for school meals, free buses, clothing for impoverished children, and study awards. After surveying what remained of London's educational services the Centre for Educational Research at the London Institute of Education concluded that the picture that emerged was of a decline in spending and services since the abolition of the ILEA (Nuttall, 1992), a comment under-lining what would happen if the education community clung to the models of schooling and educational provision which have been traditional. Thus the new configurations which educators must cope with have both pluses and minuses, demand some non-standard, creative responses, and bring into existence some new educational providers which will be built on teacher skills.

Careers structures for the future

Thus far we have considered some known factors which will shape the teacher of the future and the way educators practise. In earlier chapters we reviewed the kinds of changes which information technology will impose on teaching, and considered the new shape which educational enterprises (along with other organizations) will take – and that in particular means schools. That new mode for organizations was pithily stated by Gottliebsen (1998: 4) like this:

> Under the old arrangements, big corporations were like the *QE2*, travelling as a totally co-ordinated business operation. Now, big corporations are becoming like convoys, with a series of ships (operations) steering different courses but going in the same direction. The managing director of a 'convoy' has a much tougher job than the captain of the *QE2*.

Since schools have always copied the best organizational patterns found in industry, schools themselves will be operating like this in the near future.

In this chapter, we looked at the way an occupation (like teaching) changes when it becomes thoroughly professionalized. Hargreaves (1994; 1996: 120) has pointed out that teaching will be profoundly affected by the globalization of trade; the globalization of information, technology and communication; the acceleration of knowledge production and the speed by which it is sent around the world; the compression of time and space in the knowledge industries; and by the 'irrelevance of geography'. Above all, he refers to the 'scientific uncertainty as rates of scientific disconfirmation of previous knowledge increase and as independent electronic access to information and knowledge challenges the claims of academics and bureaucracies to specialist expertise'. He could also have included teachers here, since they surely qualify as knowledge workers. So the teacher's work-life and practices will have to change; there seems no other choice.

And all of the above will mean changes to a teacher's career, to the pattern of her working life, and particularly to her planned career path. The changes look to be profound. Who the teacher of the future will be and how she will operate is certain to be influenced by the emerging work-style of knowledge workers, especially the professional executive class, and what shape their careers will have. They will be guided by teachers who are bold enough to break ranks, as many are now doing. Teachers have always been attracted by the magnetism of the most able of the profession who are prepared to take risks, to be entrepreneurial and to function like other pace-setters.

For professionals, Walter Kiechel (1994: 2) argues, 'the job, as we know it, will cease to exist'; it is obsolete to think of an occupation as a 'regular set of duties, with regular pay, and regular hours, and a fixed place in an organization's structure'. The biggest propellant out of that mindset is the computer, information technology and international information networking. Kiechel points out that even by 1994 workers (including executives) who used a computer earned 10 per cent more than counterparts who did not. A teacher devoid of computer skills could not be employed now.

Handy agrees with Kiechel about the disappearance of the 9-to-5 day, especially for professional groups (like teachers). By the year 2000, he predicted (in 1990), less than half the workforce would be in conventional, full-time jobs. Until recently a young person 'could expect to work a set number of hours for a given number of weeks per year over a thirty-five to forty-five year period. This is no longer the case' (cited in Zbar, 1995: 5). In his *Age of Unreason*, Handy spoke of the 'shamrock organization' which has three kinds of employees – core workers who are responsible for the organization's prime mission; contractors who carry out separable segments of the organization's tasks; and a flexible labour force contracted to work in various parts of the enterprise, but never 'permanent' in the present sense of the word. Handy points out that each of those segments is differently organized, managed and paid. The tendency with this configuration is for people to put in the same number of working hours over a lifetime, but in intensive bursts of time interspersed with lean time, taken by deliberate choice or as the work-flows dictate (Handy, 1989: ch. 4).

Gottliebsen comments (1998: 4) that 'the modern senior executive must be able to isolate the core competencies of a particular business'. The areas outside that core can then be 'outsourced, often to former staff', on fixed-term contracts or through strategic alliances. This kind of work style will develop because work is no longer organized along factory lines. It is not necessary to turn up to a predetermined workplace when the work is no longer governed by a production line, a big plant and heavy immovable machinery. Already there is a shift in thinking from 'business as making things to business as providing a service', argues Kiechel (1994: 3). The evaporating jobs are being replaced by work 'done by individuals hired for a particular project', working in relatively temporary teams on assignments that have a beginning and an end, and where one is paid on the extent to which one adds value to the enterprise. A proportion of the educator profession is already operating in this mode.

Indeed, the education profession could gain the services of a number of experienced, highly educated and wise operators who want to make teaching their last, rather than their first, occupation. Handy warns (1989: 39), 'Organizations [read 'schooling providers'] may have to learn to be more flexible in the way they run things, more willing to recognize that they are buying the talents of someone but not necessarily all their time.'

As a result, knowledge workers (and therefore many teachers) will take a different view of what their career is about. A professional person will develop the idea that she is running a small business, and that she is responsible for her own employment, says Gottliebsen (1998: 4). The overarching principle, according to Kiechel (1994: 6, 7), is to think of yourself as a one-person business, a person with expert skill in a particular area which you trade within a networked society. 'The action today,' Kiechel quotes one writer as saying, 'is all about connectedness, about forming effective teams and building alliances.' Loyalty to a particular enterprise (school, school system or district) is displaced by loyalty to one's chosen profession.

Educators therefore will adapt to the several salient features beginning to characterize the life of the expert professional:

- There will be fewer managers, and colleagues will not 'like to be told what to do' largely because they were hired in the first place to deliver or apply specialist knowledge and their own expertise. Hierarchy has largely lost its point.
- Because 'one-person businesses' depend upon expertise, 'becoming better' or 'gaining promotion' means acquiring deeper and deeper knowledge and skill. The successful people are always learning, always reading, always questioning. As Kiechel (1994: 4) puts it, 'learning and career are inextricably intertwined' and even merge.
- The formal courses these professionals undertake and their learning programmes tend to be postgraduate but career-conscious, precisely targeting skill and knowledge development. The courses are crisp and modularized; earn credentials which increase the holder's marketability; are undertaken part-time or intensively; and involve highly specialized, in-depth studies. The people who take them, Kiechel (1994: 6) says, are 'older, mostly intermittent learners', acquiring 'job-specific skills' and rarely doing

a 'four-year, straight-through' degree course. Every knowledge worker undertakes such programmes, all the time. We need no reminding that on-line courses and distance-teaching modes are proliferating around the globe.

- Our ideas about financial investment in enterprises will have to change too. Machines wear out and become obsolescent or are replaced; in the industrial economy, then, ageing meant depreciation and replacement costs. On the other hand, in the information society people become better the more they use information and skill. There is depreciation when one invests in machines or buildings; but there is appreciation when one invests in people, particularly those committed to life-long learning.

- As a one-person business, the knowledge worker (and teacher) becomes responsible for her own career. It becomes unthinkable that anyone would want to spend a thirty-year career with the same company or employer, and dangerous if you are in your forties and in a large-scale organization, for both your job and the enterprise you belong to are certain to be under threat of change. Already many educators operate this way. They no longer see themselves as salaried, tenured employees, committed to spending their whole professional life wedded to one school, or to one system, to one state or territory, or even to one country.

- These knowledge workers (and teachers) do not expect to operate within tight controls imposed by organizational units whose day-to-day management is controlled centrally. As service delivery becomes more highly skilled, more of the operations and decision-making can be – and are – safely devolved to semi-autonomous units. In short, self-management generally comes with professionalization.

- In consequence, central management, centralized control of resources, and the built-in accountabilities (such as they were) which we associate with bureaucracy have passed into history, at least for professionals and for knowledge workers, replaced by the 'dispersed management' of internationalized businesses. How the enterprise, such as the school-as-provider, goes about its work is its own business, but it will be rewarded with resources and contracts only if its products and services are of an acceptably high standard. The emphasis has therefore now moved inexorably to outcomes. Every school, and every management unit, then, must give detailed attention to how it will demonstrate that its core business is being conducted well, and that it is achieving levels of performance which conform with the best standards being achieved elsewhere in the country and the world. For schools and individual teachers, this means being able to demonstrate with reliable evidence that students are learning well.

New career patterns for teachers as professionals

1 The job as we know it will cease to exist (i.e. a regular set of duties, regular pay, regular hours and a fixed place in the structure).
2 There are core workers, contractors and a flexible labour force (the 'shamrock').
3 Shift from business-as-making-things to business-as-providing-a-service.
4 Temporary teams of experts on assignments which have a beginning and an end.
5 Paid on the basis of value added to the exercise.
6 Fewer managers; hierarchy has lost its point.
7 'Becoming better' or 'being promoted' means acquiring deeper knowledge and skill.
8 Continual career-conscious, skill-targeted, modularized, part-time, postgraduate learning.
9 Appreciation, not depreciation, of human capital.
10 No wish to be salaried, tenured workers with career tied to one company.
11 Professionalization implies self-management.
12 Dispersed, networked, internationalized, outcomes-driven work-units based on collegial team-work.

Conclusion

We set out in this chapter to define who are the teachers of the future. We have suggested that teachers will work in organizations which are modelled on best business practices, that as professionals they will copy the patterns being set in other professions, and that their modes of carrying out their educational tasks will adopt the patterns developing in the occupational fields which they admire, envy and wish to emulate – not least in terms of remuneration, pay and public esteem.

The educator profession's leading practitioners and opinion-makers are deriving some creative new models for the profession out of the raw material highlighted in this chapter. They will have success, credibility, public acceptance and political support in creating them if they look for the building blocks where they have always found them, not only in the educational domain but by borrowing from the best trends in organizations in private enterprise and in allied professions which already enjoy public prestige. If we are to predict what the teacher of the future will be like and how she will carry out her professional tasks, it is realistic to construct that picture using the factors enunciated above. Individually they are all known factors, but collectively they could well build a portrait of the educator which borders on being radically new. There are huge implications here for teachers, and life-enhancing possibilities for the learners with whom they deal. This terrain is *not* for the immature, the shallow, the unworthy, the unformed or the uninformed, and society needs to be very careful about what people it commissions for this task.

Notes

1   The material in the first sections of this chapter was assembled as a result of the development work in connection with the Professional Recognition Program for teachers in the Victorian state school system. Members of the development team comprised, in addition to the author, Dr Bernadette Taylor (formerly Executive Director, Commonwealth Council for Educational Administration, and Principal of Malvern Girls High School), Dr Nancy Hillier (Principal of Annesley College, Adelaide), Mr John Gelling (formerly National Secretary of the Australian Secondary School Principals Association, and Principal of Holder High School, Canberra), Mr David O'Brien (Regional Office of the Victorian Department of School Education), and Mr Anthony Podesta (Director, McMillan Shakespeare Group of Companies).

13 A new kind of school

Principle No. 8, the last Work out your model of school or schooling 'with fear and trembling', but then talk it up, constantly and with conviction. In the last analysis, you are its advocate, and its advocacy rests with you. Put simply, why are you doing this at all?

At the end of this long excursion into what the schools of the future might look like, we might be inclined to ask the dumb questions, 'Why do we need schools anyway? Would we be better off without them?' Ivan Illich asked the same questions in his *Deschooling Society* (1970) and as a result helped to spark the Alternative School Movement of the 1970s. Society is not ready to scrap its schools without having something reliable and proven to put in their place; but it is safe to conclude that schooling provisions will evolve, and probably rapidly, into something quite different from what was known in the previous century.

Schooling obviously gives its recipients an advantage over those who have no schooling. It is therefore clearly a 'private good', favouring those who have it and justifying the existence of the schools which provide it. But if schooling simply advantages those who have it, then the beneficiaries should be prepared to pay for it. We can justify schools as private enterprises selling the means (an education) which will give a personal and competitive advantage to its customers (the students). In some cases society might want to give scholarships to those who, unable to afford the expense, may nevertheless be worth investing in for the public good. So we can justify private schools; there is a market for their services. We can also justify schools designed to cultivate talent.

But there is more to it than merely selling a good product to interested or worthy buyers. Schooling is of such importance to society that it warrants the expenditure of taxpayers' money to ensure that *everyone* is schooled. Universal education came into existence because society required a principal means of inducting people into the community, into society's culture, and in such a way that each person becomes a responsible, balanced, contributing and fulfilled member of society. The learning which enables the recipient to undertake paid employment (that is, vocational education) forms a part, but only a part, of those wider purposes of schooling. The costs to society of *not* having universal education apparently far outweigh the cost of having it. In summary, then, schooling is not only a private good, advantaging the learner; it is also a public good in that it makes everyone employable and productive and it fits the learner for life in community.

The argument in this book is that schooling need not remain trapped in one stereotyped pattern, and the twenty-first century may see to it that various modes and styles will emerge which will do the job far more effectively. We have had to resist the temptation of describing *the* school of the future, as though there will be a one-best-way as there seemed to be in the twentieth century. Rather, we might hope that the general purpose of the schooling process will be served through many providers, clothed in rich varieties of fabric.

Education in Neoteric

Even so, you and I can design something new and exhilarating out of these materials. Let us try on for size one model which we put forward for the city of Neoteric. The basic premise in this model is that the school must operate in a home-like setting, and that as far as is possible schooling is conducted in the community, and in a manner which patterns both the community and family. Thus the primal unit in our school is a symbolical house in which the learners, their tutors, their mentors and other adults work together while they are about the business of learning. It is also a unit with which the learner's parents can identify and to which they can make contributions. In fact, they could reasonably be asked to make a contractual commitment to it and to its purposes. Each symbolical house consists of about eighty-five learners to which five or six of the staff are attached, making up a home group, a group which is organized and behaves as though it lives in a home. To the extent possible, the home group is cross-age and there are adults other than teachers associated with it who in one way or another have full membership in the school family. They may include adults who have retired from full-time work.

It is an emphatic characteristic of the model that there are adults other than teachers associated with each house – as learners, as experts, as resource people, as parents, as role models, as mentors and friends, as facilitators. Being at school must feel literally like being in a family and in the community. The great divorce between school and town must be done away with, for here schooling is an activity owned by the whole community, for which the whole community is responsible, and to which all members of the community can be asked to make a contribution in some appropriate way.

Because the new model embodies school in community and schooling about community, the learning programmes make use of community facilities, trying to avoid having single-purpose amenities which are reserved for school purposes alone and which are seen as being owned by school. School will have access to the people in the community, to the skills, experience and expertise abroad in members of the wider community. It will rent, lease or pay for such access; and it will use for its purposes wherever possible already existent spaces in the community, including residential dwellings rather than purpose-built classrooms. In short, school will not be isolated in green fields, but will seek premises not far removed from the life of the community.

To be practical, schooling needs some facilities which are not normally provided elsewhere in a town or suburb, and without them it is hard to see how some of the essential parts of the learning programme could be mounted and carried out. Those facilities could include science laboratories, some information technology equipment, and some provision for the school's administrative infrastructure. These requirements will necessitate the provision of physical plant of one kind or another, though it should be much less extensive than what is now provided in a conventional school. The plant requirements will vary suburb by suburb, of course, and it is not possible to make a generalized inventory of what those facilities will be. Yet it is important that the facilities needed for schooling be planned in conjunction with urban planning as a whole. In practice, this kind of co-ordination generally does not occur except in a fairly rudimentary way, each facility (school, hospital, town centre, museum, sports centre) treated as a one-off, self-contained, sector-owned amenity designed and constructed without the planning which integrates, articulates or interrelates it with the other amenities, especially the public amenities, in the suburb, town or village.

The new school, then, is likely to need some buildings of its own, and they can be thought of as a hub or brain centre from which the school's co-ordinators work, where the administrative services are located, which contains the project resources to supplement or top up what the community has, and which may accommodate the common resources which all the houses need in order to be effective.

Thus far, we have said nothing that is radically new. It may be unusual but it is a pattern of operation found in many 'schools without walls' around the world after the innovations of the 1970s; it features in 'community schools' across the globe; and it is the basis for such complexes as the Abraham Moss Centre in Manchester, the community colleges in Cambridgeshire and Coventry, the Sutton Centre and some tertiary colleges in Britain, the Britannia Centre in Vancouver, the Erindale and Lake Tuggeranong colleges in Canberra, and the Lakes and Hub centres in Adelaide, Australia. Unusual they may be, but they work; and when they work *well*, they are educationally exhilarating places. What these examples and our model have in common is the symbiotic relationship between school and community, the shared use of facilities, the recruitment of a host of community resources (including its people) as integral parts of the educating process, and the abandonment of the great divide which has traditionally partitioned most schools off from the world around them and which physically places them in a castle of formidable buildings located on an off-shore island of green called the school grounds.

Because this new schooling pattern belongs in the community, in a sense it grows its programmes out of what the community has to offer, and it also draws its resources (like its learning areas and its rooms) from the community.

It does not need to limit itself to the *neighbourhood*, which might be too small a base from which to build really creative, mind-stretching learning, but it will certainly *start* with neighbourhood, and in doing so could well enrich that neighbourhood.

Neoteric schooling now physically resembles learning units which are houses (they could literally *be* houses, rented for the purpose), each as the home quarters for a family of learners among whom are students, teachers and adjunct adults, and numbering about eighty-five persons. The model will work for students of any age, and even across the artificial primary/secondary divide. The houses are linked and co-ordinated by a brain centre, containing facilitators, the administrative arm of the school, and any common or single-purpose amenities which are not available in the wider community. These pods use instructional sites in found space across the community, which may consist of community amenities, leased facilities, business or privately owned centres of activities and other educational centres like further education colleges. The educators attached to each house are responsible for arranging access, for articulating each student's learning programme, for monitoring the educational activities and the student's progress, and for making the educational programmes endemically coherent. And there are learning programmes built up in co-operation between the learner and the other people in the learning pod. The learnings are monitored, individually by the learner and regularly by the professional educators who are attached to the house and who operate out of it.

It may be that, in this schooling pattern, the identifiable block of buildings we now call school will disappear. Good. But it need not be so. The fundamental change is the orientation, with the way learning is conceived of, with the reaffirmation of the community's responsibility for universal, compulsory schooling, and with the redefinition of what that means for individual students and their teachers or mentors. Schooling becomes education of the community, in the community, and largely by the community.

Now feed into the equation some of the characteristics which we have arrived at in the course of this book:

- The 9-to-5 school day disappears when children can access the school at any time, and when the school's facilities remain available for an extended day.
- Students, especially senior students or those in their teens, are not required to be 'in class' all the time, although there are timetabled periods when they must all attend for some activities – like whole-class instruction times.
- Schools are spoken of as a service or a process, rather than as a geographical location, a campus.
- Every student is attached to one or several educational guides or mentors who ensure that each student's studies are coherent and accumulate into a worthwhile (or legally required) learning programme. The learning regimen produces clearly documented outcomes which are held up against officially approved benchmarks. In short, learning is not permitted to be haphazard.

- All students have one or more online educators whom they can access for consultation or advice about their learning programme.
- Although formal teaching still goes on, the emphasis in this school is upon what students learn. It is the students, then, who have the responsibility to demonstrate what they have learned by presenting exhibits of their work which give evidence of the skills and knowledge they have mastered.
- School continues to be concerned about a student's personal development, about her beliefs and values, her behaviours and her social interactions and skills. Schooling is still jealous about its learning culture. It is largely for this reason that the school makes use of student groupings which resemble 'homestead families', and why students increasingly learn in multi-grade, multi-age, multi-skill-level contexts.
- Teachers operate not so much as single instructors but in teams whose members have interlocking and complementary skills.
- The premises which the school uses consist not of traditional classrooms but have undergone physical reconstruction to incorporate in most learning spaces round tables for small-group learning, the ability routinely to access libraries, data-banks and computer gateways, to accommodate flexible time for learning, and to provide commons which are somewhat like Internet cafés.
- Part of the school's formal task is to provide systematic 'teaching' of parents so that they know how to ensure that learning-in-family, incidental learnings at home and out of school, and parent nurturing are in harmony with and reinforce the student's formal learning programme.
- Where schools own the physical premises in which they operate, those buildings are productively used for other cognate or compatible purposes, some of which are revenue-producing. Increasingly, schools use rented or leased premises to cut down on capital costs and loan servicing.
- The school's premises are open at all hours. Waves of different operators are contracted to ensure that a continuous service is appropriately available and that the use of the premises is optimized.
- Centralized, top-down, control-oriented school management has been displaced by self-managing, self-governing or networked schooling units. There are negotiated strategic alliances with other providers or part-providers to guarantee an adequate menu of curriculum offerings. Some of these providers are interstate or based overseas.
- The multi-functional, omni-capable, 'mother-hen' teacher has for the most part been superseded. The problem of teacher overload and burn-out has been solved by disaggregating what the omni-capable teacher was expected to do and by combining teaching activities into new configurations of functions. Most teachers contract to take some or all of those functions, and are paid a fee for each professional service rather than a generalized, standard salary.
- A range of adults other than teachers (such as computers advisers) have been added to the school's staff, and the role of teacher is now covered by a

range of professional educators – tutors, instructors, mentors, learning theorists, curriculum planners and experts, assessors, curriculum writers, assignment markers, editors, student counsellors.

- Some of the teachers have set themselves up in professional companies and contract their services out to the school, choosing to do that rather than being 'on a salary' or 'on the payroll'. The mode of payment and the nature of the contract does not substantially vary the way teachers operate as members of staff at the school, but there are notable variations in the way teachers work.

- Every student is expected to become literate in print skills and in digital skills, and those skills are seen as similar, complementary components of what is meant by literacy.

- Several key national and international education centres provide educational packages or modules on-line, twenty-four hours a day, and across national and state boundaries. The school's learning programmes tend to be global and international. A local programme means local applications of a programme accessed internationally. Every learning station in the school is wired to an international network.

- The curriculum, though still partly dependent on subjects and disciplines, consists of modules, chunks of worthwhile experiences, which can be connected, interconnected and formally articulated. The skills acquired through the modules are tracked with the aid of expert educators who have multi-disciplinary qualifications and are skilled in learning theory, especially child development.

- Many assessment tasks and examinations are computer-based and computer-scored. The tradition of end-of-year examination has become so out of date that it is seen as a ridiculous device. Progression is continuous, is regularly monitored and tested, and is routinely accredited.

A pattern of schooling for the twenty-first century? Why not?

Epilogue

The search for more effective models of schooling in the flux and uncertainty of worldwide change forces us to admit that we are attracted to the turbulence of change, to the beauty and excitement of transience and new growth, while at the same time deeply respecting and being committed to what is wise and universal, profound and eternal. Let me conclude, then, with two short cameos or stories.

Merlin the Wise

In the legends about King Arthur, the Knights of the Round Table are a chivalric order dedicated to finding the elusive Holy Grail which had been brought to England by Jesus' uncle Joseph of Arimathea. Those legends contain an enigmatic, shadowy, awesome figure called Merlin, the personal teacher and wise counsellor to the young Prince Arthur. Most modern versions of the Arthur stories, like the stage show *Camelot*, have trouble explaining or coming to terms with him

Merlin, the legends agree, could speak the language of trees and animals; he could commune with birds and the creatures of the wild woods; he was a living cosmology! He also had the gift not of *foresight* but of *future-sight.* There is a huge difference between the two. We use foresight when we look into the future and anticipate what we might encounter up ahead. *Future-sight*, however, is the result of being *already in* the future. It treats the future as familiar and known ground, as though it is already happening about you.

T.H. White, in his novel *The Once and Future King*, with uncanny percipi-ence therefore represents Merlin as a person who is living his life backwards. He has already lived the future, and is now an old, wise man in the process of growing young. In his teaching of the young hero-king Arthur, he talks of the future with the authority of one who has already been there, and who knows the whole of which this moment is a fleeting part.

So there is something magnificently symbolical about his end. Legend has it that Merlin had a special relationship with Nimiane, the Lady of the Lake, the one whose arm rose out of the water and held the magic sword Excalibur high when Arthur claimed it, the one who caught it again when Sir Bedevere at the dying Arthur's command hurled it back into the centre of the lake. Water has always symbolized movement, fluidity, the ephemeral and the passing. It is elusive and we cannot hold or capture it. Change is like water. The legend is obscure here, but Merlin and Nimiane became lovers, the one seducing the other, neither able to control the other, she who represents eternal changingness and he who represents eternal, unwavering wisdom locked in an embrace of ambiguity and paradox. How could the one accommodate the other? (And how can we?) Confronting the future will always be like that.

We are told that, frustrated, Nimiane, the always changing one, longed to stay conjoined with Merlin, eternal wisdom, the unchanging one. He must never to be lost, he must always be at hand. So she imprisoned him for all time in the gnarled trunk of an oak tree, that timeless ancestral tree which lives for centuries and which symbolizes a sense of place, perpetuity, silent unyielding strength and indestructibility.

And through all the years of change, he is there today. In its contorted bark and trunk, even now and usually at sunset when the light is at the right angle, you can catch the fleeting impression of his face, a sudden and unexpected epiphany, a startling awareness that future-sight is caught up and entangled within the very fabric of the here and now.

The child

The second story is a kind of daylight reverie which came from a period of silent reflection, when the writing of this book was nearly completed.

It was a glorious, warm and golden autumn day. Where I was walking through the deep woods, the trees were dropping their brilliant leaves on the path, but there were sufficient still hanging on the branches and twigs and still backlit with the morning sunlight to create an encircling of awesome colour above and around me. The carpet of fallen leaves led through an opening in the trees; and from there the path cut across a small green field and then wound up the side of a steep hill, at this time of the morning still streaked with long shadows cast by trees and even by tufts of grass and weeds.

It was what legend, poetry and folklore might call the dying of the old year, nature's gradual winding down into the cold of winter, but it was doing so with a glow of nostalgic glory. It was a typical Keatsian autumn, a 'season of mists and mellow fruitfulness', and saddening in that it passes with such an unforgettable display of passionate colours.

I had undertaken this walk, alone, in order to think through a problem which needed a solution. There was an easy answer to it – simply to do nothing, to play it safe, to stay with the crowd, to keep the head down, to rock no one's boat. Abide by convention; it is the simplest way, just to let things work themselves out, but it is usually the coward's way. The other options involved risk, and probably some personal unpopularity and discomfort; but if I did not take action to change things, then a creative opportunity to do some good would be lost.

At the top of the hill was a prominent oak tree, almost in silhouette against the sky. And as I approached it I noticed a small child there, standing beside the path, rugged against the chill morning inside a grey hooded greatcoat, so that I could not tell whether it was boy or girl.

'I'm sorry to disturb you,' I stumbled out, realizing that I was intruding on a solitude and a freedom which the child had deliberately sought out. 'I came here to try to resolve a problem, and I needed a quiet place to do it in.'

There was an awkward pause, as though two private worlds of silence, separated by age, were deciding whether to share the same space.

Then the child turned to me, and the sun caught her face, until that moment hidden inside the cowl of her greatcoat. 'I'm Angelica,' she said matter-of-factly, as though I should have recognized her. 'Problems aren't usually that hard, really.' And then, in kind of generous acceptance of me as part of her universe, she gave me a piece of advice which was startling in its simplicity and innocent wisdom, the more powerful because it came from a young child.

'It's easy really,' she said. '*Just choose what is the best thing for the future.*'

Bibliography

ABURDENE, P. and NAISBITT, J. (1993) *Megatrends for Women*. New York: Fawcett Columbine.

AMSLER, M. (1992) *Charter Schools*. Policy Briefs 19. San Francisco: Far West Laboratory for Educational Research and Development.

BAKER, H. (1997) 'The changing nature of work', *Management*, July: 5–7.

BALDRIDGE, J.V. and DEAL, T.E. (eds) (1975) *Managing Change in Educational Organizations*. Berkeley, Calif.: McCutchan.

BARNATT, C. (1997) *In Search of the Future*. London: Wiley.

BEARE, H. (1990) *An Educator Speaks to His Grandchildren*. ACEA Monograph Series 8. Melbourne: Australian Council for Educational Administration.

BEARE, H. (1992) 'What does it mean to be professional? A commentary about teacher professionalism', *Unicorn*, 18(4), November: 65–72.

BEARE, H. (1995) *What Is the Next Quantum Leap for Australian School Systems?* The 1994 Currie Lecture. Hawthorn, Victoria: Australian Council for Educational Administration.

BEARE, H. (1996) *Education for the Third Millennium*. IARTV Seminar Series 57. Jolimont, Victoria: Incorporated Association of Registered Teachers of Victoria (IARTV).

BEARE, H. (1997) 'Designing a Break-the-Mould School for the Future'. Keynote Address, ACEA Virtual Conference. Hawthorn, Victoria: Australian Council for Educational Administration.

BEARE, H. (1998) *Who Are the Teachers of the Future?* IARTV Seminar Series 76. Jolimont, Victoria: Incorporated Association of Registered Teachers of Victoria (IARTV).

BEARE, H. and BOYD, W.L. (eds) (1993) *Restructuring Schools: An International Perspective on the Movement to Transform the Control and Performance of Schools*. London: Falmer Press.

BEARE, H. and SLAUGHTER, R. (1993) *Education for the Twenty-First Century*. London: Routledge.

BENEDICT, R. (1935) *Patterns of Culture*. London: Routledge and Kegan Paul.

BENNIS, W.G., BENNE, K.D. and CHIN, R. (eds) (1970) *The Planning of Change*, second edition. New York: Holt, Rinehart & Winston.

BENNIS, W.G., BENNE, K.D., CHIN, R. and COREY, K.E. (eds) (1976) *The Planning of Change*, third edition. New York: Holt, Rinehart & Winston.

BENSON, H. (1977) *The Relaxation Response*. London: Fountain Books.

BENSON, H. (1985) *Beyond the Relaxation Response: How to Harness the Healing Power of Your Personal Beliefs.* London: Fount Paperbacks.

BENSON, H. (1996) *Timeless Healing: The Power and Biology of Belief.* Rydalmere, NSW: Hodder & Stoughton.

BERK, L.E. and WINSLER, A. (1995) *Scaffolding Children's Learning: Vygotsky and Early Childhood Education.* Washington, D.C.: National Association for Education of Young Children.

BERMAN, M. (1981) *The Re-Enchantment of the World.* Hartford, Conn.: Cornell University Press.

BERRY, T. (1988) *The Dream of the Earth.* San Francisco: Sierra Club Books.

BIERLEIN, L. and MULHOLLAND, L.A. (1992) *Charter Schools: A Viable Reform Initiative.* Tempe, Arizona: Morrison Institute for Public Policy, Arizona State University.

BIERLEIN, L. and MULHOLLAND, L.A. (1993) *Charter Schools: Expansion of a Viable Reform Initiative.* Tempe, Arizona: Morrison Institute for Public Policy, Arizona State University.

BOSKER, R.J., CREEMERS, B.P.M. and STRINGFIELD, S. (eds) (1999) *Enhancing Educational Excellence, Equity and Efficiency. Evidence from Evaluations of Systems and Schools in Change.* London: Academic Publishers.

BOULDING, E. 'Learning to image the future'. In W.G. Bennis, K.D. Benne, R. Chin and K.E. Corey (eds) (1976) *The Planning of Change*, third edition. New York: Holt, Rinehart & Winston, pp. 431–44.

BRUNDTLAND, G. (BRUNDTLAND REPORT) (1987) World Commission on Environment and Development (Chair: Gro Brundtland) *Our Common Future.* Oxford: Oxford University Press.

BUDDE, R. (1988) *Education by Charter: Restructuring School Districts.* Andover, Mass.: Regional Laboratory for Educational Improvement of the Northeast and Islands.

BUZAN, T. (1993) *The Mind Map Book.* London: BBC Books.

CALAS, M.B. and SMIRCICH, L. (1997) *Post-Modern Management Theory.* Boston: Dartmouth Publishing Co.

CALDWELL, B.J. (1998a) *Administrative and Regulatory Mechanisms Affecting School Autonomy in Australia.* Canberra: Department of Employment, Education, Training and Youth Affairs.

CALDWELL, B.J. (1998b) *Self-Managing Schools and Improved Learning Outcomes.* Canberra: Department of Employment, Education, Training and Youth Affairs.

CALDWELL, B. and HAYWARD, D.K. (1998) *Future of Schools: Lessons from the Reform of Public Education.* London: Falmer Press.

CALDWELL, B.J. and SPINKS, J.M. (1988) *The Self-Managing School.* London: Falmer Press.

CALDWELL, B.J. and SPINKS, J.M. (1992) *Leading the Self-Managing School.* London: Falmer Press.

CAMPBELL, J. (1972) *Myths to Live By.* London: Paladin.

CAMPBELL, J. (1973) *The Masks of God.* London: Paladin.

CAMPBELL, J. (1988) *The Inner Reaches of Outer Space.* New York: Harper & Row.

CAPRA, F. (1983) *The Turning Point: Science, Society and the Rising Culture.* London: Flamingo (Collins).

CARVER, F.D. and SERGIOVANNI, T.J. (eds) (1969) *Organizations and Human Behavior.* New York: McGraw-Hill.

CHUBB, J. and MOE, T. (1990) *Politics, Markets, and America's Schools.* Washington, D.C.: Brookings Institution.

COLEMAN, A.H. and OLMSTEAD, D. (1992) 'Real reform begins with chartered schools', *Detroit News,* 23 February; 3B.

COLEMAN, J.S., CAMPBELL, E.Q., HOBSON, C.J., McPARTLAND, J., MOOD, A.M., WEINFOLD, F.D. and YORK, R.L. (COLEMAN REPORT) (1966) *Equality of Educational Opportunity.* Washington, D.C.: US Government Printing Office.

CORNWELL, J. (1993) 'Just who do we think we are?' *Weekend Review (The Australian)*, 21 August: 4.

COTTON, K. (1995) *Effective Schooling Practices: A Research Synthesis.* School Improvement Research Series. Portland, Oregon: Northwest Regional Educational Laboratory.

CULVER, C.M. and HOBAN, G.J. (eds) (1973) *The Power to Change: Issues for the Innovative Educator.* New York: McGraw-Hill.

CUTTANCE, P. (1994) 'Monitoring educational quality through performance indicators for school practice', *School Effectiveness and School Improvement*, 5(2): 101–26.

DAVIDOW, W.H. and MALONE, M.S. (1992) *The Virtual Organization.* New York: HarperCollins.

DAVIES, P. (1983) *God and the New Physics.* Harmondsworth, Middlesex: Pelican.

DAVIES, P. (1992) *The Mind of God.* New York: Simon & Schuster.

DEAL, T.E. and KENNEDY, A.E. (1982) *Corporate Culture: The Rites and Rituals of Corporate Life.* Reading, Mass.: Addison-Wesley.

DENNING, P.J. and METCALFE, R.M. (eds) (1997) *Beyond Calculation: The Next Fifty Years of Computing.* New York: Copernicus.

DIANDA, M.R. and CORWIN, R.G. (1993) *An Early Look at Charter Schools in California.* SRL Occasional Paper. Los Alamitos, California: Southwest Regional Laboratory.

DOMBERGER, S. (1999) *The Contracting Organization: A Strategic Guide to Outsourcing.* Oxford: Oxford University Press.

DOWRICK, S. (1992) *Intimacy and Solitude.* Melbourne: Heinemann.

DOWRICK, S. (1993) *The Intimacy and Solitude Self-Therapy Book.* Port Melbourne: Mandarin.

DREXLER, K.E. (1986) *Engines of Creation: The Coming Era of Nanotechnology.* New York: Anchor Books (Doubleday).

DROR, Y. (1973) *Public Policy Re-Examined.* Bedfordshire: Leonard Hill Books.

DRUCKER, P. (1969) *The Age of Discontinuity.* London: Heinemann.

DRUCKER, P. (1990) *The New Realities.* London: Mandarin Paperback.

DRUCKER, P. (1993) *Managing for the Future.* London: Butterworth-Heinemann.

DUFTY, H. and DUFTY, D. (1990) *Literacy for Life.* Melbourne: Dallasta.

DYSON, F. (1981) *Disturbing the Universe.* London: Pan Books.

EDISON PROJECT (1994) *Partnership School Design.* New York: Edison Project.

EDUCATION VICTORIA (1992) *Schools of the Future Program.* Melbourne, Victoria: Education Victoria.

EDUCATION VICTORIA (1998) *Learning Technologies in Victorian Schools 1998–2001.* Melbourne, Victoria: Education Victoria.

ELIADE, M. (1987) [1957] *The Sacred and the Profane: The Nature of Religion.* San Diego: Harcourt Brace Jovanovich.

ESTES, C.P. (1992) *Women Who Run with the Wolves; Contacting the Power of Wild Woman.* London: Rider.

FEINSTEIN, D. and KRIPPNER, S. (1989) *Personal Mythology: The Psychology of Your Evolving Self.* London: Unwin Hyman.

FERGUSON, M. (1980) *The Aquarian Conspiracy: Personal and Social Transformation in the 1980s.* Los Angeles: J.P. Tarcher.

FINN, C.E. and REBARBER, T. (eds) (1992) *Education Reform in the '90s.* New York: Macmillan.

FISCHER, K.R. (1983) *The Inner Rainbow: The Imagination in Christian Life.* New York: Paulist Press.

FISKE, E.B. (1992) *Smart Schools, Smart Kids: Why Do Some Schools Work?* New York: Touchstone.

FULLAN, M. (1982) *The Meaning of Educational Change.* New York: Teachers College, Columbia University Press.

FULLAN, M. (1995) *Reshaping the Teaching Profession.* IARTV Seminar Series 50. Jolimont, Victoria: Incorporated Association of Registered Teachers of Victoria (IARTV).

GALLWEY, T. (1976) *Inner Tennis: Playing the Game.* New York: Random House.

GALLWEY, T. (1981) *The Inner Game of Golf.* London: Jonathon Cape.

GARDNER, H. (1999) *The Disciplined Mind: What All Students Should Understand.* New York: Simon & Schuster.

GATES, B. (1999) *Business @ the Speed of Thought.* Ringwood, Victoria: Viking (Penguin Books).

GELLING, J. and EVANS, B. (1993) *Developing the Principalship.* Report of the Steering Committee for the National Project on Leadership and Management Training for Principals. Canberra: AGPS.

GEORGE, C. (1972) *The History of Management Thought.* Englewood Cliffs, NJ: Prentice-Hall.

GERSTNER, L.V., SEMERAD, R.D., DOYLE, D.P. and JOHNSTON, W.B. (1995) *Reinventing Education: Entrepreneurship in America's Public Schools.* New York: Plume.

GOLDBERG, P. (1983) *The Intuitive Edge: Understanding Intuition and Applying It in Everyday Life.* Los Angeles: Tarcher.

GOTTLIEBSEN, R. (1998) 'New culture shock for executives', *Business Review Weekly,* 26 January: 4.

GREEN, S. (1998) 'The death of the eight-hour day', *The Age* (Close-Up section), 9 March: 10.

HAMMER, J. (1996) *Beyond Reengineering.* New York: Harvard Business.

HAMMER, M. and CHAMPY, J. (1994) *Reengineering the Corporation: A Manifesto for Business Revolution.* St Leonards, NSW: Allen & Unwin.

HANDY, C. (1985) *Understanding Organizations,* third edition. Harmondsworth: Penguin.

HANDY, C. (1989) *The Age of Unreason.* London: Business Books (Century Hutchinson).

HANDY, C. (1994) *The Empty Raincoat: Making Sense of the Future.* London: Hutchinson.

HANDY, C. (1996) *Beyond Certainty: The Changing World of Organizations.* London: Hutchinson.

Bibliography

HANDY, C. (1997) *The Hungry Spirit: Beyond Capitalism – A Quest for Purpose in the Modern World.* London: Hutchinson.

HANUSHEK, E. (1994) *Making Schools Work: Improving Performance and Controlling Costs.* Washington, D.C.: Brookings Institution.

HARGREAVES, A. (1994) *Changing Teachers, Changing Times. Teachers' Work and Culture in the Postmodern Age.* New York: Teachers College Press.

HARGREAVES, A. (1996) 'Transforming knowledge: blurring the boundaries between research, policy, and practice', *Educational Evaluation and Policy Analysis*, 18(2): 105–22.

HARGREAVES, D.H. (1997) 'A road to the learning society', *School Leadership and Management*, 17(3): 9–21.

HARMAN, W. (1988) *Global Mind Change.* Indianapolis, Indiana: Knowledge Systems.

HARMAN, G., BEARE, H. and BERKELEY, G. (eds) (1991) *Restructuring School Management.* Deakin, Australian Capital Territory: Australian College of Education.

HARNER, M. (1990) *The Way of the Shaman*, third edition. New York: Harper & Row.

HAWLEY, J. (1993) *Reawakening the Spirit in Work: The Power of Dharmic Management.* San Francisco: Berrett-Koehler Publishers.

HEDBERG, B., DAHLGREN, G., HANSSON, J. and OLVE, N.-G. (1997) *Virtual Organizations and Beyond.* New York: Wiley.

HENDERSON, H. (1988) *The Politics of the Solar Age: Alternatives to Economics.* Indianapolis: Knowledge Systems.

HILL, P.W. and RUSSELL, V.J. (1999) 'Systemic, whole-school reform of the middle years of schooling'. In R.J. Bosker, B.P.M. Creemers and S. Stringfield (eds) *Enhancing Educational Excellence, Equity and Efficiency. Evidence from Evaluations of Systems and Schools in Change.* London: Academic Publishers.

HUGHES, P.W. (ed.) (1987) *Better Teachers for Better Schools.* Carlton, Victoria: Australian College of Education.

HUGHES, P.W. (1991) 'Re-structuring in Australia: a personal view'. In G. Harman, H. Beare and G. Berkeley (eds) *Restructuring School Management.* Deakin, Australian Capital Territory: Australian College of Education.

ILLICH, I.D. (1970) *Deschooling Society.* London: Calder and Boyars.

JAMES, D. (1998) 'War of the worlds', *Management Today*, January/February: 4–5.

JENCKS, C., SMITH, M.S., ACKLAND, H., COHEN, D., GRINTLIS, H., HEYNES, B. and MICHELSON, S. (1972) *Inequality: A Reassessment of the Effect of Family and Schooling in America.* New York: Basic Books.

JENCKS, C., BARTLETT, S., CORCORAN, M., CROUSE, J., EAGLESSIELD, D., JACKSON, G., McCLELLAND, K., MUESER, P., OLNECK, M., SCHWARTZ, J., WARD, S. and WILLIAMS, G. (1979) *Who Gets Ahead? The Determinants of Economic Success in America.* New York: Basic Books.

JOHNSON, R.A. (1986) *Inner Work: Using Dreams and Active Imagination for Personal Growth.* San Francisco: Harper & Row.

JOHNSON, S.M. (1990) *Teachers at Work.* New York: Basic Books (HarperCollins).

JUNG, C. (ed.) (1988) *Man and His Symbols.* New York: Dell Publishing.

KAKU, M. (1998) *How Science Will Revolutionize the 21st Century.* Oxford: Oxford University Press.

KANTER, R.M. (1983) *The Change Masters: Innovation and Entrepreneurship in the American Corporation.* London: Unwin Paperbacks.

KANTER, R.M. (1989) *When Giants Learn to Dance: Mastering the Challenges of Strategy, Management, and Careers in the 1990s.* London: Unwin Paperbacks.

KANTER, R.M. (1995) *World Class: Thriving Locally in the Global Economy.* London: Unwin Hyman.

KATZENBACH, J. and SMITH, D. (1998) *The Wisdom of Teams: Creating the High-Performance Organization.* Boston, Mass.: Harvard Business School Press.

KAYE, M. (1996) *Myth-Makers and Story-Tellers.* Chatswood, NSW: Business & Professional Publishing.

KIECHEL, W. (1994) 'A manager's career in the new economy', *Fortune*, 11 April: 2–7.

KIM, T.C. and DATOR, J.A. (eds) (1994) *Creating A New History for Future Generations.* Kyoto, Japan: Institute for the Integrated Study of Future Generations.

KLITGAARD, R.E. and HALL, G.R. (1973) 'Are there unusually effective schools?', *Journal of Human Resources*, X(1): 90–106.

KOCH, R. (1998) *The Third Revolution: A Capitalist Manifesto.* London: Capstone Publications.

LANGE, D. (1988) *Tomorrow's Schools: The Reform of Educational Administration in New Zealand.* Wellington, NZ: NZ Government Printer.

LARSEN, S. (1990) *Mythic Imagination: Your Quest for Meaning through Personal Mythology.* New York: Bantam Books.

LEVINE, D.U. and LEZOTTE, L.W. (1990) *Unusually Effective Schools: A Review and Analysis of Research and Practice.* Madison, Wisconsin: National Center for Effective Schools Research and Development.

LIPNACK, J. and STAMPS, J. (1994) *The Age of the Network: Organizing Principles for the 21st Century.* New York: Wiley.

LOKAN, J. and McKENZIE, P. (eds) (1989) *Teacher Appraisal: Issues and Approaches.* Camberwell, Vic.: Australian Council for Educational Research.

LOVELOCK, J. (1988) *The Ages of Gaia: A Biography of Our Living Earth.* Oxford: Oxford University Press.

McCLENDON, J. (1974) *Biography as Theology.* New York: Abingdon Press.

McCOLSKEY, W. and EGELSON, P. (1993) *Designing Teacher Evaluation Systems that Support Professional Growth.* Greensboro: School of Education University of North Carolina.

McDONAGH, S. (1986) *To Care for the Earth: A Call to a New Theology.* London: Geoffrey Chapman.

MACKAY, Harvey (1988) *Swim With the Sharks Without Being Eaten Alive.* London: Sphere Books.

MACKAY, Hugh (1993) *Reinventing Australia.* Pymble, NSW: Angus & Robertson.

MANAGEMENT TODAY (1999) 'Editorial'. April: 10–11.

MANN, D. (1992) 'School reform in the United States: a national policy review 1965–1991', *School Effectiveness and School Improvement*, 3(3): 216–30.

MARLES, F. (1992) *Being a Member of a Profession: Implications for Teachers.* IARTV Seminar Series 15. Jolimont, Victoria: Incorporated Association of Registered Teachers of Victoria (IARTV).

MARTIN, J. (1981) *The Telematic Society.* London: Prentice-Hall.

MARTIN, J. (1996) *The Great Transition.* London: Prentice-Hall.

MILLER, C. (1987) 'Science needs new world view', *Age (Future Age)*, Melbourne, Australia, 30 March: 16.

MINTZBERG, H. (1979) *The Structuring of Organizations.* Englewood Cliffs, NJ: Prentice-Hall.

MINTZBERG, H. (1994) *The Rise and Fall of Strategic Planning.* New York: Prentice-Hall.

MULHOLLAND, L.A. and BIERLEIN, L. (1993) *Charter Schools: A Glance at the Issues.* Policy Brief. Tempe, Arizona: Morrison Institute for Public Policy, Arizona State University.

MURPHY, D. (1997) *A Return to Spirit After the Mythic Church.* Alexandria, NSW: E.J. Dwyer.

MURPHY, J. (1991) *Restructuring Schools: Capturing and Assessing the Phenomena.* New York: Teachers College Press.

NAISBITT, J. (1982) *Megatrends: Ten New Directions Transforming Our Lives.* New York: Warner Books.

NAISBITT, J. (1994) *The Global Paradox.* St Leonard's, NSW: Allen & Unwin.

NAISBITT, J. (1995) *Megatrends Asia: The Eight Asian Megatrends that are Changing the World.* New York: Warner Books.

NAISBITT, J. and ABURDENE, P. (1990) *Megatrends 2000.* New York: Warner Books.

NATIONAL COMMISSION ON EXCELLENCE IN EDUCATION (1983) *A Nation At Risk.* Washington, D.C.: US Government Printing Office.

NEVILLE, B. (1989) *Educating Psyche: Emotion, Imagination, and the Unconscious in Learning.* Melbourne: Collins Dove.

NUTTALL, D. (1992) *After ILEA: Education Services in Inner London*, London: Centre for Educational Research, Institute of Education, University of London.

OHMAE, K. (1990) *The Borderless World: Power and Strategy in the Interlinked Economy.* London: Collins.

OHMAE, K. (1995a) *The End of the Nation State.* London: HarperCollins.

OHMAE, K. (1995b) *The Evolving Global Economy.* London: Collins.

OSBORNE, D. and GAEBLER, T. (1993) *Reinventing Government: How the Entrepreneurial Spirit is Transforming the Public Sector.* New York: Penguin (Plume).

OTTO, R. (1950) *The Idea of the Holy.* Oxford: Oxford University Press.

PAPERT, S. (1993) *The Children's Machine: Rethinking School in the Age of the Computer.* New York: Basic Books.

PERELMAN, J. (1996) *Schools Out.* New York: William Morrow.

PETERS, T.J. (1987) *Thriving on Chaos.* London: Macmillan.

PETERS, T.J. (1992) *Liberation Management; Necessary Disorganization for the Nanosecond Nineties.* London: Macmillan.

PETERS, T.J. and WATERMAN, R.H. (1982) *In Search of Excellence: Lessons from America's Best-Run Companies.* New York: Harper & Row.

PICOT, B. (PICOT REPORT) (1988) Report of the Taskforce to Review Educational Administration (Chair: B. Picot). *Administering for Excellence: Effective Administration in Education.* Wellington, NZ: NZ Government Printer.

PIPHO, C. (1993) 'Bipartisan charter schools', *Phi Delta Kappan*, October: 102–3.

RAEL, J.E. (1992) *Beautiful Painted Arrow: Stories and Teaching from the Native American Tradition.* Shaftesbury, Dorset: Element.

RANSOME, P. (1996) *The Work Paradigm: A Theoretical Investigation of Concepts of Work.* London: Avebury Press.

REANNEY, D. (1991) *The Death of Forever: A New Future for Human Consciousness.* Melbourne: Longman Cheshire.

REICH, R. (1992) *The Work of Nations.* New York: Vintage Books.

REYNOLDS, D. (1994) *Advances in School Effectiveness Research and Practice.* Oxford: Pergamon.

REYNOLDS, D. and CUTTANCE, P. (eds) (1992) *School Effectiveness: Research, Policy and Practice.* London: Cassell.

REYNOLDS, D., CREEMERS, B.P.M., NESSELRODT, P.S., SCHAFFER, E.C., STRINGFIELD, S. and TEDDLIE, C. (eds) (1994) *Advances in School Effectiveness Research and Practice.* Oxford: Pergamon Press.

ROSS, K.N. and LEVACIC, R. (eds) (1999) *Needs-Based Resource Allocation in Education via Formula Funding for Schools.* Paris: UNESCO (IIEP).

RUTTER, M., MAUGHAN, B., MORTIMORE, P. and OUSTON, J. (1979) *Fifteen Thousand Hours: Secondary Schools and Effects on Children.* London: Open Books.

SADTLER, D., CAMPBELL, A. and KOCH, R. (1997) *Break Up: How Companies Use Spin-Offs to Gain Focus and Grow Strong.* New York, NY: Free Press.

SAMMONS, P., HILLMAN, J. and MORTIMORE, P. (1995) *Key Characteristics of Effective Schools: A Review of School Effectiveness Research.* London: OFSTED.

SAUTTER, R.C. (1993) *Charter Schools: A New Breed of Public Schools.* Policy Briefs 2. Oak Brook, Ill.: North Central Regional Educational Laboratory.

SAVAGE, C.M. (1996) *5th Generation Management: Co-Creating Through Virtual Enterprising, Dynamic Teaming, and Knowledge Networking.* Boston: Butterworth-Heinemann.

SAWATSKI, M. (1991) *The Profession Developing the Professionals.* Paper presented to the 23rd National Conference of the Australian Secondary Principals Association. Canberra: ASPA.

SCHEERENS, J. and BOSKER, R. (1997) *The Foundations of Educational Effectiveness.* Oxford: Elsevier Science.

SCOTT, B.W. (SCOTT REPORT) MANAGEMENT REVIEW: NEW SOUTH WALES EDUCATION PORTFOLIO (Director, B.W. Scott) (1990) *School-Centred Education: Building a More Responsive State School System.* Milsons Pt, NSW: Management Review, NSW Education Portfolio.

SENGE, P. (1990) *The Fifth Discipline: The Art and Practice of the Learning Organization.* New York: Doubleday.

SHANKER, A. (1988) 'Restructuring our schools', *Peabody Journal of Education*, 65(3): 88–100.

SHELDON, P. (1990) 'Joseph Campbell', *The Beacon*, September/October: 341–4.

SLAUGHTER, R. (1993) 'Looking for the real megatrends', *Futures*, October: 1–24.

STARRATT, R.J. (1993) *Transforming Life in Schools: Conversations about Leadership and School Renewal.* Hawthorn, Vic.: Australian Council for Educational Administration.

STEVENS, E. (1990) *Spiritual Technologies: A User's Manual.* New York: Paulist Press.

STEVENS, J. and STEVENS, L.S. (1988) *The Secrets of Shamanism: Tapping the Spirit Power Within You.* New York: Avon Books.

STOLL, L. and FINK, D. (1996) *Changing Our Schools: Linking School Effectiveness and School Improvement.* Buckingham: Open University Press.

STRINGFIELD, S., ROSS, S. and SMITH, L. (eds) (1996) *Bold Plans for School Restructuring: The New American Schools Designs.* Marwah, NJ: Lawrence Erlbaum Associates.

SWIDLER, L. (1988) *Yeshua: A Model for Moderns.* Kansas City: Sheed & Ward.

SWIMME, B. (1996) *The Hidden Heart of the Cosmos.* Marknoll, NY: Orbis Books.

TEILHARD DE CHARDIN, P. (1959) *The Phenomenon of Man.* London: Fontana.

THOMAS, J.M. and BENNIS, W.G. (eds) (1972) *Management of Change and Conflict.* Harmondsworth: Penguin.

Bibliography

TILLEY, T.W. (1990) *Story Theology.* Collegeville, Minnesota: Liturgical Press.

TOFFLER, A. (1981) *The Third Wave.* London: Pan Books.

TOFFLER, A. (1985) *The Adaptive Corporation.* London: Pan Books.

TOWNSEND, T., CLARKE, P. and ANSCOW, M. (eds) (1999) *Third Millennium Schools: A World of Difference in Effectiveness and Improvement.* Lisse: Swets & Zeitlinger.

UNICEF (1995) *The State of the World's Children 1994.* Paris: UNICEF.

VYGOTSKY, L. (1978) *Mind in Society: The Development of Higher Psychological Processes.* Boston, Mass.: Harvard University Press.

WEICK, K.E. (1976) 'Educational organizations as loosely coupled systems', *Administrative Science Quarterly*, 21, March: 1–19.

WERTHEIM, M. (1999) *The Pearly Gates of Cyberspace.* Sydney: Doubleday.

WILBER, K. (1983a) *Eye to Eye: The Quest for a New Paradigm.* Garden City, NY: Anchor Books.

WILBER, K. (1983b) *A Sociable God.* London: New Science.

WILLIAMS, S. and BUECHLER, M. (1993) *Strategic Investment: Tough Choices for America's Future.* In Brief (a policy brief for the National Governors' Association, 16 April). Washington, D.C.: National Governors' Association.

WINK, W. (1992) *Engaging the Powers: Discernment and Resistance in a World of Domination.* Minneapolis: Fortress Press.

WOHLSTETTER, P. and ANDERSON, L. (1994) 'What can US charter schools learn from England's grant-maintained schools?', *Phi Delta Kappan*, February: 486–91.

WOLF, F.A. (1989) *Parallel Universes: The Search for Other Worlds.* New York: Simon & Schuster.

WRISTON, W. (1992) *The Twilight of Sovereignty: How the Information Revolution is Transforming Our World.* New York: Maxwell Macmillan International.

YUNGBLUT, J.R. (1992) *Shaping a Personal Myth to Live By.* Rockport, Mass.: Element.

ZBAR, V. (1995) *New Trends in Organization and Management.* IARTV Seminar Series 43. Jolimont, Victoria: Incorporated Association of Registered Teachers of Victoria (IARTV).

ZOHAR, D. and MARSHALL, I. (1994) *The Quantum Society: Mind, Physics, and a New Social Vision.* London: Flamingo.

Index

Aburdene, P. 23
academic curriculum/subjects 5, 26, 27
accountability 75, 113, 128–43;
    accountability task 142–3;
    information about student learning
    131–2; performance indicators
    132–42; reporting to the community
    served by the school 129, 130–1;
    stakeholders 128–30, 134, 135;
    student-learner and 143; system
    accountability 130
accreditation/registration 105, 173, 177
acculturation into society 20–2, 82, 105,
    106, 158–60
action plans 71, 124–7
age-grade structures 88–9
age-related curriculum 150
agrarian society 25–8
alliances, strategic 153, 190
Alternative School Movement 186
American culture/values 16
Amsler, M. 117, 119, 120
annual report 71, 129, 132
appraisal function 110–11
army 27
Asia/Pacific area 12
assessment 17, 157, 164, 168, 191
audiences (for reporting) 128–30, 134,
    135; see also stakeholders
Australia 76, 114, 115–16
Australian Schools Commission 98

babies, having 15
backward mapping 103–4, 125
Barnatt, C. 92
basic human needs 13
Beare, H. 19, 36, 37–8, 40, 99
belief systems 15, 16, 17, 21–2; enabling
    19; myth-making 50–3; power of
    18–19
benchmarking 138–9
Benedict, R. 49
Benson, H. 49
Berman, M. 55
Berry, T. 56
Bierlein, L. 116
bio-regional stories 56
Board of Trustees 119
books 17
borderlessness 153–4; see also
    globalization
Bosker, R. 164
Boulding, E. 101
brain 41–2
brain centre/hub 92–3, 188, 189
Britain 98, 115, 117
brokers of educational services 80, 154,
    163–5
Brundtland Report 5–6
Budde, R. 116
buddy systems 171
bureaucracy 29, 60
Bush, G. 95–6
Buzan, T. 172

cabled city 147
Caldwell, B. 67, 116
Campbell, J. 21, 51
Canada 142
Canberra High School 6
Capra, F. 38–9
careers 15, 155; teachers' career
    structures for the future 180–4
categories 133
central education barn 92–3, 188, 189
ceremonial learnings 159
Champy, J. 69

change 1–8, 144; cameos 191–3;
    emerging school 2–8; new approaches
    to 107; resistance to 25
charter schools 71, 113–27; charter
    school movement 115–18; objectives
    and action plans 124–7; profiles and
    vision statements 120–4; school and
    its stakeholders 118–20
Chernobyl disaster 59
'child' cameo 192–3
Chinese 16
Chubb, J. 33
cities 12–13, 29; wired city 147
citizenship: planetary 159; responsible
    19–20, 21–2
clades 37
class groups 88–9
class system 26
climate for learning 164
clones 37
Coalition of Essential Schools 136–7
code of professional practice 175, 177
cognitive development 160–2
Coleman Report 96
collaborative learning 44, 110, 154–5
collegiality 171
colligative systems 57
common learnings 159
commons 56
community 82, 90; accountability to
    community served by the school 129,
    130–1; educational houses 93, 187,
    189; learning in and about 158–63;
    new school model 187–9
community facilities 3
competition 5, 67
compulsory elementary schooling 28
computers 14, 16, 148; transportable
    147; *see also* information technology
concern for individual client 176
Confucianism 16
connections 43–5, 52; *see also* networks
consciousness 45–6
consumerism 20
consumption, inequalities in 13
contractors 181
Copernicus, N. 42
core, strategic 72, 73, 75
core competencies 181
core workers 181
Cornwell, J. 41
cosmogenesis 36
costs 4, 80; meeting 75–7, 81–2

Cotton, K. 164
credo 120–4
cultural development 160–2
cultural learnings 159
culture 18–22; enculturation 20–2, 82,
    105, 106, 158–60
curriculum 1, 113, 144–65;
    characteristics of effective schooling
    163–5; instrumentalism and 18;
    international 16–17, 60–1; IT and
    knowledge society 145–8; learning in
    and about community 158–63; myth-
    making 47–53; network and student-
    as-knowledge-worker metaphors
    153–8; new ways of knowing and
    36–53; nodular and modular 89, 156,
    191; planning 100; production- line
    schooling 31; quantum approaches
    42–6; rebuilding the approach to
    150–3; schools and accommodation
    to knowledge society 148–50;
    scientific method and 38–42; teaching
    functions and 168
customer-driven government 67–8
Cuttance, P. 164

data-bases, access to 145–6
data collection 134–8
Davies, P. 36
decentralization 68, 119, 183
Delfin Corporation 87–8
demand levels 139
Denning, P.J. 92
Descartes, R. 42
design of schooling process 85–98;
    access to IT for all 91–5; additional
    design features 90–1; greenfields site
    87–90; school effectiveness movement
    95–8
Detroit Public Schools Empowerment
    Plan 117
developed countries 13
digital skills 147, 191
direct professional-to-client relationship
    176
discipline procedure 175–6
disciplines/subjects 89, 151, 156, 160–2
dispersed management 68, 119, 183
diversity 37
dollar allocations 4
Dror, Y. 132–3, 137
Drucker, P. 18, 23, 57, 61
Dufty, D. 52

Dufty, H. 52
dynamism 37, 44–5
Dyson, F. 37

e-book 146–7
early childhood 91
earth/planet: concern for 5–6, 12, 13–14;
    living system 17, 41, 54–7
economically-oriented policies 5, 97–8
Edelman, G. 41–2
Edison Project 92
education: as industrial sector 77–8; as
    service 78
education centres 191
education credit (voucher) 2
education departments 30, 33–4
education markets 4, 68
Education Victoria 114, 142
educators 3, 4, 17, 89; curriculum of the
    future 162–3; incompatibility with
    school's credo 122; inspirational 18;
    mentoring and assessing 157–8; new
    kind of school 189, 190–1;
    professionalism 177; teams 156, 163,
    182, 190; *see also* teachers
effective schooling 95–8, 163–5
elementary schooling, universal 28
Eliade, M. 43
elitism 26
emerging school 2–8
empiricism 39–40
employment 33; education for 31, 81–2,
    104, 105, 106; future trends 14–15,
    155; teachers' work patterns 80–1
empowerment 51, 67
enabling belief system 19
enabling state 66
enculturation 20–2, 82, 105, 106, 158–60
Encyclopaedia Britannica 145
end-of-cycle review 71
enterprise: post-industrialism and 32–5;
    schools as enterprises 2, 33, 53, 68,
    90, 164–5
enterprise networks 65–82; framework for
    education sector 77–82; meeting the
    costs 75–7; new logic for government
    services 65–8; post-modern
    management for schools 68–75
environment 5–6, 12, 13–14; *see also*
    earth/planet
environmental movement 44
equity 91
essential services 78–9

expectations, high 164
expert opinions 138
expert professionals 182–4
expressive arts 52, 106

facilities *see* school buildings/facilities
factory metaphor 28–32, 151
faith factor 49
families 15
fees for service 173, 176
Feinstein, D. 51
Ferguson, M. 36
feudalism 27
film 146
financial rewards 71, 177
Fischer, K.R. 48
Fitzroy North Primary School 122–4
flexible labour force 181
foresight 192
formal professional development 173–4,
    177; educators of the future 182–3
formal schooling 90, 91
'found space' 3, 93
full-service school centres 3
fundamentalists 15
funding 72, 75–7; accountability and
    financiers 129; charter schools
    119–20; split-level 76–7, 81–2
future-sight 192
futures 101–2; *see also* planning
'future's child' 11–17

Gaebler, T. 66–8
Gaia 41
Galbraith, J.K. 57
Gardner, H. 156
Gates, B. 69, 144, 145, 148
gateway 92–3, 188, 189
George, C. 107
global co-operation 3, 4, 5
globalization 11–12, 57–61, 70, 153–4
Gottliebsen, R. 180, 181, 182
government: national 5, 76, 97; new logic
    for government services 65–8;
    regulator of essential services 78–9
graduate profession 166, 172, 173
grain production 12
grammar schools 26, 27
grant-maintained schools (GMS) 115,
    117, 118
greenfields site 87–90

Hall, G.R. 96–7

Hammer, J. 151
Hammer, M. 69
Handy, C. 57, 98, 154, 155, 181, 182
Hanushek, E. 72
Hargreaves, A. 180–1
Hargreaves, D. 3
Harman, W. 57
Harner, M. 49
Hayward, D.K. 67
headteachers *see* Principals
healing 49
Henderson, H. 55, 56
Her Majesty's Inspectors (HMI) 79
hierarchy 151, 182; of schools 30
Higher Education Contribution Scheme
    (HECS) 34
Hill, P.W. 158
history 56
holism 43–5, 55
home: as learning location 3, 90;
    home/school partnership 165
Hong Kong 92
houses, educational 93, 187, 189
Hughes, P.W. 167
human capital, investment in 183

Illich, I. 186
images 48–9; recurring 23–4
implementation 124–7
incentives 71
Indians 16
individual-isolating society 42–3
Industrial Revolution 28–32, 38
industry: education as 77–8
inequality, global 13–14
information technology (IT) 62–3, 181;
    and the knowledge society 145–8;
    school design and access to 91–5
Inner London Education Authority
    (ILEA) 98, 179–80
inputs 137
instrumentalism 18
intermediate educational precincts 94
International Baccalaureate 179
International Congress on School
    Effectiveness and Improvement
    (ICSEI) 96
international courts of justice 13
international curriculum 16–17, 60–1
international education centres 191
Internet 44, 145, 148
investment in human capital 183
Islam 16

Jencks, S. 96
Jung, C.G. 51

Kaku, M. 41
Kaye, M. 24
key learning areas 18, 76
Kiechel, W. 181, 182
KISS (keep it simple, stupid!) 131
Klitgaard, R.E. 96–7
knowledge 16, 36–53; myth-making
    47–53; new approach to knowing and
    38–42; quantum approaches 42–6;
    scaffolding 157; teachers' prior
    knowledge 173–6
knowledge society: IT and 145–8;
    schools and accommodating to
    148–50
knowledge workers 14; careers 182–3;
    student-as-knowledge-worker 153–8
Krippner, S. 51

larger single-site schools 111
Larsen, S. 45, 50, 51
leadership 165
learning 4, 16, 90, 153, 157; active and
    inert 146; climate for 164;
    collaborative 44, 110, 154–5; for
    community membership 158–60; data
    collection on student learning 131–2;
    expert professionals and career 182;
    focus on 164; life-long 90, 91, 155–6;
    new kind of school 190; outcomes
    120; quantum approaches and 44–5;
    transformational 18–22; *see also*
    curriculum
learning organization 109–10, 165
learning programmes 189; devised by
    student 143; plurality of 152–3
legislation 126
Leibnitz, G.W. 41
Levacic, R. 2
Levine, D.U. 164
Lezotte, L.W. 164
life expectancy 11
life-long learning 90, 91, 155–6
linear curriculum 150
Lipnack, J. 94
living systems 17, 41, 54–7, 110
local school districts 118
longitudinal data 131
Lovelock, J. 40, 41, 57

machine metaphor 24, 41–2, 54–5

Mackay, H. 107
major transformations 24–5
management: charter schools 113–27;
    dispersed 68, 119, 183; self-
    management 33, 97–8, 114, 183, 190
managerialism 97–8
managers 182
Mann, D. 1–2
manufacturing 28–9, 33
market metaphor 32–5, 151–2
market-oriented schooling 4, 68
Marshall, I. 43, 44, 45, 46, 54
Martin, J. 88
masks 49–50
mass education 28–32, 38, 151
master plan 71
materialism 39
McClendon, J. 48
McDonagh, S. 55
meanings 20–2
mechanization 28
media 50
megatrends 23, 100
mental models 110
mentors 171
'Merlin the Wise' cameo 192
metaphors 23–35; factory 28–32, 151;
    machine 24, 41–2, 54–5; market 32–5,
    151–2; network *see* network
    metaphor; pre-industrial society 25–8
Metcalfe, R.M. 92
mid-cycle reviews 71
military spending 13
mind-map, professional 172–6
Mintzberg, H. 107–9
mission 120–4; accomplishment of 70–1;
    articulation of 71
mission-driven government 67
models 101
modular curriculum 89, 156, 191
Moe, T. 33
monastery 26–7
money 29–30
monitoring 164
monoculture 21
morality 5
mothers, working 16
Mulholland, L.A. 116
multi-campus schools 111
multinational corporations 58, 60, 61–2
multiple realities 45
Murphy, D. 42–5

myths: new ways of knowing 47–53;
    personal histories 20–2

Naisbitt, J. 23, 57, 100
nation-states 29, 58, 59
National Commission on Excellence in
    Education 97
national education centres 191
national governments 5, 76, 97
neighbourhood 188–9; educational
    houses 93, 187, 189
network metaphor 54–64, 152–3;
    reworking the curriculum 153–8
networked organization 72–5
networks 44, 54–64, 90; emerging school
    3; enterprise networks *see* enterprise
    networks; globalization 57–61;
    information technology 62–3, 145,
    147, 148; living planetary system
    54–7; permanence and transience
    61–2; systems of educational units 95
Neville, B. 48, 49, 52
New American Schools corporation 96
new school model 187–91
New South Wales, Australia 115
New Zealand 115, 116–17, 118–19
Newtonian physics 42
nodular curriculum 89, 156
nouveau riche 30
Nuttall, D. 180

Oak Ridge School 124
objectives 124–7
objectivity 39–40
OFSTED 179
Ohmae, K. 57, 59–60
oil production 12
operating structures 110–12
operating units 72–5
Oppenheimer, R. 37
optimal level 139
organizational structure 61–2, 68–75, 137
Osborne, D. 66–8
Otto, R. 18
outcomes 116; reporting 128–43

Papert, S. 88
parents 76–7; accountability to 129;
    nurturing and teaching 190
Pareto, V. 41
past practice 138
pedagogy 168
Perelman, J. 151

performance appraisal 169–70
performance indicators 125, 132–42;
    listing audiences 134, 135; naming
    categories 133; selecting indicators
    134 8; setting a standard 138 9; sub-
    optimizing 139–42
permanence 61–2
personal development/formation 190;
    curriculum and 159, 160–2; funding
    and 76–7, 82; one of the purposes of
    schooling 82, 104, 105–6
personal mastery 109
personal mythologies 20–2, 48
personality 49–50
personalized services 177
Peters, T.J. 107, 131
Philadelphia, USA 117
Picot Report 115, 116
Pipho, C. 117
planet *see* earth/planet
planetary citizenship 159
planned levels 139
planning 99–112; for accountability
    141–2; action plans 124–7; futures
    101–2; new approaches to change
    107; operating structures 110–12;
    procedure 99–101; purposes of
    schooling 104–6; tactical and
    strategic 107–10, 125; techniques
    102–4; urban 87–90, 188; *see also*
    design of schooling process
plant, physical *see* school
    buildings/facilities
politics 13
population, sub-optimization by 140
population growth 12
portable computers 147; *see also*
    information technology
portfolio, student's 137
positivism 39
possible futures 101–2
post-industrialism 18, 24–5, 32–5, 97
post-modern management 68–75
post-secondary education 31
preferable futures 102
pre-industrial patterns of schooling 25–8
prevention 68
primary (direct) indicators 134
Principals 33, 34; operating structures
    110–11
print skills 147, 191
prior knowledge/learning 173–6
private good, schooling as 186

private schools 26, 30, 76, 186
private sector 66
privatization 66, 179
probable futures 101–2
problem-solving skills 160–2
procedures 137
process, schooling as 79, 98
production-line schooling 28–32, 38, 151
professional companies 81, 179, 191
professional standards 138
professionalization of teaching 80–1,
    166–85; credentials 172; professional
    mind-map 172–6; teachers'
    contributions to the profession 169;
    transition from trade to profession
    177–8
profiles 120–4
Programme Evaluation and Review
    Technique (PERT) 125
programmed learning 159–60
progressive education 152
projections 103
providers of services 66; government as
    provider 66; and regulators 78–9;
    schools as providers of schooling
    process 79, 163–5
provincial governments 76
public good, schooling as 186–7
public schools 30
purposeful teaching 164
purposes of schooling 81–2, 104–6

qualifications 31; teachers 166, 172, 173,
    177
quantitative analysis 40
quantum world-view 40–1, 42–6

Rael, J. 50
rationality 38, 40
reality 90; multiple realities 45–6
Reanney, D. 45
recurring imagery 23–4
reductionism 39
re-engineering 33
registration 105, 173, 177
Regulations 126
regulator, government as 78–9
Reich, R. 57, 59, 60, 69, 70, 153–4
relationships 43–5, 52; *see also* networks
rented space/facilities 2–3
research 174
resistance to change 25
resourcing *see* funding

responsible citizenship 19–20, 21–2
restructuring 33
results orientation 67
reviews 71; cycle of 132
rewards, financial 71, 177
Reynolds, D. 164
rites of passage 20, 158–9
Ross, K.N. 2
rural industry 14
Ruskin, J. 158
Russell, V.J. 158
Rutter, M. 96

Sadtler, D. 61
Sammons, P. 164
Sautter, R.C. 118, 119, 120, 128
Sawatski, M. 171
scaffolding knowledge 157
scenarios 102–4
Scheerens, J. 164
school buildings/facilities 1, 62; central
    educational barn 92–3, 188, 189;
    design 85–7, 88, 100; emerging school
    2–3; intermediate educational
    precincts 94; neighbourhood
    educational houses 93, 187, 189;
    school of the future 188, 190
school charters *see* charter schools
school day 89, 157, 189
school effectiveness 163–5; movement
    95–8
school effects policies 96–7
school life, teachers' contribution to 168–9
school-as-provider 79, 163–5
school reform movement 151
school-site council 118–19
school system 90
schooling: as a process 79, 98; as public
    and private good 186–7; purposes of
    81–2, 104–6
Schools Authority 6
Schools Council 98
Schools of the Future programme 114,
    115–16
scientific co-operation 14
scientific method 38–42
sea 14
second opinion 174
Second World War 59
secondary education 31
secondary (indirect) indicators 134–6, 137
self 43
self-dismemberment 61–2

self-image 48
self-interest 5
self-management 33, 97–8, 114, 183, 190;
    see also charter schools
Senge, P. 109–10
separation of powers 78–9
sequenced learning 159–60
service agencies 81, 179, 191
services 15, 60; education as a service 78;
    essential 78–9; new logic for
    government services 65–8; new school
    model 179–80; paying for 80;
    professionalization of teachers 181–2;
    schools as brokers of educational
    services 80, 154, 163–5
shamans 49–50
shamrock organization 181
Shanker, A. 117
shared vision 110, 164
similar cohort 138
Singapore 14, 92
single-site schools, larger 111
Sizer, T. 136
skills, professional 173–6
Slaughter, R. 19, 36, 37–8, 40
small schools 111
'smart home' 14
social welfare network 13, 58
society, acculturation into 20–2, 82, 105,
    106, 158–60
Solar Age 55
space colonies 14
specialization 174, 177
spin-off companies 73
Spinks, J.M. 116
split-level funding 76–7, 81–2
staff *see* educators, teachers
stakeholders: accountability and 128–30,
    134, 135; charter schools and 118–20
Stamps, J. 94
stand-alone enterprises 2, 33, 90
standards: decline in 97; setting 138–9
Starratt, R.J. 121
steering 66–7
Stevens, E. 52
Stevens, J. 48
Stevens, L.S. 48
stories *see* myths
strategic alliances 153, 190
strategic core 72, 73, 75
strategic planning 107–10, 125
strategic thinking 108–10
Stringfield, S. 96, 121

structures: operating structures 110–12;
    organizational structure 61–2, 68–75,
    137
student-as-knowledge-worker metaphor
    133–8
student learning *see* learning
students: new kind of school 189–90;
    responsibility for own learning
    programmes 143; rights and
    responsibilities 165; stakeholders
    128–9
subjects/disciplines 89, 151, 156, 160–2
sub-optimization 139–42
Sub-Saharan Africa 13
supercities 12–13, 29
superpositions 45
supervision 110–11, 171
supplementary data 131
survival levels 139
Swidler, L. 47
Swimme, B. 42
symbolical houses 93, 187, 189
system, school as 95
system accountability 130
systems thinking 109

tactical planning 107–10, 125
task, sub-optimization by 140–1
taxation 58
teachers 4, 80–1, 113, 166–85; careers
    structures for the future 180–4; and
    information about student learning
    131–2; new kind of school 190–1;
    new school model 178–80; post-
    industrialist era 34–5;
    professionalism 172–8; reworking the
    curriculum 157–8; roles and
    functions 168–71; training 100, 166,
    173; *see also* educators
teaching, purposeful 164
team learning 44, 110, 154–5
teams 44; professional 174–5;
    teachers/educators 156, 163, 182, 190;
    temporary 182
Teilhard de Chardin, P. 36
television 16, 146
theories 41
thinking curriculum 158
Tilley, T.W. 46
time, sub-optimization by 140
TOE ('theory of everything') 36
Toffler, A. 24, 31–2, 72
tolerance 5

trade 58
training 15; teachers 100, 166, 173
transempirical language 47
transformational learning 18–22
transience 61–2
trend lines 23, 99–100, 102–4

United Kingdom (UK) 98, 115, 117
United States of America (USA) 98,
    116, 117–18; culture and values 16
universal education 186; elementary
    schooling 28; secondary schooling 31
urban planning 87–90, 188
urbanization 29–31, 43
users-pay approach 17, 34, 68
utilitarianism 5

value added 182
values 15
Victoria, Australia 114, 115–16
video 146
Vietnam War 59
village schools 28–9
virtual reality 146
vision 49, 107–8; shared vision 110, 164
vision statements 120–4
vocationaleducation31,81–2,104,105,106
voucher, education 2

Waterman, R.H. 131
Weick, K.E. 48
welfare networks, international 13, 58
White, T.H. 192
whole-earth conspiracy 36
Wilber, K. 40, 44, 46, 57
Wink, W. 19–20
wired city 147
Wolf, F.A. 57
women 14–15
work patterns, teachers' 80–1
working rules 126–7
world-views 11–22; enabling beliefs 19;
    future's child 11–17; major
    transformations 24–5; personal
    histories with meanings 20–2; power
    of belief systems and world-views
    18–19; responsible citizens 19–20
Wriston, W. 59

Yungblut, J.R. 20

Zohar, D. 43, 44, 45, 46, 54